EXPLORATIONS IN SOCIOLOGY

British Sociological Association conference volume series

Sami Zubaida (editor)	1	*Race and Racism*
Richard Brown (editor)	2	*Knowledge, Education and Cultural Change*
Paul Rock and Mary McIntosh (editors)	3	*Deviance and Social Control*
Emanuel de Kadt and Gavin Williams (editors)	4	*Sociology and Development*
Frank Parkin (editor)	5	*The Social Analysis of Class Structure*
Diana Leonard Barker and Sheila Allen (editors)	6	*Sexual Divisions and Society: Process and Change*
Diana Leonard Barker and Sheila Allen (editors)	7	*Dependence and Exploitation in Work and Marriage*
Richard Scase (editor)	8	*Industrial Society: Class, Cleavage and Control*
Robert Dingwall, Christian Heath, Margaret Reid and Margaret Stacey (editors)	9	*Health Care and Health Knowledge*
Robert Dingwall, Christian Heath Margaret Reid and Margaret Stacey (editors)	10	*Health and the Division of Labour*
Gary Littlejohn, Barry Smart, John Wakeford and Nira Yuval-Davis (editors)	11	*Power and the State*
Michèle Barrett, Philip Corrigan, Annette Kuhn and Janet Wolff (editors)	12	*Ideology and Cultural Production*
Bob Fryer, Alan Hunt, Doreen MacBarnet and Bert Moorhouse (editors)	13	*Law, State and Society*
Philip Abrams, Rosemary Dean, Janet Finch and Paul Rock (editors)	14	*Practice and Progress: British Sociology 1950–1980*
Graham Day, Lesley Caldwell, Karen Jones, David Robbins and Hilary Rose (editors)	15	*Diversity and Decomposition in the Labour Market*
David Robbins, Lesley Caldwell, Graham Day, Karen Jones and Hilary Rose (editors)	16	*Rethinking Social Inequality*
Eva Garmarnikow, David Morgan, June Purvis and Daphne Taylorson (editors)	17	*The Public and the Private*
Eva Garmarnikow, David Morgan, June Purvis and Daphne Taylorson (editors)	18	*Gender, Class and Work*
*Gareth Rees, Janet Bujra, Paul Littlewood, Howard Newby and Teresa L. Rees (editors)	19	*Political Action and Social Identity: Class, Locality and Ideology*
*Howard Newby, Janet Bujra, Paul Littlewood, Gareth Rees and Teresa L. Rees (editors)	20	*Restructuring Capital: Recession and Reorganization in Industrial Society*

*Sheila Allen, Kate Purcell, Alan Waton and Stephen Wood (editors)	21	*The Experience of Unemployment*
*Kate Purcell, Stephen Wood, Alan Waton and Sheila Allen (editors)	22	*The Changing Experience of Employers: Restructuring and Recession*
*Jalna Hanmer and Mary Maynard (editors)	23	*Women, Violence and Social Control*
*Colin Creighton and Martin Shaw (editors)	24	*The Sociology of War and Peace*
*Alan Bryman, Bill Bytheway, Patricia Allatt and Teresa Keil (editors)	25	*Rethinking the Life Cycle*
*Patricia Allatt, Teresa Keil, Alan Bryman and Bill Bytheway	26	*Women and the Life Cycle*
*Ian Varcoe, Maureen McNeil and Steven Yearley (editors)	27	*Deciphering Science and Technology*
*Maureen McNeil, Ian Varcoe and Steven Yearley (editors)	28	*The New Reproductive Technologies*
David McCrone, Stephen Kendrick and Pat Straw (editors)	29	*The Making of Scotland*
*Stephen Kendrick, Pat Straw and David McCrone (editors)	30	*Interpreting the Past, Understanding the Present*
*Lynn Jamieson and Helen Corr (editors)	31	*State, Private Life and Political Change*
*Helen Corr and Lynn Jamieson (editors)	32	*Politics of Everyday Life: Continuity and Change in Work and the Family*
*Geoff Payne and Malcolm Cross (editors)	33	*Sociology in Action: Applications and Opportunities for the 1990s*
*Pamela Abbott and Claire Wallace (editors)	34	*Gender, Power and Sexuality*
*Robert Reiner and Malcolm Cross (editors)	35	*Beyond Law and Order: Criminal Justice Policy and Politics into the 1990s*
Pamela Abbott and Geoff Payne (editors)	36	*New Directions in the Sociology of Health and Illness*
Claire Wallace and Malcolm Cross (editors)	37	*Youth in Transition: The Sociology of Youth and Youth Policy*
Malcolm Cross and Geoff Payne (editors)	38	*Social Inequality and the Enterprise Culture: Towards a New Sociology of Work*

**Published by Macmillan*

£45-00

Beyond Law and Order

Criminal Justice Policy and Politics into the 1990s

Edited by
Robert Reiner
Lecturer in Criminology
Department of Law, London School of Economics

and

Malcolm Cross
Principal Research Fellow
Centre for Research in Ethnic Relations
University of Warwick

M

First published 1991

Published by
MACMILLAN ACADEMIC AND PROFESSIONAL LTD
Houndmills, Basingstoke, Hampshire RG21 2XS
and London
Companies and representatives
throughout the world

Phototypeset by Vine & Gorfin Ltd
Exmouth, Devon

Printed in Hong Kong

British Library Cataloguing in Publication Data
Beyond law and order: criminal justice policy politics into the 1990s. — (Explorations in sociology, 35).
1. Great Britain. Criminal law. Justice. Administration
I. Reiner, Robert II. Cross, Malcolm III. Series
364.941
ISBN 0–333–54280–0 (hardcover)
ISBN 0–333–54281–9 (paperback)

Series Standing Order

If you would like to receive future titles in this series as they are published, you can make use of our standing order facility. To place a standing order please contact your bookseller or, in the case of difficulty, write to us at the address below with your name and address and the name of the series. Please state with which title you wish to begin your standing order. (If you live outside the UK we may not have the rights for your area, in which case we will forward your order to the publisher concerned.)

Standing Order Service, Macmillan Distribution Ltd, Houndmills, Basingstoke, Hampshire, RG21 2XS, England.

Contents

Notes on the Contributors

Nigel Brearley was educated at Essex and Sheffield Universities, and the London School of Economics. He is currently Research Officer in the Sociology Department at the Polytechnic of Central London, engaged in a project studying the work of detectives.

Dee Cook is Lecturer in Criminology at Keele Centre for Criminology. Her publications include several articles on the investigation and punishment of tax and social security fraud, and 'Women on Welfare' (in P. Carlen and A. Worrall (eds), *Gender, Crime and Justice*, 1987). She is author of *Rich Law, Poor Law: different responses to tax and supplementary fraud*, 1989) and editor (with Pat Carlen) of *Paying For Crime*: 1989). She is currently researching discipline and punishment through welfare; income inequality and sentencing; financial crime.

Malcolm Cross is currently Principal Research Fellow at the Centre for Research in Ethnic Relations at the University of Warwick. He is a former Chairperson of the British Sociological Association, and the Social Research Association. He has written *Caribbean Echoes and British Realities: Blacks, Asians and the Colonial Encounter* (1990), *Urbanisation and Urban Growth in the Caribbean* (1979), *West Indian Social Problems: A Sociological Perspective* (1970), and numerous papers on urban labour markets and ethnic minorities. He has edited a number of volumes, and is editor of *New Community*.

Nicholas Dorn is Development Director of the ISDD (Institute for the Study of Drug Dependence), London. He has done consultancy in Pakistan, the Philippines, and in relation to Afghanistan. Publications include *Policing the Drug Distribution Business* (in press) with Karim Murji and Nigel South. His postgraduate studies were at Middlesex Polytechnic and Kent University. He currently directs various research and policy studies with funding from the private sector and from three government departments (Home Office, Department of Health, Department of Education and Science), including a study of drug distribution and enforcement.

Les Johnston is Senior Lecturer in Social Sciences, Polytechnic South West (Exmouth) and Honorary Research Fellow, Centre for Police and Criminal Justice Studies, University of Exeter. He is author of *Marxism, Class Analysis and Socialist Pluralism* (1986), as well as articles on police organisation, police accountability, and police complaints, and is currently engaged in writing a book on privatisation and policing: *Privatization and the New Policing* (1991).

Roy D. King is Professor of Social Theory and Institutions at University of Wales – Bangor. He is also Director of the Centre for Social Policy Research and Development. Educated at the Universities of Leicester, Cambridge and London he has been Research Officer at the Medical Research Council and the Institute of Education, London; Lecturer and Senior Lecturer at the University of Southampton; Ford Foundation Fellow at Yale Law School; and Visiting Professor in Sociology at University of Wisconsin – Madison. Major publications include *Patterns of Residential Care; A Taste of Prison; Albany: Birth of a Prison – End of an Era; The Future of the Prison System*. He is currently researching the survival strategies of prisoners and their families with Dr Kathleen McDermott under an ESRC grant.

Kate Lyon is Lecturer in Applied Social Studies in the Department of Social Work, University of Bristol. She was formerly Lecturer in Criminology, University of Bath. She graduated in Sociology at the LSE, and has been a Research Officer in the Home Office Research Unit, and a Course Director for NACRO. She is currently doing research on women's imprisonment.

Kathleen McDermott is Research Fellow at the Centre for Social Policy Research and Development, University College of North Wales. Her current research with Roy King is on 'Coping with Custody: A Study of Survival Strategies Used By Prisoners' Families'. Prior to this research, she and Roy King conducted a 4-year study on 'Security, Control and Humane Containment'. Her higher education was at City University of New York and the University of California – Berkeley. She is the author of 'We Have No Problem: The Experience of Racism in Prison' (*New Community*, 16 (2), 1990) and is co-author with Roy King of 'Mind Games: Where the action is in prisons' (*British Journal of

Criminology, 28 (3), 1988); 'British Prisons 1970–1987: The Ever-Deepening Crisis', (*British Journal of Criminology*, 29 (2), 1989); and 'A Fresh Start: The Enhancement of Prison Regimes' (*The Howard Journal of Criminal Justice*, 28 (3), 1989).

Kathleen Magee graduated from Queen's University Belfast with a degree in Social Studies and Political Science in July 1986. In 1987 she was employed as a Research Assistant on an ESRC-funded project on the RUC directed by John Brewer. A book on this research, *Inside the RUC*, is due out in 1990, co-authored with John Brewer. She has taught Sociology since 1986, and lectured to RUC officers at the police training college in Northern Ireland. She is currently completing a thesis on the occupational culture of the RUC.

R.I. Mawby is Principal Lecturer in Social Policy at Polytechnic South West. He graduated from LSE in 1970 and received an MSc from LSE in 1971. He subsequently carried out research with Sheffield University, receiving his doctorate in 1978, and has lectured at the Universities of Leeds and Bradford. His most recent books are *Crime Victims: Needs, Services and the Voluntary Sector* (1987), *Volunteers in the Criminal Justice System* (1990), *A Special Constable* (1990), (all with Martin Gill), and *Comparative Policing Issues: An International Perspective* (1990). His current research interests include comparative policing, neighbourhood watch and victim experiences.

Tim May began his career in the retail and manufacturing sectors, and then read sociology at the LSE where he was awarded the 1985 Hobhouse prize for undergraduate studies. Following this, he undertook an MSc in Social Research Methods at Surrey University, during which time he worked at the Centre for Criminological Research, Oxford. He then worked as a Researcher at Plymouth Polytechnic for three years – the product of which was submitted as a Ph.D – and is now a Lecturer in Sociology and Social Policy at Polytechnic South West. He is the author of a forthcoming book *Probation: Politics, Policy and Practice*.

Karim Murji is a Research Criminologist at the Institute for the Study of Drug Dependence. He studied at Essex University and as a postgraduate at LSE, where his research was on race and policing. At ISDD he works on research projects about drug markets and on inter-agency referral schemes.

Philip Rawlings is Lecturer in the Department of Law at Brunel University, and previously in the Department of Law at University College, Aberystwyth; LL.B. (Hull), Ph.D. (Hull). He is co-author of *Imprisonment in England and Wales: A Concise History* (Croom Helm, 1985), *Tenants' Rights* (1986) and of a forthcoming book of essays on recent work in legal history (1990). He is author of *Drunks, Whores and Idle Apprentices: The Biographical Literature of Crime in the Eighteenth Century* (forthcoming, 1990). Research interests include police and policing, and the history of crime and criminal justice in the early modern and modern periods.

Robert Reiner lectures in Criminology in the Law Department, LSE. He was formerly Reader in Criminology at Bristol and Brunel Universities. He is author of *The Blue-Coated Worker* (1978), *The Politics of the Police* (1985), and numerous articles and chapters on policing, crime and justice. He is currently completing research on contemporary chief constables, and on custody officers. He is co-editor of *Policing and Society: An International Journal*, and Review Editor of *The British Journal of Criminology*.

Nigel South is a Research Sociologist at the Institute for the Study of Drug Dependence, London. He studied at the University of Essex and, for his Ph.D., at Middlesex Polytechnic where he is also a Research Associate of the Centre for Criminology. He is the author of *Policing for Profit* (1988), co-editor of *A Land Fit for Heroin?* (1987) and will be co-author of *Policing the Drug Distribution Business* (1991/2). He has carried out research on a variety of criminological and social policy issues and taught in the UK and the USA, most recently at the State University of New York at Plattsburgh.

Kevin Stenson presently teaches criminology and sociology at Buckinghamshire College of Higher Education and at Goldsmiths College, London University. He has also taught part-time and as a visiting lecturer at Birkbeck College, London, Syracuse University (London Programme) and North Western University, Illinois. He studied sociology at Middlesex Polytechnic, the University of Leeds and Brunel University, where he completed a

Ph.D. in 1989. He has published a number of articles and reviews in criminology, sociology and social work journals. He is conducting (with Fiona Factor) an ethnographic study of the relation between young Jewish people, community organisations and the police. He is editing *The Politics of Crime Control* (1991) with Dave Cowell.

Sandra Walklate is Principal Lecturer in Sociology, Liverpool Polytechnic. She is co-author with M. Brogden and T. Jefferson of *Introducing Policework* (1988), and author of *Victimology: The Victim and the Criminal Justice Process* (1989). She is currently involved in evaluating 'Industry Watch' on Merseyside in conjunction with Merseyside Police. She graduated from the University of Lancaster.

Introduction: Beyond Law and Order – Crime and Criminology into the 1990s

Robert Reiner and Malcolm Cross

During the late 1970s widespread anxieties about economic, social, cultural and moral change in British society came to be crystallised into one primary symbol: 'law and order'. The image of a society in the grip of muggers, hooligans, terrorists, violent pickets, and other folk-devils condensed and made concrete pervasive yet vaguer fears of national decline. (The definitive analysis of this remains Hall *et al.*, 1978, for all its flaws; cf. Sumner, 1981; Waddington, 1986). It is true that such 'respectable fears' have a long history, and appear to be a perennial feature of modern societies (Pearson, 1983). However, this does not mean that there are not times when they become peculiarly intense, and indeed may have a rational basis (Reiner, 1986, 1990a).

During the 1980s scepticism about straightforward interpretations of crime statistics became more common. This was largely due to publicity given to the important series of national British Crime Surveys done by the Home Office Research Unit (Hough and Mayhew, 1983 and 1985; Mayhew, Elliott and Dowds, 1989). There have also been a number of influential local crime surveys (Kinsey, 1985; Farrington and Dowds, 1985; Jones, Maclean and Young, 1986; Bottoms, Mawby and Walker, 1987; Bottoms, Mawby and Xanthos, 1989). These crime surveys have clearly established that officially recorded levels and patterns of crime bear a problematic relationship to underlying trends in victimisation and offending behaviour, as critical criminologists have long pointed out (for example, Box, 1981). However, they also show there is substance in the popular perception of increasing crime in the recent past, and that fear of crime is both pervasive and has a rational kernel in the experience of people living in the most vulnerable areas of society. This has prompted the conversion of some leading critical criminologists to a new 'left realist' position, which regards crime as a significant social problem blighting the lives of the weakest groups in the population (Taylor, 1981; Lea and Young, 1984; Kinsey, Lea and Young, 1986; Young, 1986; Phipps, 1986).

'Law and order' as a political issue had already been 'stolen' by the Tories, however (Downes, 1983). During the 1979 General Election campaign, much emphasis was placed on the Labour government's supposed softness, and indeed connivance, in the undermining of law and morality. As Mrs Thatcher put in one much publicised speech: 'Labour Ministers do not seem to understand their own responsibilities in the unending task of upholding the law in a free society' (19 May 1979, televised campaign meeting in Birmingham). Labour's approach, she continued, was 'the path to social disintegration and decay'. She pledged that 'across that path we will place a barrier of steel'.

In putting 'law and order' at the centre of the political stage Mrs Thatcher was, as she saw it, only responding to widespread social anxiety. As she put it in an early speech as Tory leader, 'We will not make law and order an election issue, the British people will.' One central element in the articulation of popular concern about 'law and order' was the increasingly high-profile lobbying activity of criminal justice professionals themselves, especially the police. The growth during the 1970s of a 'bobby lobby' has been widely documented (Reiner, 1980, 1982; Kettle, 1980), and the Police Federation and several chief constables became increasingly prominent media figures. Starting in the early 1970s, and first explicitly elaborated in the Police Federation's 1975 'law and order' campaign, police lobbying became a significant factor in the 1979 election campaign and the overall policies of 'Thatcherism' (Taylor, 1980, 1987; Brake and Hale, 1989). Mrs Thatcher's previously cited 'barrier of steel' speech was delivered the night before the Police Federation published in every daily newspaper a prominent advertisement putting its views on 'law and order'. Throughout the campaign there was a similar symbiosis between Conservative statements and those of a number of police bodies. The advertising was not a waste of Federation members' money. An ITN poll on the night of the 1979 Election found that 23 per cent of voters had switched to the Tories 'on law and order'. This was a bigger proportion than for any other issue apart from 'prices' (Clarke and Taylor, 1980).

Once in office the Conservatives began to implement their

promised package of measures, all of which were intended to reduce crime by strengthening the deterrent impact of the criminal justice system. There were to be more police – better paid, and equipped with enhanced technology and legal powers. Punishment was also to be beefed-up. Tougher sentencing was promised, with sharp shocks (mainly not short) for serious or recalcitrant offenders.

The treatment began in earnest from the moment the Conservatives took office in 1979. On the first working day after the Tory election victory, the leaders of the Police Federation were summoned to Downing Street to be told that the pay increase and formula recommended by the Edmund-Davies committee were to be implemented immediately. (Labour had also undertaken to do this, but in two stages, the second of which was not yet due.) This ushered in a long honeymoon period in relations between the police and the government. Until recently the generous implications of the Edmund-Davies agreement have been followed without demur, pay levels have remained relatively generous, and police numbers have boomed. The total strength of police forces in England and Wales increased from 89 226 in 1979 to over 93 000 in 1981. However, the increase slowed down in the later 1980s: in 1988 police strength was 94 982. Expenditure on policing has also gone up rapidly. It was £1035m in 1977–8, more than double this by 1982–3 (£2370m) and had gone up again to £3825m by 1988–9.

Punishment has also been accentuated in line with Conservative promises. The latest volume of *Criminal Statistics* says: 'the proportionate use of custody for adults sentenced for indictable offences increased each year from 15 per cent in 1979–80 to 19 per cent in 1985–7 but fell to 18 per cent in 1988' (*Criminal Statistics 1988*, London: HMSO, 1989, p. 139). The average length of sentence has also gone up for most types of offender. For example, 'for males aged 21 and over sentenced to immediate imprisonment for indictable offences at all courts, the average sentence has risen from 11.9 months in 1984 to 14.0 months in 1986 and 15.2 months in 1988. Excluding persons sentenced to life imprisonment the proportion of those given 4 years or more has risen from 4 per cent in 1984 to 7 per cent in 1988, whilst the proportion given sentences of under 6 months has fallen from 39 per cent in 1984 to 31 per cent in 1988' (*Ibid*, p. 140). Expenditure on the prison service has increased by 66 per cent since 1978–9, and on prison building by

100 per cent. It is projected that between 1985 and 1995 twenty-eight new prisons will have opened, with 25 000 new prison places added.

But despite much bitter medicine the patient has got worse. Crime and disorder, far from abating, have increased well beyond the levels with which the Conservatives beat Labour in 1979. The number of notifiable offences recorded by the police was 2 377 000 in 1979 (excluding criminal damage under £20), but by 1988 this had gone up to 3 550 000. Recorded crime increased every year during the 1980s (apart from a tiny dip between 1982 and 1983). The only substantial exception is the last year's figures, which show a drop from a 1987 total of 3 716 000 (and which the government have tried to make much of as a harbinger of success). In addition, the 1980s were characterised by a variety of forms of violent disorder, unprecedented in post-war British experience, whatever echoes there may be of more remote periods. These range from the inner-city uprisings of 1980, 1981 and 1985, with their profound reverberations on the criminal justice system, through a number of bitter industrial disputes (notably the 1984–5 miners' strike), to a more recent collection of moral panics about a variety of leisure-time problems: football hooligans, rural 'lager louts', 'acid house' parties. Altogether, the criminal record of the 1980s is one which should embarrass a government elected on a 'law and order' platform.

As the failure of the 'law and order' package to achieve its avowed objective of reducing crime became increasingly apparent, so the government's stance began, slowly but perceptibly, to do a U-turn. The tough elements of the programme remained in place, notably the enhanced police capacity to deal with public disorder, and the prison building plans. But alongside these, indeed partially eclipsing them, there developed a set of new rhetorics and realities.

The key theme in the new Conservative rhetoric on 'law and order' which emerged during the second half of the 1980s is the recognition that the criminal justice system by itself, and more broadly any aspect of government policy, can have only a limited part to play in the control of crime. The sources of crime, and therefore the sources of crime control, lie in broader social processes, as critics of the government's original 'law and order' package had always argued. 'Society', banished by Mrs Thatcher to a conceptual limbo, has in effect been brought back in.

However, it has done so in the particular guise of the 'community', with all its imprecise aura of vacuous virtue. 'Community' is the buzzword of the government's U-turn, relegating the tough 'law and order' approach of its early years to a back seat. As Douglas Hurd put it in a recent Home Office booklet summing up current strategy, *Tackling Crime*, it 'looks beyond the formal structures of the criminal justice system to the role of the wider community – businesses, voluntary organisations and everyone as citizens – in preventing crime before it happens'. 'Community' approaches are found everywhere in its pages: community policing, community crime prevention, punishment in the community. The common theme is of official agencies hiving-off aspects of their work. Their place is taken by citizen volunteers, charitable organisations, and privately paid-for services. The detailed ways in which these processes of voluntarisation and privatisation work themselves out in a variety of contexts is explored by most of the chapters in this book (for example, Johnston, Rawlings, Mawby and Gill, Lyon, May, and Walklate). As Douglas Hurd expresses it in his Foreword to *Tackling Crime*: 'Since 1983 there has been a welcome upsurge in the number of citizens who in different ways are active against crime. We owe a substantial debt to all those who work in the criminal justice services. In addition, businessmen, teachers, parents, local government councillors and officials, volunteers of many kinds now share the same interest.' Partnership and cooperation, between official agencies, and between the official system and private individuals, are the order of the day.

There are several sources of this new modesty about the role of government and official agencies in the maintenance of 'law and order'. First and most obvious is the apparent failure of the original strategy of boosting the strength and powers of the official system. This has made it necessary to go beyond 'law and order', spreading responsibility to the 'community', and hopefully tapping its resources into the bargain.

The policy U-turn was facilitated by research and advice from the civil service side of the Home Office. An understanding of the limitations of a purely deterrent approach to crime control was already prevalent among Home Office civil servants and researchers in the late 1970s, and the then Head of the Research and Planning Unit, Ron Clarke and his colleagues led the formulation of a coherent alternative under the banner of 'situational crime prevention' (Clarke and Mayhew, 1980; Clarke and Hough, 1980). Thus a systematic policy analysis and prescription was waiting in the wings as the government became ripe for conversion when its unabashed 'law and order' thrust began to appear impotent.

This conversion was also eased by the fact that the tough approach, with the heavy costs it entails, was always potentially at odds with the government's overall concern to limit public expenditure. As early as 1983 the Home Office indicated its commitment to applying the Financial Management Initiative to the criminal justice system, with the issuing of Circular 114 to police forces, and a package of changes aimed at improving management information and control of resources within the prison system. In recent years bargaining over pay and expenditure within all criminal justice agencies has become ever more volatile and conflict-ridden. During 1989 there were clear signs, for example, that the police militancy of the late 1970s which had culminated in the Edmund-Davies inquiry and pay settlement, was about to return. The Police Federation Annual Conference condemned the trend towards policing 'for profit, not people', while in November it declared 'out and out war' with the government over a dispute concerning rent allowances. An article in its magazine *Police* announced: 'this law and order government's honeymoon with the police is over'.

However, the movement towards privatisation and voluntarism in criminal justice is more than just a parochial one based on the shifting political exigencies of Thatcherism. They are in fact international phenomena of long-standing, with deeper structural sources (Spitzer and Scull, 1977; Scull, 1977; Shearing and Stenning, 1983, 1987; Cohen, 1985; Rosenbaum, 1986; Skolnick and Bayley, 1986; South, 1988; Shapland and Vagg, 1988; Matthews, 1988; Robinson, 1988; Nelken, 1989). Two leading North American authorities on private policing have suggested that 'what we are witnessing . . . is not merely a reshuffling of responsibility . . . but the emergence of privately defined orders . . . that are in some cases inconsistent with, or even in conflict with, the public order proclaimed by the state' (Shearing and Stenning, 1987, pp. 13–14). An alternative interpretation, in line with the implications of Foucault's influential work, sees the apparent hiving-off of state control as more effectively spreading discipline throughout the social order (Foucault, 1977; Cohen, 1979).

In the British context there are certainly indications that in many stances citizen involvement is essentially a means of co-optation into the agendas and perspectives of official state agencies. Prime examples are neighbourhood watch, police-community consultation, and lay-visiting to police stations (Donnison *et al.*, 1986; Morgan, 1989; Kemp and Morgan, 1989).

Moreover, the process of apparently devolving responsibility from official agencies to citizens has proceeded alongside an apparent counter-trend towards increasing central control within the criminal justice system itself. In policing, for example, several commentators have underlined the trend towards *de facto* nationalisation (Reiner, 1989; Dorn *et al.*, in this volume), while there has been explicit floating of various schemes for enhancing efficiency through greater centralisation or the formation of national units (such as Sir Peter Imbert's plan for a British equivalent of the FBI). There is also much greater official concern to assess and plan criminal justice *as a system*. In the words of the Home Office: 'the criminal justice system needs to operate as a whole, with a coherent and systematic approach' (*Tackling Crime*, p. 70). This concern for centralisation and coordination has a similar root to privatisation, namely the control of resources. It is also a response to the perceived internationalisation of serious crime and order problems, especially with the growth of European integration, and has parallels in other countries (Anderson, 1989).

The 1990s are likely to be characterised by a continuation of these profound and complex changes in the criminal justice sytsem. On the one hand there is the developing theme of privatisation, voluntarisation and partnership with the public which is at the forefront of government rhetoric. This signals a recognition of the need to go 'beyond law and order'. On the other hand, the strength and power of the official system continues to be enhanced, and to become even more tightly controlled from the centre. To the extent this is explicitly acknowledged it is justified by the need to secure value for money through effective managerial and financial accountability, and to ensure a coordinated response to national and international problems and pressures.

In these contradictory trends the criminal justice system is no different from a number of other spheres of social policy. In education, for example, the 1988 Reform Act stipulates both a

National Curriculum and local management. In the health service, community care and attempts to impose greater autonomy on general practitioners and hospitals runs in parallel with attempts to enhance the control of what doctors prescribe, mainly for cost-cutting reasons. In local government itself, 'accountability' is harnessed to an unprecedented package of restrictions on what councils can be accountable for. In managing the labour market, the trend is towards encouraging 'enterprise' and imposing centrally determined standards for vocational training. The hallmark of the Conservative government is a profound contradiction between central direction and public engagement.

At the same time public confidence in the system of justice seems to be plummeting, according to the evidence of opinion polls. The last year of the 1980s was a vintage one for scandals, with the major *cause célèbre*, the Guildford Four, casting doubt on the legitimacy of all parts of the criminal justice process. Opinion poll evidence also charts the growing public awareness of the system's limited capacity to protect them from criminal victimisation.

While the present line of government policy is much more sophisticated and realistic than its original simplistic 'law and order' approach, it remains limited by a fundamental flaw. 'Society (a.k.a. the 'community') has come back in as a potential partner of the formal system in controlling crime. But it does not feature in any significant way in the picture presented of the causes of crime. Crime and disorder are seen primarily as products of opportunities for almost random or spontaneous acts. There is no hint of any acceptance of a relationship between other areas of government policy and rising crime. On the contrary, comments on crime causation by government spokespersons go out of their way to deny such a relationship (see, for example, John Patten's 'Crime: A Middle Class Disease?', *New Society*, 13 May 1988, pp. 12–13). Yet the bulk of research on the issue suggests clear empirical support for the plausible links between growing unemployment and economic inequality (which have resulted from Conservative economic and social policy) and rising levels of crime and disorder (Farrington *et al.*, 1986, Box, 1987. But cf. Carr-Hill, 1989). The bracketing-off of crime control from social and economic policy, which still features in the Conservative approach, despite its seductive overtures to the 'community', remains the Achille's heel of the current strategy.

Bad times for crime tend to be good times for the criminal justice professions, and similarly for criminological research (as Marx anticipated in his ironic remarks on the 'productivity' of the criminal, 'the criminal produces not only crimes but . . . the professor who gives lectures on criminal law': Marx, 1964, p. 375). The late 1960s and early 70s had been a time of enormous intellectual effervescence and excitement in criminology, as 'new' criminologists of a variety of ideological and methodological hues attacked the orthodoxy of empiricist, policy-oriented 'correctional' research on the causes of crime (Cohen, 1981; Rock, 1988). However, the cost of this was that the phase which was dominated by what Jock Young has subsequently characterised as 'left idealism' (Young, 1986) produced little by way of research or understanding of the concrete phenomena of crime and control institutions.

This changed profoundly in the 1980s. Opportunities for criminological research expanded, as criminal justice agencies especially the police) became fearful for their legitimacy and opened their doors more to outside researchers as well as expanding their own research activities. Funding for criminological research became a priority within the shrinking budget for social science research. The Economic and Social Research Council has financed three major initiatives in this field during the 1980s: on crowd behaviour (cf. Gaskell and Benewick, 1987), Crime and the Criminal Justice System (cf. Downes, 1990), and on the Police and Criminal Evidence Act (cf. McKenzie, Morgan and Reiner, 1990, and Dixon *et al.*, 1990, for examples). The Home Office has funded more research of its own and from outsiders. New independent research institutions have been established, such as the Police Foundation (Weatheritt, 1989; Morgan and Smith, 1989), and existing ones have expanded their support in this area.

Much of this work has been narrowly focused on policy-oriented questions, and has not advanced understanding (let alone critique) very far. (It has been what Jock Young somewhat pejoratively labels 'administrative criminology': Young, 1986). But the best of this efflorescence of research has not only advanced knowledge but also reform. The celebrated study of the Metropolitan Police by the Policy Studies Institute, for example, is a striking demonstration of how officially sponsored research can produce important and valuable results (Smith *et al.*, 1983). The various volumes of work by the Home Office Research and Planning Unit also testify to the crudity of assuming that official work will lack wider value (for example, Heal, Tarling and Burrows, 1985; Hope and Shaw, 1988). However, while empirical research has flourished, theorising – the attempt to integrate the fruits of this research with wider perspectives and develop a coherent framework of understanding – has atrophied. The only theoretical development which has stimulated widespread debate is 'new left realism', which is essentially a rationale for the trend towards policy-oriented research. (Lea and Young, 1984; Kinsey, Lea and Young, 1986; Matthews and Young, 1986; *Contemporary Crises*, 1988, vol. 2; Young, 1988, are examples of 'realism'. Critical discussions from different perspectives include Scraton, 1987, and Stenson and Brearley in this volume). What is clear is the shift in focus of criminological work from the largely theoretical and programmatic work of the 1970s to a predominance of more empirical and policy-focused research. This has been associated with a shift in the political stance of radical criminology as well, with a tendency for a reformist position to replace undiluted negative critique of the working of criminal (in)justice institutions (Kettle, 1984, 1985).

These trends in crime, criminal justice and criminology during the 1980s are all reflected and analysed by the chapters in this volume. They are a selection of papers which were originally delivered at the British Sociological Association Annual Conference, held at Plymouth Polytechnic on 20–23 March 1989, with the overall theme 'Sociology in Action'. The conference was organised by a committee which included Malcolm Cross and arranged in a number of streams intended to demonstrate the relevance of current sociological research for policy debate in a variety of areas. These papers result from the criminal justice stream, which was convened by Robert Reiner.

The papers between them offer research results and policy analysis which illuminate the current developments in crime and criminology that have been outlined above. Half the papers address the police and policing issues in the broadest sense. This reflects the increasing emphasis there has been on policing research in the 1980s, as the police institution and policing have been pushed into the centre of policy debate and public concern about 'law and order' and the criminal justice system (Reiner, 1985, 1989; Morgan and Smith, 1989).

Johnston (Chapter 1) and Rawlings (Chapter 2) describe and analyse the 'creeping privatisation' of the policing function, which has become the central current concern of police organisations. Johnston argues that we are witnessing a profound alteration, 'a renegotiation of the public/private mix' and the emergence of a 'new policing'. He offers a theoretical analysis of the sources of this process and its consequences for understanding of the state, citizenship and social justice. Rawlings gives a wide-ranging overview of the shifting trajectory of the Conservatives' policy on policing, charting the disenchantment with the apparent failure of the original gung-ho 'war against crime', and the subsequent embrace of the view that, in Mrs Thatcher's words 'combating crime is everybody's business . . . it cannot be left solely to the police'.

As policing entered the centre of the political stage, chief constables became prominent and controversial public figures. In Chapter 3 Robert Reiner presents a social portrait of this hitherto neglected but increasingly important power elite. Their emergence as a coordinated and coherent national elite, with distinctive sociological characteristics, is examined on the basis of an empirical study of contemporary chief constables.

A major influence on the development of policing in Britain has been the experience of attempting to control the bitter strife in Northern Ireland (Hillyard, 1981; Hillyard and Percy-Smith, 1988, ch. 7). Magee's Chapter 4 is derived from an innovative study of *routine* policing in Northern Ireland, involving observational fieldwork with the Royal Ulster Constabulary. She describes the development of the present policing predicament facing the RUC, and demonstrates the tensions which arise from a dual role of paramilitary and routine policing. This has important implications for the contradictory mainland trends towards both more militaristic and more community-oriented policing.

One of the key sources of the current discussions about the reorganisation of police forces into a more centrally coordinated or national pattern has been anxiety about the growth of professional international crime, especially involving drugs. Chapter 5 by Dorn, Murji and South is the result of extensive research into drug markets and their control. It offers an analysis and critique of recent debates about police reorganisation, and their roots in misconceptions and moral panics about the trade in drugs.

An important advance in recent years has been the recognition that the concept of policing covers a much wider range of social agencies and processes than the police themselves. Dee Cook in Chapter 6 reports comparative study of the enforcement policies of the Inland Revenue in relation to tax evasion, and the Department of Social Security concerning benefit fraud. Her research clearly demonstrates the proverbial 'one law for the rich and another for the poor' which Conservative policy has accentuated. This is important not only for issues of social justice, but because it fractures the 'community' which the government is purporting to draw into crime prevention.

The trend towards voluntarisation has been manifest in a number of fields of criminal justice policy. In Chapter 7 based on a study of the role of the voluntary sector in various parts of the system, Mawby charts the development of community involvement, and distinguishes a variety of forms of it. The main focus of the Chapter is on the contrasting social characteristics of three groups of volunteers: special constables, probation volunteers, and victim support. The research underlines the need to break up the protean word 'community' and recognise the crucial differences between types of volunteer and their involvement in the formal system.

Tougher sentences were a core part of the original 'law and order' package, and despite the more recent attempts to develop the variety of 'punishment in the community', the prison system will remain central. As with other parts of the public sector, the government has attempted to bring it in line with the general pursuit of the 3 E's, 'economy, efficiency and effectiveness'. The vehicle for this was the 1987 package of management and work system changes, called 'Fresh Start', which amounts to the most comprehensive administrative reorganisation of prisons within the last century. King and McDermott's study of its impact (Chapter 8) suggests that it has not yet accomplished its objectives, and indeed in some respects has been counter-productive. Their sober evaluaton has important implications for all aspects of the criminal justice system, where similar innovations have been attempted.

The new emphasis on 'punishment in the community' signalled by the 1988 Green Paper *Punishment, Custody and the Community* places the probation service in a central role. However, it also implies a shift towards the overt control aspects of the probation function, away from its traditional social work ethos. Tim May, in Chapter 9, gives a comprehensive analysis of the beleaguered condition of the probation service in an era where the stress has been on punishment rather than rehabilitation. It provides a useful overview of the changing role and ideology of the service as the politics of penological discourse have changed.

Recent developments (including the Green Paper) also involve a growth in inter-agency working, and collaboration between state and voluntary or private agencies in the field of probation and the handling of offenders. In Chapter 10 Kate Lyon discusses these trends in relation to juvenile justice. It is based on a case-study of one alternative-to-custody scheme for serious young offenders, and shows the problems of collaboration between statutory and voluntary services.

One of the central planks of government policy has become the emphasis on *prevention* of crime, and the role of victims and the public at large as potential victims, in accomplishing this. Chapter 11 is Sandra Walklate's theoretical critique of the ideological assumptions about victims and crime causation which underlie government strategy and the rhetoric of community crime prevention. She is also critical of the work of the 'left realists' in this area, which mirrors some of the government's confusions. One of the points emphasised is the folly of separating crime control from social and economic policy, which the government does in its attempts to deny any link between unemployment, social divisions and crime.

'Left realism' has been the only attempt to develop a theoretical framework for crime control policy. Stenson and Brearley in Chapter 12 offer a constructive critique of the left realist approach, and a sympathetic analysis of its development. They argue that its origins in a set of reactions to the 'new right' and concrete policy issues has resulted in eclecticism, inconsistency and incompleteness. They suggest that a potentially fruitful theoretical foundation would be a radical reading of the work of Durkheim. In particular this would recognise the importance of the process of 'moral education' for policies concerned with crime prevention and control, but without embracing the reactionary backlash of Conservative policy. This points to the important yet neglected agenda of how moral cultures which do not encourage crime and disorder, but which are not simply repressive, can develop.

The chapters in this volume demonstrate that there has been on all sides a movement away from blunt partisan conflict and unproductive rhetoric about 'law and order'. However, central questions remain unresolved, notably the connection between criminal justice and wider social and economic matters. Profound changes are occurring, not only in Britain but elsewhere, in relations between the state, formal criminal justice organisations, and groups in the community. The studies reported here do indicate that criminological and more general sociological research have much to offer in understanding and resolving future policy developments. The government is attempting to move beyond its original 'law and order' approach, which it has come to accept as simplistic. (Criminologists might be forgiven for muttering a collective 'told you so'!). But its rediscovery of the social in the guise of the 'community' remains partial and contradictory. The essays in this book should help chart the way 'beyond law and order'.

REFERENCES

ANDERSON, M. (1989) *Policing the World*, Oxford: Oxford University Press.

BOTTOMS, A., MAWBY, R. and WALKER, M. (1987) 'A Localised Crime Survey in Contrasting Areas of a City', *British Journal of Criminology*, 27.

BOTTOMS, A., MAWBY, R. I. and XANTHOS, P. (1989) 'A Tale of Two Estates', in D. Downes (ed.), *Crime and the City*, London: Macmillan.

BOX, S. (1981) *Deviance, Reality and Society*, London: Holt, Rinehart & Winston.

BOX, S. (1987) *Crime, Recession and Unemployment*, London: Macmillan.

BRAKE, M. and HALE, C. (1989) 'Law and Order', in P. Brown and R. Sparks (eds), *Beyond Thatcherism*, Milton Keynes: Open University Press.

CARR-HILL, R. (1989) Review of S. Box 'Recession, Crime and Unemployment', *British Journal of Criminology*, 29, 2, pp. 186–8.

CLARKE, R. and HOUGH, M. (eds) (1980) *The Effectiveness of Policing*, Farnborough: Gower.

CLARKE, R. and MAYHEW, P. (eds) (1980) *Designing Out Crime*, London: HMSO.

CLARKE, A. and TAYLOR, I. (1980) 'Vandals, Pickets and Muggers', *Screen Education*, 36.

COHEN, S. (1979) 'The Punitive City', *Contemporary Crises*, 3, 4.

COHEN, S. (1981) 'Footprints in the Sand: A Further Report on Criminology and the Sociology of Deviance in Britain', in M. Fitzgerald, G. McLennan and J. Pawson (eds), *Crime and Society*, London: Routledge.

COHEN, S. (1985) *Visions of Social Control*, Cambridge: Polity.

DIXON, D., BOTTOMLEY, K., COLEMAN, C., GILL, M., and WALL, D. (1990) 'Safeguarding the Rights of Suspects in Police Custody', *Policing and Society*, 1, 2, pp. 115–41.

DONNISON, H., SCOLA, J. and THOMAS, P. (1986) *Neighbourhood Watch*, London: Libertarian Research and Education Trust.

DOWNES, D. (1983) *Law and Order: Theft of An Issue*, London: Fabian Society/Labour Campaign for Criminal Justice.

DOWNES, D. (ed.) (1991) *Crime and Criminal Justice*, London: Macmillan, (forthcoming).

FARRINGTON, D. and DOWDS, E. A. (1985) 'Distentangling Criminal Behaviour and Police Reaction', in D. Farrington and J. Gunn (eds), *Reactions to Crime*, Chichester: Wiley.

FARRINGTON, D., GALLAGHER, B., MORLEY, L., ST. LEDGER, T. J. and WEST, D. J. (1986) 'Unemployment, School-Leaving and Crime', *British Journal of Criminology*, 26, 4.

FOUCAULT, M. (1977) *Discipline and Punish*, London: Allen Lane.

GASKELL, G. and BENEWICK, R. (eds) (1987) *The Crowd in Contemporary Britain*, London: Sage.

HALL, S., CRITCHER, C., JEFFERSON, T., CLARKE, J. and ROBERTS, B. (1978) *Policing the Crisis*, London: Macmillan.

HEAL, K., TARLING, R. and BURROWS, J. (eds) (1985) *Policing Today*, London: HMSO.

HILLYARD, P. (1981) 'From Belfast to Britain', *Politics and Power 4: Law, Politics and Justice*, London: Routledge.

HILLYARD, P. and PERCY-SMITH, J. (1988) *The Coercive State*, London: Fontana.

HOPE, T. and SHAW, M. (eds) (1988) *Communities and Crime Reduction*, London: HMSO.

HOUGH, M. and MAYHEW, P. (1983) *The British Crime Survey*, London: HMSO.

HOUGH, M. and MAYHEW, P. (1985) *Taking Account of Crime*, London: HMSO.

JONES, T., MACLEAN, B. and YOUNG, J. (1986) *The Islington Crime Survey*, London: Gower.

KEMP, C. and MORGAN, R. (1989) *Behind the Front Counter: Lay Visitors to Police Stations*, Bristol University Law Faculty: Centre for Criminal Justice.

KETTLE, M. (1980) 'The Politics of Policing and the Policing of Politics', in P. Hain (ed.), *Policing the Police 2*, London: Calder.

KETTLE, M. (1984) 'The Police and the Left', *New Society*, 6 December.

KETTLE, M. (1985) 'The Left and the Police', *Policing*, 1, 3.

KINSEY, R. (1985) *Merseyside Crime and Police Surveys*, University of Edinburgh: Centre of Criminology.

KINSEY, R., LEA, J. and YOUNG, J. (1986) *Losing the Fight Against Crime*, Oxford: Blackwell.

LEA, J. and YOUNG, J. (1984) *What Is To Be Done About Law and Order?*, Harmondsworth: Penguin.

McKENZIE, I., MORGAN, R. and REINER, R. (1990) Helping the Police With Their Enquiries: The Necessity Principle and Voluntary Attendance At The Police Station', *Criminal Law Review*, January.

MARX, K. (1964) *Theories of Surplus Value*, London: Lawrence & Wishart.

MATTHEWS, R. (ed.) (1988) *Informal Justice*, London: Sage.

MATTHEWS, R. and YOUNG, J. (eds) (1986) *Confronting Crime*, London: Sage.
MAYHEW, P., ELLIOTT, D. and DOWDS, L. (1989) *The 1988 British Crime Survey*, London: HMSO.
MORGAN, R. (1989) ' "Policing By Consent": Legitimating the Doctrine', in R. Morgan and D. Smith (eds), *Coming to Terms With Policing*, London: Routledge.
MORGAN, R. and SMITH, D. (eds) (1989) *Coming To Terms With Policing*, London: Routledge.
NELKEN, D. (ed.) (1989) 'Criminal Justice At The Margins', Special issue of *The Howard Journal of Criminal Justice*, 28, 4.
PEARSON, G. (1983) *Hooligan*, London: Macmillan.
PHIPPS, A. (1986) 'Radical Criminology and Criminal Victimisation', in R. Matthews and J. Young (eds), *Confronting Crime*, London: Sage.
REINER, R. (1980) 'Fuzzy Thoughts: The Police and Law and Order Politics', *Sociological Review*, 28, 2.
REINER, R. (1982) 'Bobbies Take The Lobby Beat', *New Society*, 25 March.
REINER, R. (1985) *The Politics of the Police*, Brighton: Wheatsheaf.
REINER, R. (1986) 'Policing, Order and Legitimacy in Britain', in S. Spitzer and A. Scull (eds), *Research in Law, Deviance and Social Control*, Greenwich, Connecticut: JAI.
REINER, R. (1989) 'Where the Buck Stops: Chief Constables' Views On Police Accountability', in R. Morgan and D. Smith (eds), *Coming To Terms With Policing*, London: Routledge.
REINER, R. (1990a) 'Crime and Policing', in S. MacGregor and B. Pimlott (eds), *Tackling The Inner Cities*, Oxford: Oxford University Press.
REINER, R. (1990b) 'Policing and Public Order in 1989', in P. Catterall (ed.), *Contemporary Britain: An Annual Review*, Oxford: Blackwell/Institute of Contemporary British History.
ROBINSON, C. D. (ed.) (1988) 'Dynamics of the Informal Economy', Special Issue of *Social Justice*, 15, 3–4.
ROCK, P. (ed.) (1988) *A History of British Criminology*, Oxford: Oxford University Press.
ROSENBAUM, D. P. (ed.) (1986) *Community Crime Prevention: Does It Work?'*, Beverly Hills: Sage.
SCRATON, P. (ed.) (1987) *Law, Order and the Authoritarian State*, Milton Keynes: Open University Press.
SCULL, A. (1977) *Decarceration*, Englewood Cliffs, New Jersey: Prentice Hall (2nd edn, Cambridge: Polity Press, 1984).
SHAPLAND, J. and VAGG, J. (1988) *Policing By The Public*, London: Routledge.
SHEARING, C. and STENNING, P. (1983) 'Private Security: Implications For Social Control', *Social Problems*, 30, 5.
SHEARING, C. and STENNING, P. (eds) (1987) *Private Policing*, Beverly Hills: Sage.
SKOLNICK, J. and BAYLEY, D. (1986) *The New Blue Line*, New York: Free Press.
SMITH, D. *et al.* (1983) *Police and People in London*, London: Policy Studies Institute.

SOUTH, N. (1988) *Policing for Profit*, London: Sage.
SPITZER, S. and SCULL, A. (1977) 'Privatisation and Social Control', *Social Problems*, 25.
SUMNER, C. (1981) 'Race, Crime and Hegemony', *Contemporary Crises*, 5.
TAYLOR, I. (1980) 'The Law and Order Issue in the British General Election and Canadian Federal Election of 1979', *Canadian Journal of Sociology*, 5, 3.
TAYLOR, I. (1981) *Law and Order: Arguments For Socialism*, London: Macmillan.
TAYLOR, I. (1987) 'Law and Order, Moral Order: The Changing Rhetorics of the Thatcher Government', *Socialist Register 1987*, London: Merlin.
WADDINGTON, P. A. J. (1986) 'Mugging As A Moral Panic', *British Journal of Sociology*.
WEATHERITT, M. (ed.) (1989) *Police Research: Some Future Directions*, Aldershot: Gower.
YOUNG, J. (1986) 'The Failure of Criminology: The Need For A Radical Realism', in R. Mathews and J. Young (eds), *Confronting Crime*, London: Sage.
YOUNG, J. (1988) 'Radical Criminology in Britain', in P. Rock (ed.) *A History of British Criminology*, Oxford: Oxford University Press.

1 Privatisation and the Police Function: From 'New Police' to 'New Policing'

Les Johnston

INTRODUCTION

In the past, debate on policing has been preoccupied with two issues. First, there has been prolonged discussion about whether the police function should be defined in terms of law enforcement (Kinsey *et al.*, 1986), social service functions (Punch and Naylor, 1973), or order maintenance (Wilson, 1968; Reiner, 1985). Second, there has been debate about the form which that function, however defined, should take: whether police intervention should be maximal/pro-active (Alderson, 1979) or minimal/reactive (Kinsey *et al.*, 1986). Despite the sophistication of some of this work, consequent debate has tended to remain polarised between what are, ultimately, rather crude models of policing. The police are seen either as a reactive force (the so-called 'fire-brigade' model), or as a pro-active service (the community policing model), or as some, usually pathological, combination of the two (Gordon, 1984).

Whether intentionally or not, this debate allows it to be assumed that analysis of the form and function of policing is encompassed by an analysis of the public police. What this fails to take into account is the extent to which policing is a social function which can be carried out by private, as well as public agents. It follows that policing should be defined in terms of its practices rather than in terms of its personnel (Cain, 1979).

Historically speaking, there is good reason to argue that public policing (the 'new police'), when it emerged, was itself 'out of step with the historical lineage of policing forms' (South, 1987, p. 72). In the century prior to the establishment of the new police, that lineage involved a complex of voluntary activity, including associations for the prosecution of felons, private patrols, armed guards, thieftakers and various quasi-military associations (see South, 1987; Rudé, 1985; Shubert, 1981). The existence of private policing in the twentieth century is, therefore, hardly novel.

In the course of this chapter I shall argue that the boundaries between public and private responsibility for law enforcement, crime control and order maintenance are, again, being redrawn. In effect, we are witnessing a renegotiation of the public/private mix and the consequent emergence of a 'new policing'. The chapter is divided into three sections. Section One examines privatisation in the context of formal policing organisations. Section Two considers private initiatives carried out by groups of citizens, either with or without police approval. Section Three outlines some of the theoretical issues and policy considerations such developments signify.

PRIVATISATION AND POLICING ORGANISATIONS

Privatisation, as Le Grand and Robinson (1984) remind us, is more than merely the replacement of the state by the market. State involvement can take the form of provision, subsidy or regulation of a service and, in principle, privatisation can involve a reduction in one or more of these. In practice, things are rather more complicated: a reduction in state provision might, for instance, be combined with maintenance of, or even increase in state regulation. (An example would be the various 'state subsidized and state-regulated . . profit-making half way houses, diversion programs and . . prisons' in the USA: Marx, 1987, p. 188.) Furthermore, privatisation can be effected through various types of non-state body: private companies, private individuals, charities, voluntary bodies, consumers' groups and so on. In short, it can take a variety of forms and its characteristics are by no means self-evident.

Currently, in the policing context, privatisation is likely to occur in several ways. One of the most obvious involves public police agencies either hiring out personnel, or charging for the provision of services. At present, the Post Office Investigations Department is seeking approval from the Department of Trade and Industry to establish a security firm, which will hire out its services to private clients. The head of POID, an ex-Metropolitan Police commander, has stated 'we are trying to Bupa-ise the police. We will be doing what the police can or will not do because of their limited resources' (*Observer*, 21 August 1988). Such developments raise serious legal and ethical questions – in this case, about personnel having access to criminal records whilst working on behalf of private interests.

Ethical questions also arise about charging for police services. Some police forces have introduced charges for certain burglar alarm services. Though this might be said to amount to a reduction in public subsidy for a service, police authorities already have a right under Sec. 15(1) of the 1964 Police Act to charge for 'special service'. Although the Act does not define a 'special service', typically, charges are made for police presence at sports fixtures and similar events. Debate arising from a recent legal case (Harris v Sheffield United), coupled with the fact that nothing in the Act precludes events such as political meetings being defined as 'special', has opened up the issue of whether, and in what circumstances, charges are appropriate. So far, legal judgement has applied the principle of 'public benefit' to cases, though, in practice, charges seem to be applied on an *ad hoc* basis by police authorities, and in any case public and private domains (and their respective benefits) are increasingly difficult to disentangle (Weatherill, 1988).

Another form of privatisation involves attempts to 'hive off' those sectors of the police service which have commercial potential. Recently the Home Office appointed County Natwest, a merchant bank, to study the prospects for running the Police National Computer, the Directorate of Telecommunications and the Forensic Science Service, as business agencies under a chief executive, within the civil service. Certainly, privatisation of either the national computer or the forensic services would raise major concerns about public accountability, impartiality and confidentiality.

However, the issue has to be seen in broader terms than the mere 'hiring out', 'charging for' or 'hiving off' of services. For one thing, privatisation of police services has to be located in the context of privatisations occurring in other parts of the criminal justice system. The idea of using civilian gaolers, for instance, is part of a broader strategy of 'civilianisation' of certain police posts – itself a form of de-regulation, in so far as it removes some of the restrictions which, in the past, prevented civilians from doing police work. It is also intended to alleviate the drain on police personnel arising from the increased use of police cells for remand prisoners. And at the same time, of course, the government is pledged to introduce an element of privatisation into the building and management of new remand centres.

This example illustrates that privatisation has to be seen as a totality within the criminal justice system. Moreover, the Green Paper outlining the remand proposals (Home Office, 1988b) carries important messages for the police service. The document insists that there is no matter of principle at stake over the privatisation of remand, because contracting out is a well-established feature of Home Office operations. Significantly, the example given to justify this view is the use of private security companies at residential training establishments, and at the Harmondsworth Immigration Detention Centre. As the services which the industry provides in these establishments are, however, fundamentally, police services, one can only assume that there will be no issues of principle at stake, were any future discussion of the privatisation of police services to occur.

The role of the private security sector confirms that privatisation should be viewed as a totality, the industry having not only a police role, but a growing influence on penal policy. Private security companies are prominent in two of the major consortia bidding for contracts to build and manage remand prisons and there is a powerful elite within penal policy-making, sympathetic to the industry. (The chairman of the Commons Home Affairs Committee is John Wheeler, Director General of the British Security Industries Association. The previous chairman was Sir Edward Gardner, who is now heading Contract Prisons plc. Group 4 and Racal-Chubb are also prominent in the consortia bidding for private prison contracts.) In view of this, it is not surprising that 'Punishment, Custody and the Community' gives a role to the industry in proposals for house arrest and electronic tagging, a role which might, in due course, expand:

> Private sector security organisations may be able to play a part in some aspects of the new arrangements, e.g. by monitoring curfews, but it would be difficult for them *yet* to take on the wide-ranging responsibilities involved in supervising offenders throughout the country. (Home Office, 1988a, p. 17, emphasis added)

And if we take into account recent suggestions that community-based alternatives to custody might be reorganised on free market lines, it is possible to envisage a space opening up which would permit much greater private sector involvement.

In a policing context, concern has also been expressed about the emergence of private patrols in residential streets, schools, and town centres. A recent survey suggests that there may be as many as 1000 of these throughout the country. Some are carried out by municipal employees and groups of concerned civilians, but the vast majority are undertaken by private security companies (Boothroyd, 1989). Controversy also arose when in January 1989 Sealink announced that it was dispensing with the service of 100 British Transport Police officers at eight large ports and replacing them with a mixture of private security personnel, local police and special constables from whom, it believed, it would get better service. Significantly, John Wheeler has suggested that any private sector challenge to the British Transport Police's monopoly arising out of a future British Rail privatisation, 'is something that should be looked at' (*The Independent, 21 February 1989*).

Alan Eastwood, Chairman of the Police Federation, has referred to examples of this sort as 'straws in the wind'. Some indication of which way that wind is blowing might be gained from a brief consideration of the American experience. Here the degree of private security penetration of policing is considerable, and 'moonlighting' – the employment of off-duty public police officers by private security companies, or by other private and quasi-public bodies – is commonplace. Estimates suggest that 20–30 per cent of public police officers are engaged in off-duty employment (usually in uniform); something which raises serious conflicts of interest (Reiss, 1988). In this respect, the Hallcrest Report notes that 'some police officer-run security firms had their best business volume in their own precinct or district' (Cunningham and Taylor, 1985, p. 205).

Contracting out of services is also relatively advanced in the USA, where the industry is already involved in duties such as parking enforcement and traffic control, and is expanding into prisoner transfer, court security, non-injury accident investigation, special events policing, prison security and crime prevention services. In some cases, communities have contracted privately for total police protection (Cunningham and Taylor, 1985, p. 186; Meadows, 1984, p. 58).

Links between public and private sectors are well established in many cities. In New York City, the Police Department has made an arrangement with security officers in a city store enabling them to provide surveillance, make arrests, transport suspects to holding facilities, make record checks and enter criminal history information (Stewart, 1985). Increasingly, private personnel are granted Special Police Officer status. Such schemes exist in Baltimore, New York and California and require the completion of a rudimentary training programme. But, again, ethical problems arise when private citizens have public powers and access to public records. Significantly, in the Hallcrest study, 65 per cent of responding organisations had access to conviction records on at least a monthly basis, the FBI accepting fingerprint applications from non-criminal justice agencies at a charge of $12 per card (Cunningham and Taylor, 1985, ch. 4).

American examples confirm that the private sector has expanded, but what is the extent of that expansion and how is the industry structured? Estimates of the size of the industry are notoriously unreliable. For one thing, categories used for determining who should be defined as an employee of private security vary between countries. For another, estimates of expenditure vary dramatically according to which set of figures one selects. For this reason one British commentator concludes that 'it is extremely difficult (if not currently impossible) to give any guaranteed accurate estimate or assessment of the size of . . . the private security sector' (South, 1988, p. 25: see also Shearing and Stenning, 1981, pp. 198–9).

Having said that, such figures as there are, confirm a rapid expansion during the last decade. This has been especially striking in North America where some estimates suggest a 2:1 ratio of private to public personnel and where, as Hallcrest indicates, the $21 billion spent on private security exceeds the combined totals for local, state and federal agencies (Cunnigham and Taylor, 1985, ch. 1).

Some writers see 'fiscal crisis' as the key factor in this expansion, escalating demand and dwindling resources, giving rise to what Stewart calls 'a critical gap . . between the police service and the public's perception of need'. In a situation where police forces are concerned with 'demand shedding', 'prioritisation', 'screening' and the like, it is suggested that private security fills a vacuum: 'When demand drives the available service into scarcity, the market begins to look for substitution of alternative, less expensive services' (Stewart, 1985, p. 759).

Certainly, fiscal crisis has had an impact on growth, though other writers would emphasise the need to locate the development of private security in the context of historical changes in the structure of property ownership and social control (Shearing and Stenning, 1981; Spitzer and Scull, 1977). Equally, it is important to look at the structural properties of the industry itself. First and foremost, it is multinational, concentrated and centralised. Canadian private security, for example, has been said to have a 'branch plant' character, a large proportion of the contract security industry being controlled by foreign-based (mainly US) companies (Shearing and Stenning, 1981). In Britain the market is dominated by a small number of major international companies. Taking figures for 1985 (Jordan & Sons, 1987), the largest companies in terms of market share are Chubb (25 per cent); Securicor, a British company with up to 30 per cent of its personnel employed abroad (15.5 per cent); and Group 4, a Swedish company (7.5 per cent). These three companies dominate different sectors of the market – Chubb (locks and safes); Securicor (transport); Group 4 (guards and patrol) – despite increasing tendencies towards diversification. Though, in a very competitive marketplace, some new firms are expanding rapidly, much of the remainder of the British industry is specialised and localised, employing small numbers of personnel. In the late 1970s, for example, 84 per cent of those working in the private security sector were employed by just nine companies (Home Office, 1979).

In 1985, the size of the UK market stood at £581.5 million, representing an increase of 11.8 per cent on 1984 figures. Almost 50 per cent of that figure was taken up by intruder alarms, the fastest growing sector. It is important to emphasise that the market is a dynamic one where overall expansion is likely to continue, but where 'it is less easy to predict how individual components of the whole will fare' (South, 1988, p. 30). For example, contract security companies are already seeking to make themselves less despendent upon labour-intensive activities such as guarding and cash-in-transit services. In the long term it is likely that the electronics and telecommunications side of the industry will expand at the expense of the labour-intensive side, though the speed at which such tendencies might occur is uncertain.

One thing which has dominated discussion, in the light of these developments, is the question of how public police and private security organisations relate to one another. Hallcrest, in discussing the roles of private and public personnel, concludes that 'private security officers perform very few of the common activities of police officers' (Cunningham and Taylor, 1985, p. 91). This conclusion is intended as a rejoinder to the earlier Rand Report, which defined private security principally in terms of guard forces and contract guard services. In effect, Rand is seen as having placed undue attention on the crime detection and prevention aspects of the industry, ignoring its non-crime aspects: 'The major functions of private guards are to prevent, detect and report criminal acts on private property' (Kakalik and Wildhorn, 1972, p. 19). In Hallcrest's view, Rand then compounds that fault, by finding private personnel woefully inadequate with respect to the performance of these functions, and by calling for greater licensing and regulation.

Rand's definition of the private security role is certainly too narrow. In contrast, a number of authors have drawn attention to the preventative functions undertaken by the private sector, functions which have, until the recent past, been underdeveloped in public policing. Equally, however, there is wide agreement that prevention has different meanings in the public and private domains:

> While the preventative role of the public police is almost universally referred to in terms of 'crime prevention', private security typically refer to their preventative role as one of 'loss prevention', therby acknowledging that their principal concern is the protection of their clients' assets (Shearing and Stenning, 1981, p. 212; see also Cunningham and Taylor, 1985, pp. 90–1; South, 1988, pp. 44–53).

At the same time, of course, it has to be admitted that the private sector does not just prevent loss. It also protects clients and employees in public places (Reiss, 1987). At the New Jersey Bell Telephone Company in Newark, for example, a cordon of private security guards rings the building each night at 5.00pm. Guards stand at twenty-five-yard intervals for three blocks in order to provide safe passage for commuters wishing to reach railway stations (Tucker, 1985).

It would seem, then, that there is both overlap in, and demarcation between, the respective functions performed by public and private bodies. Public officers have a relative monopoly over tasks such as interrogation, whilst private security personnel enjoy similar control over locks and keys. In between, however, there is a continuum of activities, many of which cut across the public-private divide: alarm responses; escort duties; traffic control; control of access and movement. Alongside that grey area, there exists another, equally opaque one populated by quasi-public institutions (university, transport and public utility police forces). And the balance between public, quasi-public and private performance of these duties is, at present, subject both to constant change and to varying forms of interdependence (Marx, 1987).

This raises a question, of course, about the complementarity of these different bodies. The dominant (consensual) view sees private security as 'filling a vacuum' left by the shortfall of public policing. Despite the expansion of private security, however, relations between public and private sectors are, more often than not, based on mutual suspicion or avoidance. In the Hallcrest survey two-thirds of law enforcement managers reported that they did not even maintain a list of private security managers in their areas. And despite the constant interchange of personnel between the sectors, relations are still characterised by lack of mutual respect, poor communication and little cooperation. This reality sits uncomfortably alongside the image of the private sector as the 'junior member' in a cohesive public–private partnership geared to the maintenance of social order. Whether that partnership is conceived in bland 'social service' terms, or whether it is seen as the manifestation of an emerging 'disciplinary society', reality is likely to be more complex and variable.

PRIVATISATION, CITIZENSHIP AND SECURITY

Privatisation can also be brought about when private citizens take over some of the responsibility for public security. Clearly, such 'active citizenship' can range from purely individual acts of self-protection (such as installing locks in houses) to collective activities of different sorts. In this section I shall consider two types of collective activity, roughly differentiated according to their degree of autonomy from public police.

(a) 'Responsible' Citizenship and Community

The first form of activity can be located within a framework of 'community policing', where the object is to construct a partnership between police and public. Various modes of active citizenship are officially sanctioned as legitimate and responsible components of this strategy (such as membership of the Special Constabulary or participation in neighbourhood watch schemes).

Assessment of such community-based approaches can be aided by an examination of social change in localities and neighbourhoods. Consider one analysis of community initiatives in the control of crime (Clarke, 1987). Clarke maintains that community solutions do not manage crime, they simply serve to provide a sense of control within the community. Policing, he suggests, has passed through three stages. Prior to the development of the new police, communities managed crime themselves. Then the public police took over responsibility for crime control. Despite this police monopoly, however, a considerable degree of informal social control continued to be exercised within working-class communities. Indeed, the fact that only a small number of officers was required to manage the population, confirms the effectiveness of such informal mechanisms. Since 1939, however, this situation has changed in two ways. First, urban, working-class communities have been destroyed by redevelopment policies. Second, citizenship has expanded. People know their rights and make more and more demands for formal 'due process' to be exercised. The conjunction of these two processes has eliminated the basis for informal social control. As the structural preconditions of community policing are now no more, community initiatives can, at best, restore only a sense of control. The third stage results, therefore, in the elimination of informal mechanisms from crime control and culminates in the 'disintegration of the system which has managed social control for the past century' (Clarke, 1987, p. 396).

How valid is the argument that informal social control has been eradicated, and policing consequently transformed, by the twin impact of community disintegration and citizenship? It is interesting to compare Clarke's thesis with Shapland and Vagg's study of 'self-policing' in urban and rural localities, for it is their contention that 'members of the public . . . are themselves engaging in a great deal of "policing" work' (Shapland and Vagg, 1987, p. 54; see also Shapland and Vagg, 1988). In this study, a considerable amount of informal activity (watching, noticing, direct action) was seen to take place both in urban and rural localities. The authors, however, make two significant comments about the character of this activity. First, though 'remarkably prevalent' in both urban and rural localities, it was less evident in the former than in the later. This observation suggests that urban renewal may have a negative impact on informalism, as Clarke argues. Second, it is noted that people's problems, nuisances and crimes are highly localised: 'The precise manifestation of a particular problem . . . was very localised; to one street, or even part of a street' (Shapland and Vagg, 1987, p. 55). Informal responses were, therefore, themselves also highly localised.

Recognition of the continued existence of informal social control in urban locations suggests that Clarke's thesis needs to be qualified. Urban renewal had an impact on informal social control, but did not eradicate it. Indeed, according to some interpretations it may have privatised it, the construction of high-rise 'vertical streets' destroying certain forms of communal space. However, this version of privatisation can, itself, be pushed too far:

> There was only the privatised space of the family unit, stacked one on top of each other, in total isolation, juxtaposed with the totally public space which surrounded it, and which lacked any of the informal social controls generated by the neighbourhood. (Cohen, 1984, p. 114)

Cohen is suggesting here that the physical infrastructure of redevelopment reinforced the privatised world of social relations discovered by sociologists of the post-war period. But such a view can all too easily invoke a glorious past of communal working-class solidarity, where social order was enforced by some nebulous form of collective class consciousness. (For three different forms of critique of this view, see Cronin, 1984; Johnston, 1986; Pahl and Wallace, 1988). Neither the 'solidaristic' past, nor the 'privatised' present, allow for the complexity of urban social relations.

The point is that redevelopment is one of several variables (including environmental design, housing type and tenure, ethnic composition of the community, age structure, population density, quality of local political organisation, and so on) which will shape the particular character of informal social control in any locality. And there is likely to be considerable diversity in the ways in which, and the extent to which, such control is exercised in particular places.

This raises two problems. The first is for the police. If the character of informal social control is variable and localised, the street being 'too large a unit' for people to watch (Shapland and Vagg, 1987, p. 56), uniform policies of crime prevention, like neighbourhood watch (and the structures of consultation that exist alongside them – notably police consultative committees) are probably, more often than not, misdirected. What may be required are specific forms of police–public partnership tailored to the characteristics of informalism in local areas.

The second issue concerns how citizenship should be assessed. Clarke sees it as inimical to informalism because people stand on their rights and demand that the police exercise 'due process'. Citizenship may be a good thing, but it is negative in its effects, in so far as it is concerned with individual rights, to the exclusion of social values. It is, in effect, another manifestation of privatised social relations. According to this view, active citizenship would be inherently individualistic: bolting your doors, buying a dobermann, or peeking from behind the curtain at your fragment of the street. Whether or not one agrees with this assessment, Clarke raises an important question. Can citizenship have a social content? The second form of activity to be considered here would suggest an affirmative answer, though one which raises considerable controversy.

(b) Autonomous Civil Activity

Some reactions to crime, or to fear of crime, involve citizens in autonomous forms of 'self-policing': those which are undertaken, in the main, without the cooperation or involvement of public police organisations. Typical of such activities are the citizen street patrols, subway patrols and block watches which have emerged in the USA, some examples of which have begun to appear in Britain. (The most extreme examples in the UK are, of course, the Northern Ireland punishment squads: see Thomson, 1988.)

Early American research suggested that the desire for mobilisation in such groups was strongest among males, the young, the less well educated and blacks (Marx and Archer, 1973; Marx and Archer, 1976). But in Britain, the few groups which have come to light display a wide diversity of personnel and objectives. One of the most recently formed, in Grimethorpe, South Yorkshire, deploys between sixty and eighty volunteers, every night of the week, on all-night patrol of residential streets. Here, the main object is to deter property crimes. Other groups, however, have different functions. A group operated in North Mosely in order to respond to problems posed by the growing number of prostitutes and kerb-crawlers in the area. Its membership was middle class, consisting of professionals, housewives, and local business people, both white and Asian, and it patrolled on six nights a week to discourage prostitutes, pimps and their clients from frequenting the streets. In contrast, some street patrols have developed as self-defence organisations. Such a group appeared in Waltham Forest as an offshoot of the Pakistani Welfare Society, patrolling at weekends in groups of six or seven to check on the homes of those subjected to racial attack. One writer, commenting on these last two groups, says 'they are the police's natural constituency. They believe in law and order, have always supported the police, and only as a last resort have they taken to the streets' (Henshaw, 1986).

In some cases, however, groups have emerged which are not part of the police's natural constitutency. On Merseyside, for example, there have been cases of violent acts being directed at heroin-pushers under circumstances where police–community relations are, to say the least, strained. In a recent interview, a prominent member of Toxteth's black community remarked on the problem of heroin-dealing on the streets.

> They come here because they know there are less police and they are less likely to get done . . . we move them on, we take their money until they get fed up and move off . . . the community gives them a good hiding . . . Effectively, we police it ourselves. (*The Independent*, 15 October 1988)

Classic vigilantism of the sort found in the USA more than a century ago occurred where there was no developed criminal justice system. Today, the situation is different and modern vigilantist activity appears to emerge when two circumstances arise. First, communities believe that public tranquillity is under threat from escalating crime and disorder. Second, they believe that the criminal justice system is not dealing with the crisis: either because it is unable to do so (a case of 'infinite demand' coupled with 'finite resources'), or because it is unwilling to do so (due to organisational inefficiency or misplaced priorities).

In these circumstances there is often widespread support for such forms of active citizenship. In Marx and Archer's study of groups in the Boston area in the early 1970s, 55 per cent of the white population and 69 per cent of the black population supported the idea of citizen patrol. More recent American studies of the Guardian Angels confirm this level of support. In a study carried out in New York, 61 per cent of civilians (13 per cent of transit police; 12 per cent of New York Police Department officers) wished there were more Angels, and 67 per cent (27 per cent transit police; 28 per cent NYPD) believed their presence made the subways safer. Only 4 per cent of civilians (43 per cent transit police; 52 per cent NYPD) opposed their actions (Ostrowe and DiBiase, 1983). Another study found no clear evidence that Angels street patrols had any direct impact on crime levels (though the same could be said for police foot patrols: Clarke and Hough, 1984: Kelling, 1983). Nevertheless, over 60 per cent of respondents said that they felt safer as a result of patrols. Indeed, most police officers and city officials saw Angels patrols as beneficial and nearly half wanted them to continue (Pennell *et al.*, 1985).

The emergence of such groups in Britain raises two serious issues. The first concerns the relationship between participation and accountability. Twelve years ago, Laurie Taylor wrote an article in which he considered the prospects for, and the desirability of, vigilante activity in Britain (Taylor, 1976). In the context of the period (economic crisis, fear of 'ungovernability' and the panic about 'mugging'), Taylor's assessment of vigilantism is partly negative: it is uncontrolled, arbitrary in its effects, unaccountable to any authorised body; its members are inexperienced, unscreened, untrained and may risk breaking the law; and, in the political climates of 1976, it is likely to be hi-jacked by the forces of racism.

But, for all that, Taylor refuses to see vigilantism in entirely negative terms. After all, he asks, is not self-help likely to be the best response available to many people (especially the poor) when faced with crime? And is it not the case that in contrast to a criminal justice system which is often experienced as bureaucratic, insensitive, unresponsive and inefficient, vigilantism may have certain 'democratic resonances' attached to it?

Taylor's ambivalence about vigilantism is entirely justified. It is reasonable that people should participate in the provision of their own security. The danger is, of course, that such participation is difficult to control. Some versions of active citizenship are, to say the least, dangerous. Wilson, for instance, argues that citizen street patrols can serve a useful communal function by discouraging disorderly behaviour, though his conception of such behaviour is disturbingly broad: 'A gang can weaken or destroy a community by standing about in a menacing fashion and speaking rudely to passers-by without breaking the law' (Wilson and Kelling, 1982, p. 36). In one sense, of course, Wilson is right. Active citizenship needs to be defined as social citizenship. But it also has to be limited by some public constraint: at the very least by some reference to the criminal law.

A second issue concerns the narrow focus of citizenship in the British context. It is all very well to invoke civic values, but some of the most likely recruits for citizen street patrols will be, as in the USA, young, male, lower-class blacks. These are precisely the groups who experience the greatest degree of alienation from civil institutions and from the organisations which are supposed to represent their interests (Ben-Tovim *et al.*, 1986; Lea and Young, 1984). Significantly, the US National Institute of Justice report on the Guardian Angels commented favourably, and at some length, on its attempt to construct a positive role model for young people in the community:

> The most significant factor of the Guardian Angels may be that they represent a group of young people generally recognized as contributing to the crime problem . . . the involvement of youth in crime prevention is a significant feature of the Guardian Angels. (Pennell *et al.*, 1985, p. 24)

In comparison with this, the Home Office's response to the arrival of the Angels in Britain – persuade potential recruits to join the Special Constabulary – speaks volumes about the limited way in which the British establishment defines active citizenship in respect of young people.

CONCLUSION: THEORETICAL AND POLICY CONSIDERATIONS

In a sense, the conclusion to this chapter may be summed up in a single statement: 'Without a theory of what policing is, it is impossible to develop coherent policies about it.' I have tried to demonstrate that policing consists of a complex of public and private/formal arrangements. Neither the form nor the function of the policing complex can be defined in simple terms, and its content is variable across time and space. This suggests that there is a need for much more theoretical analysis to be directed towards locating policing across both public and private domains, and then for consideration to be directed towards assessing the feasibility and desirability of different types of 'mixes'. To date, relatively little work has addressed the issue in this way, and policing research remains far too 'publicly' oriented. It is vital that this imbalance be corrected as soon as possible, because if it is not, there is every indication that the policing mix will be restructured by default, rather than by a body of public policy, informed by rigorous research. For the remainder of this chapter I shall consider a few of the issues that might be at stake in future analysis.

First, consider the issue of self-policing. Wilson argues that 'the essence of the police role in maintaining order is to reinforce the informal control mechanisms of the community itself' (Wilson, 1982, p. 34). Now one might have reservations about Wilson's application of this principle, and to the particular conception of order that preoccupies him, but there is much to be said for the principle that formal policing has to build upon existing informal practices. Indeed, Shapland and Vagg make a similar point: 'Members of the public . . . are themselves engaging in a great deal of "policing" work, and . . . wish the police to complement and extend what they themselves are currently doing' (Shapland and Vagg, 1987, p. 54). This fact, coupled with the localised nature of much informal activity, suggests that policing policy, if it is to be effective, needs to be highly specific in its focus, taking into account the particular character of social relations in given localities.

Such a focus suggests that we need to know much more about the social variables affecting the character of self-policing in a locality. In Britain there is a relative paucity of such material, whereas in America, by contrast, debates on citizen 'coproduction' of public security have begun to explore the content of self-policing. (In Britain, there is only a small amount of literature that touches on this issue: see, for example, Hough and Mayhew, 1985, pp. 47–9; Smith, 1986, ch. 7; Jones *et al.*, 1986, pp. 24–7.) Coproduction can involve a range of practices: individual/household activities undertaken with police cooperation (property marking, joining the police auxiliary), or without such cooperation (bars, bolts, alarms, staying indoors); group activity undertaken with police cooperation (liaison groups, police-sponsored patrols), or without it (citizen patrols, autonomous block watches: see Percy, 1979).

In the American research, some attempt has been made to look at the relationship between such productive activity and social variables such as age, income, race, housing tenure and victimisation, in the hope that data produced can have relevance for policy: 'If planners were aware of what characteristics are related to what form of coproduction, policies could be developed to mesh the actions of service bureaucracies with communities with these characteristics' (Rosentraub and Harlow, 1983, p. 451).

Certainly, analysis of this sort raises interesting questions in the present climate. Should high-income areas, having greater capacity for private self-protection enjoy the same level of public police services as low-income areas? Under conditions of limited resources and differential standards of coproduction, should police services be allocated unequally in order to ensure greater equity between consumers?

But the American research is limited in two respects. First, there is a problem about the type of analysis carried out. To date, the best of this research (for example, Warren, Harlow and Rosentraub, 1982) has hypothesised that different forms of productive activity (such as activity involving cooperation with the police, as opposed to that carried out autonomously) will have different implications for policy. The problem is, however, that the different categories may not be mutually exclusive for individuals or groups of individuals. In Britain, for example, there have been members of neighbourhood watch schemes who have also been involved in citizen street patrols, and this should be no surprise, given what we know about individuals' patterns of social and political participation. What this suggests is a need, not just for quantitative data, but for qualitative research on the different combinations of productive activity that make up patterns of self-policing in a locality.

A second problem is that coproduction research has tended to adopt an excessively 'administrative' focus. Frequently, the assumption is that the crime problem can be dealt with as soon as policy-makers activate the newly discovered tripartite structure of coproduction (public police, private security and active citizens):

> [L]aw enforcement, given these new developments, is best understood as a problem of public administration [which can examine] the possible benefits from various possible permutations of public agency/private sector relationships. (Henderson, 1987, pp. 49 and 55)

The problem is that this administrative focus is bereft of any politics. As such, it is unable to explore the political, ethical and legal factors which will determine whether any particular coproductive practice is, in point of fact, either administratively feasible (for there are, as I have indicated, potential conflicts between public and private agents), or politically desirable.

There is a need, also, not only for more empirical research on areas such as self-policing and private security, but for research which is willing to explore the various theoretical issues raised by the 'new policing'. In conclusion I shall refer to three areas worthy of future theoretical consideration.

First, there is the question of the relationship between public and private spheres. I said at the beginning of this chapter that privatisation was more than merely the absence or withdrawal of the state from a given activity. In the context of policing and criminal justice, it is clear that privatisation may, in fact, coincide with an expansion of the state's role. This point is well illustrated in *Punishment, Custody and the Community* (Home Office, 1988a), where two processes occur simultaneously. On the one hand, the role of the private security sector is expanded through its involvement in the supervision of offenders in the public sphere. On the other hand, the proposals for house arrest and electronic tagging enable the state to invade the most private of all institutions, the household. Privatisation is not, then, a zero-sum game.

Such developments have implications for how we theorise the state (public) and market (private) spheres. Existing concepts (extended state, free economy/strong state, authoritarian state) invariably misrecognise the extent to which authority in contempory societies is exercised through a complex and fluid mix of public and private institutions and practices. A graphic illustration of this fact is the emergence of a private security sector in the People's Republic of China (Wildeman, 1988).

Examples of this sort suggest that the boundaries between public and private aspects of criminal justice and law enforcement will change. Those boundaries will also become less and less distinct. Such processes require careful theoretical consideration if public policy is to have any meaningful impact on their development. As yet, there seems little sign of this occurring. In the case of policing policy, for example, fundamental assumptions about the police role are often at odds with existing developments. Compare, for instance, the primacy accorded to pro-action and foot patrol in liberal policing theory, with evidence that these roles are already being usurped by the private sector. Shearing and Stenning suggest that in North America, foot patrol is now almost the exclusive preserve of private security. The private sector's monopolisation of this role, together with its domination of the preventative one, indicates that modern policing is 'gradually being restructured in such a way as to bring it more closely in line with Peel's dream', but through private means, rather than public ones (1981, p. 217).

The second issue is citizenship. When Douglas Hurd invoked the principles of active citizenship in the fight against crime, he did not anticipate the arrival of the Guardian Angels in Britain. But their arrival, together with the phenomenon of citizens 'taking to the streets', serves to remind us that in a society like ours, citizenship can develop in ways other than those intended by governments. The traditional liberal view of citizenship is one where the citizen is a passive bearer of rights. But where the state is unable or unwilling to meet expressed demands for services, active citizenship is likely to increase. This may be no bad thing. But in circumstances where substantive inequalities between different categories of citizen are also prevalent, active citizenship is likely to expose and politicise conflicts between competing sets of 'rights', without offering any just means of resolving them. Such a situation will persist until a concept of 'active citizenship' is constructed which is informed by principles of social justice (cf. Mouffe, 1988: Hoover and Plant, 1989).

This last point suggests a third area of concern, underpinning the other two, for any analysis of the relationship between the state, private bodies and citizens should be informed by principles of social justice. Privatisation, in the various forms discussed here, throws up complex issues of justice. If policing policy is to become more attuned to the specific characteristics of localities, questions arise about the relationship between the different definitions of law enforcement and justice such local specificity implies. What is the correct relationship between national and local accountability? How should the principle of universalism in law enforcement and justice be balanced with the need for responsiveness to varying local needs? How can the 'informal' and 'instrumental' standards of justice employed by private bodies be reconciled with public standards?

The 'new policing' is likely to expose the contradictions between these differing conceptions of justice more and more. In Britain, theorists of the left and centre-left are being forced to reassess relations between public and private spheres in new and radical ways. Much of this has involved the abandonment of 'statist' conceptions of service delivery and the resurrection of hitherto forbidden concepts ('citizenship', 'the market'). Perhaps it is now time for such radical attention to be directed at the policing system which will confront us in the twenty-first century. One thing is certain. Ignoring the changes will not make them go away.

REFERENCES

ALDERSON, J. (1979) *Policing Freedom*, Plymouth: Macdonald & Evans.

BEN-TOVIM, G., GABRIEL, J., LAW, I. and STREDDER, K. (1986) *The Local Politics of Race*, London: Macmillan.

BOOTHROYD, J. (1989) 'Nibbling Away at the Bobby's Patch', *Police Review*, 13 January.

CAIN, M. (1979) 'Trends in the Sociology of Police Work', *International Journal of the Sociology of Law*, 7, pp. 143–67.

CLARKE, M. (1987) 'Citizenship, Community and the Management of Crime', *British Journal of Criminology*, 27, 4, pp. 384–400.

CLARKE, R. and HOUGH, M. (1984) *Crime and Police Effectiveness*, Home Office Research Study No. 79, London: HMSO.

COHEN, P. (1984) 'Subcultural Conflict and Working Class Community' in Butterworth, E. and Weir, D. (eds) *The New Sociology of Modern Britain*, London: Fontana.

COHEN, S. (1985) *Visions of Social Control*, Cambridge: Polity Press.
CRONIN, J. E. (1984) *Labour and Society in Britain 1918–79*, London: Batsford.
CUNNINGHAM, W. C. and TAYLOR, T. (1985) *Private Security and Police in America* (The Hallcrest Report), Portland: Chancellor Press.
GORDON, P. (1984) 'Community Policing: Towards the Local Police State?', *Critical Social Policy*, 10, pp. 39–58.
HENDERSON, J. H. (1987) 'Public Law Enforcement, Private Security and Citizen Crime Prevention: Competition or Cooperation?', *Police Journal*, 60, pp. 48–57.
HENSHAW, D. (1986) 'Vigilante Groups Move in to Fill the Law and Order Vacuum', *Listener*, 23 January.
HOME OFFICE (1979) *The Private Security Industry: A Discussion Paper*, London: HMSO.
HOME OFFICE (1988a) *Punishment, Custody and the Community*, London: HMSO.
HOME OFFICE (1988b) *Private Sector Involvement in the Remand System*, London: HMSO.
HOOVER, K. and PLANT, R. (1989) *Conservative Capitalism in Britain and the United States*, London: Routledge.
HOUGH, M. and MAYHEW, P. (1985) *Taking Account of Crime*, Home Office Research Study No. 85, London: HMSO.
JEFFERSON, T. and GRIMSHAW, R. (1984) *Controlling the Constable*, London: Muller.
JOHNSTON, L. (1986) *Marxism, Class Analysis and Socialist Pluralism*, London: Allen & Unwin.
JONES, T., MACLEAN, B. and YOUNG, J. (1986) *The Islington Crime Survey*, London: Gower.
JORDAN & SONS LTD. (1987) *Britain's Security Industry*, London: Jordan & Sons Ltd.
JUDGE, T. (1988) 'Is There a Profit To Be Made Out of Policing?', *Police*, December, pp. 12–16.
KAKALIK, J. S. and WILDHORN, S. (1972) *Private Police in the United States: Findings and Recommendations: Volume 1*, Rand Corporation for US Dept. of Justice, Washington: Government Printing Office.
KELLING, G. (1983) 'On the Accomplishments of the Police' in M. Punch (ed.), *Control in The Police Organisation*, Cambridge, Mass.: MIT, pp. 152–68.
KINSEY, R., LEA, J. and YOUNG, J. (1986) *Losing the Fight Against Crime*, London: Blackwell.
LEA, J. and YOUNG, J. (1984) *What is to Be Done About Law and Order?*, Harmondsworth: Penguin.
LeGRAND, J. and ROBINSON, R. (eds) (1984) *Privatisation and the Welfare State*, London: Allen & Unwin.
MARX, G. T. (1987) 'The Interweaving of Public and Private Police in Undercover Work', in C. D. Shearing and P. C. Stenning (eds), *Private Policing*, California: Sage, pp. 172–93.
MARX, G. T. and ARCHER, D. (1973) 'The Urban Vigilante', *Psychology Today*, January, pp. 45–50.
MARX, G. T. and ARCHER, D. (1976) 'Community Police Patrols and

Vigilantism', in H. J. Rosenbaum and P. C. Sedeberg (eds), *Vigilante Politics*, University of Pennsylvania Press, pp. 129–57.

MEADOWS, R. (1984) 'Private Security and Public Safety: Developments and Issues', *Journal of Security Administration*, 7 (2), pp. 51–61.

MOUFFE, C. (1988) 'The Civics Lesson', *New Statesman and Society*, October, pp. 28–31.

OSTROWE, B. B. and DiBIASE, R. (1983) 'Citizen Involvement as a Crime Deterrent: A Study of Public Attitudes Toward an Unsanctioned Civilian Patrol Group', *Journal of Police Science and Administration*, 11 (2) pp. 185–93.

PAHL, R. E. and WALLACE, C. D. (1988) 'Neither Angels in Marble nor Rebels in Red: Privatisation and Working Class Consciousness', in D. Rose (ed.), *Social Stratification and Economic Change*, London: Hutchinson, pp. 127–52.

PENNELL, S., CURTIS, C. and HENDERSON, J. (1985) *Guardian Angels: An Assessment of Citizen Response to Crime*, US Dept. of Justice, Washington: Government Printing Office.

PERCY, S. L. (1979) 'Citizen Coproduction of Community Safety', in R. Baker and F. A. Mayer (eds), *Evaluating Alternative Law Enforcement Policies*, Lexington, Mass.: Lexington Books.

PUNCH, M. and NAYLOR, T. (1973) 'The Police: A Social Service', *New Society*, 24.

REINER, R. (1985) *The Politics of the Police*, Brighton: Wheatsheaf.

REISS, A. J. (1987) 'The Legitimacy of Intrusion into Private Space', in C. D. Shearing and P. C. Stenning (eds), *Private Policing*, California: Sage, pp. 19–44.

REISS, A. J. (1988) *Private Employment of Public Police*, US Dept. of Justice, Washington: Government Printing Office.

ROSENTRAUB, M. S. and HARLOW, K. S. (1983) 'Private/Public Relations and Service Delivery: The Coproduction of Personal Safety', *Policy Studies Journal*, 11 (3) pp. 445–57.

RUDE, G. (1985) *Criminal and Victim*, Oxford: Clarendon Press.

SHAPLAND, J. and VAGG, J. (1987) 'Using the Police', *British Journal of Criminology*, 27, 1, pp. 54–63.

SHAPLAND, J. and VAGG, J. (1988) *Policing By the Public*, London: Routledge.

SHEARING, C. D. and STENNING, P. C. (1981) 'Modern Private Security: Its Growth and Implications', in M. Tonry and N. Morris (eds), *Crime and Justice: An Annual Review of Research Volume 3*, University of Chicago Press, pp. 193–245.

SHUBERT, A. (1981) 'Private Initiative in Law Enforcement: Associations for the Prosecution of Felons, 1744–1856', in V. Bailey (ed.), *Policing and Punishment in Nineteenth-Century Britain*, London: Croom Helm, pp. 25–41.

SMITH, S. J. (1986) *Crime, Space and Society*, Cambridge: Cambridge University Press.

SOUTH, N. (1987) 'Law, Profit and "Private Persons": Private and Public Policing in English History', in C. D. Shearing and P. C. Stenning, *Private Policing*, California: Sage, pp. 72–109.

SOUTH, N. (1988) *Policing for Profit*, London: Sage.

SPITZER, S. and SCULL, A. (1977) 'Privatisation and Capitalist Development: The Case of the Private Police', *Social Problems*, 25 (1), pp. 18–29.

STEWART, J. K. (1985) 'Public Safety and Private Police', *Public Administration Review*, pp. 758–65.

TAYLOR, L. (1976) 'Vigilantes – Why Not?', *New Society*, 4 November, pp. 259–60.

THOMSON, A. (1988) 'Paramilitaries Operate a Shoot-to-Cripple Policy', *Listener*, 3 March, pp. 7–8.

TUCKER, W. (1985) *Vigilante: The Backlash Against Crime in America*, New York: Stein & Day.

WARREN, R., HARLOW, K. and ROSENTRAUB, M. S. (1982) 'Citizen Participation in the Production of Services: Methodological and Policy Issues in Coproduction Research', *Southwestern Review*, 2 (3), pp. 41–55.

WEATHERILL, S. (1988) 'Buying Special Police Services', *Public Law*, pp. 106–27.

WILDEMAN, J. (1988) 'When the State Fails: A Critical Assessment of Contract Policing', Paper presented to the annual meeting of the American Society of Criminology, Chicago, Illinois.

WILSON, J. Q. (1968) *Varieties of Police Behaviour*, Cambridge, Mass.: Harvard University Press.

WILSON, J. Q. and KELLING, G. L. (1982) 'Broken Windows', *The Atlantic Monthly*, March, pp. 29–38.

2 'Creeping Privatisation'? The Police, The Conservative Government and Policing in the Late 1980s

Philip Rawlings

THE ELECTION OF A 'LAW AND ORDER' GOVERNMENT

Recently it has been argued not only that senior police officers and police organisations engage in political debate, but also that their opinions have an important influence on government policy. The tendency of this work has been to portray the police as having broadly a pro-Conservative and an anti-Labour bias in their opinions (Hall, 1979; Reiner, 1980, 1985b). The problem with this is that the Left has been out of government for a decade, and yet the public opposition of senior police officers and police organisations to government policy has increased rather than abated. This chapter looks at the degeneration of what in 1979 seemed to be the start of an harmonious relationship between the police and the Tory government.

The Tories under Thatcher won the election in 1979 on a manifesto which pledged the 'reduction of waste, bureaucracy and over-government', but whatever implications this policy had for other parts of the state few believed that it would be applied to the police. The bipartisan consensus over policing had been shattered in the 1970s as the Tories criticised Labour over the rise in recorded crime and the Grunwick dispute, and they entered the election with a tough attitude to 'law and order' as a key feature of their campaign. The symbols of their commitment to this policy were attacks on the Labour government's cuts in the police budget, and promises that 'The next Conservative government will spend more on fighting crime even while we economise elsewhere' (Commons Debates, 12 July 1977, col. 231, 27 July 1977, col. 1738–39; Conservative Central Office, 1977, 1979). This drew support from, among others, the Police Federation and the commissioner of the Metropolitan Police (Mark, 1977; and generally, Clarke and Taylor, 1980; Clarke, Taylor and Wren-Lewis, 1982). Since 1979 ministers have publicly declared their resolve to carry through these promises. For instance, in 1985 Thatcher told the Conservative Party Conference, 'The government will continue steadfastly to back the police. If they need more men, more equipment, they shall have them'; and in 1988 she boasted that, 'Today the police service is bigger, better paid, better equipped, and more thoroughly trained than at any time in the past' (*Police Review*, 23 May 1986; *The Times*, 26 May 1988). The evidence seems to support these assertions: full implementation of the Edmund-Davies pay award, as opposed to the staggered implementation proposed by the Labour administration; an increase between 1979 and 1988 of just over 12 000 officers, or roughly an 11 per cent rise in numbers; more police powers under the Police and Criminal Evidence Act 1984 and the Public Order Act 1986; and Home Office support, sometimes in the face of opposition from local police authorities (Spencer, 1985; Loveday, 1986), for increases in weaponry and for training in 'public order' policing. But, in spite of all this, from about 1983 the government has attracted greater public criticism from individual police officers and police organisations than any previous administration.

As the Conservatives approached the end of their first term in office they realised that despite the promised drop in crime as a result of their 'law and order' policies, crime had actually risen. So the government was, as an editorial in the *Guardian* later put it, 'painfully aware that, if it shouts too raucously for a great war against crime, people will start asking: what has been happening for eight years?' (*Guardian*, 7 March 1986; Taylor, 1987). On top of this the Tories had found difficulties in trying to fulfil their promises to cut public expenditure because, in part at least, rising unemployment had increased social security expenditure and the cuts implemented by the Labour government had reduced the opportunities for 'easy' savings. So the big spending services became targets for cuts, especially those like the police with high staffing costs. Ironically the Edmund-Davies award made the police particularly vulnerable because it guaranteed higher than average pay awards and limited government control over those awards.

So the Conservatives sought to move away from the 1979 formula that more spending on the police leads to less crime. In its place they argued that crime was due to factors which were beyond the control of the government and the police. In 1986 the Home Secretary told the Police Federation Conference, 'The truth is that, however many laws we change, however much equipment we provide, however many police officers we put on the streets, these measures will not alone turn back the rise in crime' (*Police*, June 1986; also, ibid, September 1987). Crime came to be attributed to a lack of individual moral discipline, or, as Norman Tebbit put it, 'the post-war funk which gave birth to the permissive society, which in turn generates today's violent society' (N. Tebbit, in Taylor, 1987). Therefore, the solutions lay in the hands of offenders, parents, teachers, those who controlled television, videomakers and even potential victims and their neighbours. Crime prevention and detection was not the exclusive preserve of the police: 'Combatting crime,' according to Thatcher, 'is everybody's business, everybody's responsibility. It cannot be left solely to the police' (*The Times*, 26 May 1988; also Hurd in *Police*, September 1986; *Guardian*, 22 October 1987).

The way was cleared for the imposition of the Financial Management Initiative so familiar in some other state institutions. In January 1983 Whitelaw, the Home Secretary, had warned the police that a review was about to begin 'against the essential policy requirement that resources should only be increased where both the need for them, and their value in use, is proven' (*The Job*, 28 January 1983). So it came as no surprise when in November 1983 Circular 114/1983, sent by the Home Office to all police forces, declared that, 'the constraints on public expenditure . . . make it impossible to continue with the sort of expansion which has occurred in recent years'. The aim was to bring the police within the government's 'determination to secure better value for money throughout the public sector' (Commons Debates, 20 May 1984, WA col. 124). According to the Circular the police 'should make the most effective use of the substantial resources now available to it'. This was not merely an invitation to chief officers, it was backed by the sanction of a Home Office refusal to increase the budget or the authorised establishment (the number of officers each force is authorised by the Home Office to employ) of a recalcitrant force, and HM Inspectors of Constabulary were to report to the Home Office on whether in each force 'resources are directed in accordance with properly determined objectives and priorities'.

VALUE FOR MONEY?

Police officers of all ranks – or at least their representative organisations and those periodicals aimed at a police audience – have responded to these developments with a rarely equalled unanimity. Broadly, they cling to the idea that more police does mean less crime so that the issue of establishment levels has become central to their critique of the government's policy. Although few officers would say that the police should be given a free hand over resources, the import of their argument often tends to be that the police are the experts on crime so only they know how it can best be tackled, and, therefore, their views on resources should be paramount. In addition, not far below the surface of some expressions of opinion a feeling of anger can be detected at what is regarded as a betrayal by the government, and this has perhaps made the police all the more fierce in their criticisms.

The anger of police organisations has been increased by a failure to consult with them on major issues. Before publishing Circular 114/1983 the Home Office only consulted with the Tripartite Working Party, which, besides the Home Office, consists of the Association of Chief Police Officers (ACPO), the Association of County Councils and the Association of Metropolitan Authorities. The Police Federation (PF), whose members form the bulk of police officers, and the Superintendent's Association (SA) were excluded, and neither believed that the presence of ACPO amounted to an adequate representation of their members. Similarly, both the PF and the SA were annoyed by the failure in 1988 of the Home Office to consult on controversial proposals to dismiss 'lazy or careless officers'; Alan Eastwood, chair of the PF, angrily commented that even though he had been speaking to the Home Secretary on that very subject only two days before the proposals were announced, the first he had heard of them was through the BBC (*Police Review*, 7 October 1988). Indeed, since the mid-1980s the PF has often regarded the government's attitude to them as part of its general reluctance to consult with trade unions and as representing a desire to undermine the strength of the PF so that pay might more easily be held down (*Police*, March 1984). The PF has responded by adopting increasingly aggressive stances during negotiations over pay and rent allowances. In 1988 delegates at its annual conference warmly applauded a suggestion that the time when the police should consider taking industrial action over pay was drawing near (*The Times*, 23 July 1988). Uniquely ACPO joined in the attacks on the government's failure to consult following the unilateral imposition in 1988 of an 8.5 per cent pay rise on senior officers (*Guardian*, 16 November 1988). The police have represented the effect of the government's strategy over pay as inevitably leading to the pre-Edmund-Davies problems of low recruitment and high wastage: 'The thin blue line will stretch even further, but like a piece of elastic, it will eventually break . . . All the good done by Edmund-Davies will be wasted – we will be in a worse position than we've ever been in before' (*Police* Review, 20 May 1988).

The introduction by Circular 114/1983 of new management techniques has also led to problems. It is true to say that the techniques, generally called 'Policing by Objectives' (PBO) – a sort of extended version of Drucker's 'Management by Objectives' (Drucker, 1955) – are supported by many senior police officers, and, therefore, the inclusion in Circular 114/1983 of directions to the police to improve their efficiency was not wholly unsupported. Yet even the enthusiasts express important reservations. Newman introduced new management strategies into the Metropolitan Police before Circular 114/1983 was issued; nevertheless he began to complain about the levels of establishment in his force towards the end of his period in office (Newman, 1986b; *The Job*, 6 February 1987). Tony Butler, an assistant chief constable and author of *Police Management*, recently remarked:

> We are no different to a company making baked beans. People come to us for a product and, in some areas, we have competitors like the security industry. But we are a public service and not simply subject to market forces. I cannot

just cancel a patrol because it is too expensive – although we do have to strive to deliver the service in a cost-effective way. (*The Independent*, 8 August 1988. Also Wilkinson, 1989)

ACPO has criticised PBO on the grounds that it undervalues social-work-type policing (*Guardian*, 18 June 1987). Although chief constables seem to feel obliged to refer in their annual reports to the setting of objectives and to management skills, reading these reports often gives the distinct impression that many are unconvinced about how such policies translate into practice. Moreover, chief officers in particular have claimed that the vagueness of the measurement standards used to assess a force's performances means that the Home Office can avoid consultation and reasoned argument, thereby diminishing the autonomy of police forces and increasing its own power: in the words of Peter Wright, chief constable of South Yorkshire and president of ACPO, 'It is the sort of vacuum in which these decisions are taken which is worrying. We are not aware of the content of the measure that is used; it just happens that way' (*Police Review*, 13 January 1989, 24 February 1989, 14 July 1989). But once again the underlying issue is that while the government maintains that PBO will lead to a more efficient and effective use of resources and, almost as a sort of by-product, will tend to hold down the numbers of police officers and so reduce costs, police organisations regard its primary objective as being the cutting of expenditure through a reduction in the number of police officers without any real concern about the effect this may have on policing (*Police Review*, 20 May 1985; *Police*, April 1987). So when the PF chose 'Value for Money' as the theme for their 1988 Conference this was meant not as a call to greater efficiency from the membership, but as a statement of fact; a month before Eastwood had declared, 'All the talk is of cost. None of the thought is of value. Let us say to a Government that lectures us upon value for money in the police service: "Good God, what more do you want?" ' (*Guardian*, 1 April 1988).

THE END OF 'TRADITIONAL POLICING'?

Government ministers have reacted to police criticisms about establishment levels by quoting figures which show how these have been raised since 1979. In reply to such figures Roger Birch, then president of ACPO, said in 1988, 'The additional manpower provided since [1979] has been absorbed largely in bringing strengths up to levels agreed appropriate to the situation which prevailed fifteen or sixteen years ago. The demands of policing have changed beyond all recognition since that time' (*Police*, June 1988). Newman argued that the increases were swallowed up by the loss of officers on duty caused by cutbacks in overtime which were a result of budgetary constraints (Newman, 1987; *Police Review*, 19 June 1987), and others have accused the Home Office of distorting the figures by including increases in the number of civilians employed in police forces (*Police Review*, 26 May 1989).

An important part of the police argument is that more officers are required because of changes in policing during the 1980s, and to demonstrate this attempts have been made to provide evidence for the view that police officers are overstretched. Stress has become a major issue: Peter Hayes, deputy chief constable of South Yorkshire and secretary of the central advisory unit on stress, said recently, 'In many parts of the country, the workload on police offiers has reached the point where it can honestly be described as intolerable.' In response to requests from the PF and SA, ACPO set up a working party on stress-related illness, and many forces have their own occupational health units in which stress-related illness is given particular attention (*The Observer*, 28 October 1988; *Guardian*, 30 November 1988; *Police Review*, 26 February 1988, 14 July 1989). However, the police have sought to show that their work has not simply increased, but that it has also become more dangerous. One way in which this has been done is through the highlighting of assaults on officers, and with the cooperation of chief officers the *Police Review* has recently begun to collaborate figures and to construct 'league tables'.

In order to explain how these changes in the amount and type of their work have come about, the police have certainly referred to what both they and the government regard as a general moral decline in Britain. However, although statements on this subject made by James Anderton, the chief constable of Greater Manchester Police, have been given a great deal of prominence in the media, in general the police have tried to steer away from a viewpoint which implies that they have little control over crime, and instead they have laid emphasis on the allegation that the government's policies have undermined their effectiveness and created new crime phenomena.

First, there is resentment at both an increase in legislation affecting the police and a lack of consultation with them prior to its introduction. The Police and Criminal Evidence Act 1984 has been widely attacked, and the fact that officers routinely make assertions to police audiences such as 'PACE makes it virtually impossible for police to investigate the hard core of the criminal fraternity' (*Police Review*, 23 December 1988) without feeling the need to explain these statements, gives an indication of the depth of feeling. The Act is seen as moving the police from an 'order maintenance' function to the sort of 'legalistic' style which, they believe, has obstructed policing in the USA. So Imbert, the commissioner of the Metropolitan Police, believes that 'an unintended and unforeseen consequence of PACE was that the balance has tilted too far in favour of the suspect' (Imbert, 1988; also, Newman, 1985). Similarly, ACPO has sought to explain falling detection rates by claiming that although the number of arrests has actually risen over the past few years, the effect of the Act has been to reduce the number of offences to which people are willing to admit (*The Independent*, 31 July 1987; HM Chief Inspector, 1987). It has also been claimed that the Act requires more sergeants in police stations to act as custody officers, but that the Home Office has failed to compensate for the loss of these officers from other duties (*Police Review*, 19 May 1989). Another recent major piece of legislataion created an independent prosecution system, the Crown Prosecution Service (CPS), which has come in for vigorous criticism. The head of the London branch of the PF called it the 'Criminals' Protection Society'; the *Police Review* published stories from police officers in which the CPS was blamed for the acquittal of 'guilty' people; and Leslie Curtis of the PF claimed that plea bargaining by the CPS was undermining police morale (*Police Review*, 21 July 1989; *Guardian*, 20 May 1987). But most hated of all seems to be the Police Complaints Authority, referred to as the 'Prosecute Coppers Association', of which the police are, according to Eastwood, 'heartily sick' and which attracted a motion of no confidence at the PF's 1989 Conference (*Police Review*, 26 May 1989).

Second, the police have tried to connect establishment levels to increases in violent crime. One delegate to the Scottish Police Federation Conference in 1988 said of the financial objections to increased establishments, 'But what choice is there? The choice of a further escalation in crime and lawlessness in society or making a society in which members of the public can be free to go about their daily business without fear or favour?' (*Police Review*, 6 May 1988). The police have argued that not only has the amount of crime risen, but also its nature and geographical location have changed, with the result that what are regarded as understaffed rural police forces have become exposed. Symbolic of this is the 'rural riot'. While the government acknowledges the existence of rural riots, the tendency has been to attribute them to a lack of individual moral discipline. Hurd told the PF Conference in 1988 that the problem lay in 'too many young people with too much money in their pockets, too many pints inside them but too little self-discipline and too little notion of the care and responsibility which they owe to others. (*Police Review*, 27 May 1988). The police view differs in an important way. In a report prepared for ACPO in 1988 and based on questionnaires filled in by each police force, Brian Hayes, the chief constable of Surrey, recorded 250 'incidents of serious disorder' in 1987, which he defined as incidents involving more than twenty people who were committing public order offences, assault or criminal damage and to which more than ten officers were called from outside the sub-divisonal area. Hayes accepted Hurd's view about the role of drink, but laid more emphasis on the view that the problem was aggravated by the lack of officers on the spot to cope with large-scale disturbances:

> A reasonable show of strength at the outset may remove the problem completely, avoiding damage, violence, and disruption to local people. This will clearly need additional manpower to reverse the trend of directing ever-increasing resources at larger centres of population to cope with more predictable demands, which have denuded many rural areas of adequate cover . . . If little or no extra resources are made available to shire counties because of the competing claims of Metropolitan forces, it is difficult to see how the problem can be tackled seriously. If this occurs, then the consequences in terms of the quality of life outside our cities are serious. (*The Independent*, 23 September 1988; *Police Review*, 10 June 1988)

The Home Office took the report seriously and set up their own small research project (Tuck, 1989). This was critical of ACPO's methodology, challenging, for instance, the way the label 'rural' had been attached to incidents taking place in densely populated areas such as the Thames Valley. Moreover, it did not really agree that the situation was getting beyond the ability of the police to respond. This, and what were regarded as some bizarre notions about low-alcohol drinks, led Alan Eastwood of the PF to dismiss the report as 'codswallop'.

It seems no coincidence that a summary of Hayes's confidential report was widely leaked shortly after the Home Office had announced in June 1988 what the police regarded as grossly inadequate increases in establishment levels for the following year. The report seemed to justify the instant denunciation of those increases by Birch, president of ACPO. He remarked that they 'cannot even scratch the surface' of rural crime, and added:

> Part of the problem of violence and disorder in our towns and villages stems from the fact that police manpower does not meet the many challenging demands of the 1980s. As a consequence our towns and villages are no longer adequately patrolled. Unchecked high spirits so often turn into hooliganism and crime. (*Police*, June 1988)

For Birch, rural riots revealed the importance of what he called 'traditional policing'. He argued that officers on the beat could prevent problems from arising, or at least could give an early warning if trouble broke out. Although he acknowledged that this sort of policing was 'heavily demanding on manpower', he urged 'the Government to grasp the nettle of finishing the job it started by providing sufficient manpower to put policemen back on the streets' (*Police*, June 1988; *Police Review*, 14 October 1988). The value of the 'rural riot' for the police in their argument with the government has been that it spreads the fear of large-scale disorder from the Labour-controlled inner-city areas to the Tory shires.

Third, low establishment levels and an emphasis within the PBO system on detection rates have been blamed by many police forces for their use of 'screening' strategies in which only crimes rated as 'solvable' are investigated (*Police Review*, 26 June 1987; *Strategy '83*, no. 4). This has, it is claimed, undermined efforts to establish good police–community relations, which was supposedly one of the key objectives of post-Scarman policing. Birch, as president of ACPO, argued that, 'If we can no longer devote time and resources to minor problems, which to the person involved may be the biggest thing in their lives, then we shall lose our human face' (*Police Review*, 6 February 1987). However, when Anderton made a similar criticism, Douglas Hurd replied by saying that Anderton's own Greater Manchester force had shown that the best way of dealing with autocrime – 'one of the biggest crimes in the city' – was 'not by having more uniformed bobbies on the beat . . . What you have is plainclothes people, and they target particular areas and produce results' (*Police Review*, 26 June 1987). One response from the police to this has been that, 'there has been little research to establish if the potential presence of a uniformed officer prevents crime. If we returned to the days when there were enough constables to man every beat, when there was less opportunist crime because of the very possibility of a bobby coming round the corner, would not crime almost disappear?' (*Police Review*, 2 October 1987). Another reaction has been to focus on the fear of crime, which the Home Office's own researchers have identified as important (Maxfield, 1984), and to claim that more officers on the beat would reduce this fear: as one delegate at the SA Conference in 1987 put it:

> Cost effectiveness . . . is not the issue: the issue is the perception of the public's fears and the effectiveness of the service to allay those fears . . . [T]he only way the public feel they can have confidence [in walking the streets] is by being visibly assured of protection and support. That can only be given by the uniformed officer. (*Police Review*, 2 October 1987; also East, 1988)

MRS THATCHER'S FAVOURITE CHUNK OF SOCIETY

During 1988 these various criticisms made by the police of government policy were often being drawn together under the umbrella of an accusation that the long-term objective was to privatise parts of the service. Police organisations seemed to see this accusation as a valuable way of putting their case across to a wider audience. By this time the apparently relentless policy of pushing through a broad privatisation programme was regarded by many people as evidence that the government was guided not by rational arguments and objectives, but by ideological dogma. By presenting the policy on the police as ultimately directed towards privatisation the police sought to draw support for their criticisms by connecting them to this broader and increasingly popular critique of the government. The police argue that the restrictions on their budgets and establishment levels, the increase in police work and their inability to perform adequately the tasks which they believe the public sees as of first importance, have opened up gaps which are being filled by the private security industry and vigilante groups. Hence, Eastwood claims that what is happening is the 'creeping privatisation of the police service'. And the accusation is that this is a deliberate objective of the government's policy, for, as an editorial in *Police Review* argued, 'If the police can no longer cope with law and order, how long will it be before the responsibility for its maintenance is handed to Mrs Thatcher's favourite chunk of society, the private sector?' (*Police Review*, 21 October 1988). This conclusion draws credence from, among other things, the plans to privatise the Police National Computer and to make police forces pay for forensic services (*Guardian*, 14 March 1989; *Police Review*, 17 February 1989, 27 February 1989, 3 March 1989, 10 March 1989, 21 July 1989; *The Independent*, 27 February 1989), the fact that the chair of the important Home Affairs select committee, Conservative MP John Wheeler, is also president of the British Security Industry Association (*Police Review*, 19 May 1989), and the endorsement by the influential right-wing Adam Smith Institute of the privatisation of street policing (Elliott, 1989). From within the industry it was confirmed that private security firms were expanding rapidly into 'areas which were previously regarded as the exclusive province of the police' (*Police Review*, 14 July 1989). Furthermore, the police and the police press have produced a stream of examples of privatisation in operation: residents hiring security firms to patrol their streets or forming their own patrols; the replacement of British Transport Police at Sealink ports by security firms; the use of security guards at MOD premises, probably including MI5 and MI6 offices; the appearance of the Guardian Angels on the London Underground (*Police Review*, 7 October 1988, 21 October 1988, 13 January 1989, 10 March 1989, 14 April 1989; *Sunday Mirror*, 11 December 1988, 1 January 1989; *Observer*, 30 October 1988; *Guardian*, 28 January 1987, 8 March 1989).

While recognising that commercial suppliers of burglar alarms and the like may have a function, the reaction of many within the police has been to denounce the expansion of the private sector into patrol work: 'Increased privatisation is not the answer to the crime problem and in the best interests of the public further expansion of non-police involvement should be firmly resisted. The primacy of the police role must be sacrosanct' (*Police Journal*,

58 (1985), p. 96). Similarly, Alan Eastwood has remarked recently, 'the expansion of the private security industry into the realm of public policing is something to be deplored, to be resisted and to be stopped'. But it has been recognised that such expressions of opinion are not enough, so evidence purportedly showing the disadvantages of extending the role of the private sector has been produced. David Owen, chief constable of North Wales Police, compiled a report for ACPO in 1988 in which he pointed out that the private security industry was unaccountable and he claimed both that many firms were corrupt and that even the large, well-respected companies employed people with criminal records (*Police Review*, 26 August 1988; also, Bridgman, Olding and Grossland, 1988). This report was leaked and was immediately followed by articles in the police press which supported Owen's findings. The flavour of these can be gathered from the opening assertion of a series published in *Police Review*: 'The private security industry is flourishing, wide open and riddled with former criminals' (*Guardian, 8 March 1989; Observer, 5 March 1989; Police Review*, 26 August 1988, 24 February 1989, 3 March 1989, 10 March 1989; *Police*, March 1989). At the same time, the police have expressed an understanding of the motives of those who would resort to private security firms, arguing that many 'would not need to if there were realistic police establishments' (*Police Review*, 26 August 1988). Moreover, the hiring of security firms to patrol streets has been taken to show that the public endorses the view that more officers means less crime.

The police also feel that the principle of privatisation is being applied within the police service. Although civilians have always been employed in police forces, the government have made the transfer of work from police officers to civilians a key feature of their drive for a more effective use of resources (Home Office Circulars 114/1983 and 105/1988; Loveday, 1989). Typically this is depicted by the police as merely an exercise in cost-cutting rather than an attempt to improve policing; in the words of Curtis of the PF, 'it seems that civilians are a good idea because they are cheaper than policemen' (*Police*, June 1984). The PF believes that far from the new civilian staff releasing more officers for the beat, they are actually replacing officers, and that, in spite of promises to the contrary, forces with a good record on civilianisation receive no better treatment from the Home Office (*Police*, March 1985;

Police Review, 20 May 1988). Civilians are being employed in work which the police see as central to operational policing, for instance as scene-of-crime officers and fingerprint officers, and since many are still members of NALGO, which refuses to give up the right to strike, concern has been expressed that operations are potentially at risk from this policy. Furthermore, it is argued that civilians are employed to do specific jobs and are less flexible than police officers, that there is uncertainty as to who has control over the civilian staff so that the chief constable's authority is diminished, and that poor pay and the lack of a proper career structure means that civilians are difficult to recruit and, once trained, difficult to keep (*Police Review*, 24 May 1988, 1 July 1988, 28 October 1988, 26 May 1989, 7 July 1989).

There has also been some distrust of the Home Office's motives for encouraging the recruitment of more special constables (Commons Debates, 18 February 1988, col. 1143). Officially the specials are to be used only in emergencies and not as a way of saving money by replacing regular officers, but the definition of an 'emergency' is said to have become quite wide in some forces. The PF alleges, and many senior officers privately acknowledge, that shortages of regular officers and the reduction of overtime have led to more than half of the police forces in England and Wales using specials to make up the shortfall (*Guardian*, 26 April 1989).

Like the PF, many chief officers are arguing that civilianisation will not solve the problems facing the police and that more regular officers are needed. For example, John Hall, the chief constable of Humberside Police, wrote in his 1988 *Annual Report*:

> Faced with a seemingly inexorable rise in public demand for police services, it is apparent that civilianisation of police posts is only a partial solution. Although other ways of increasing the efficiency and effectiveness of existing resources have been or are being explored, I remain firmly of the opinion that a substantial increase in the police authorised establishment is vital to maintaining an acceptable standard of public service. (Hall, 1988. Also Graham, 1988; Morris, 1988; Over, 1988; Smith, 1988; Wright, 1988)

DEFINITION AND CONTROL

Up to the mid-1980s the police publicly urged the development of their paramilitary capabilities (Rawlings, 1985), but as financial restrictions began to bite they recognised that emphasis on this area was undercutting other policing activities. Moreover, large-scale paramilitary operations were difficult to justify, not just to those communities which were targeted, but also to those which had been stripped of their officers (Waddington, 1985). This is not to say that the police wish to relinquish, or to resist further extensions of, their paramilitary gains – far from it – but there has been some reaction, particularly after the miners' strike in 1984–5. Officers showed a dislike of 'serving as Maggie Thatcher's private army' and doing the NCB's 'dirty work'; even Anderton was worried that the police were acquiring 'the image of a heavy-handed mob stopping people from going about their lawful duties' (Morris, 1987; *Police Review*, 24 May 1985; Rawlings, 1985; Commons Debates, 10 April 1986, col. 217). Of course, a cynic might view such post-strike remarks simply as attempts to deflect criticisms about the use of aggressive police tactics.

Nevertheless, many in the police have become concerned about the service's declining image. Polls by the *Daily Express*, the Consumers' Association and MORI in 1989 showed public dissatisfaction with the police in many, although not all, areas of their work and a marked decline in public support since 1981. Even the *British Social Attitudes* survey, which Eastwood regarded as revealing 'a high degree of public support' because it indicated that the police enjoy a greater share of public confidence than any other group, revealed that only 51 per cent of the public trusted the police to act in the public interest (*Police Review*, 31 March 1989, 21 July 1989, 14 April 1989; Jowell, Witherspoon and Brook, 1988). Significantly, the Metropolitan Police commissioned a report in 1988 on how the force might improve its public image from Wolff Olins, a public relations agency, and as a result launched a campaign called the Plus Programme (*Police Review*, 14 April 1989, 21 April 1989).

In spite of their doubts about opinion polls, the police have come to recognise that public opinion can play an important part in their critique of the government's policies. The forthcoming report on the Operational Policing Review undertaken by the PF, SA and ACPO, which is likely to be the most concerted attack on the government's policies so far, draws on public as well as police opinion. Indeed during the late 1980s on public platforms the police have tended to concentrate on the idea that 'traditional policing' is being undermined by the government. However, although the 'traditional' element implies the cosy reassurance of 'Dixon of Dock Green' policing methods, what the phrase means has been kept deliberately vague: 'policing' is regarded by the police as the work which they do and, therefore, only they can really define what it entails. Curtis of the PF did give a hint that 'traditional policing' had a hard-edged nature when in 1987 he said that the lack of police officers meant that it was not always possible to provide 'effective preventive policing' and that this led to 'no-go' areas; he added, 'the traditional measured tread of the beat bobby has given way to tiptoeing in eggshells. Conventional policing cannot operate for fear of repercussions' (*Guardian*, 31 May 1987). But the phrase 'traditional policing' also implies a critique of a government which is seen as undermining the autonomy of the police by increasing central control through tighter auditing and inspection strategies supported by sanctions based on finance and establishment levels. However, by arguing that the government has undermined 'traditional policing' the police have unwittingly placed on the agenda the fundamental, and previously unasked, questions about what the police should do. As the police focus on the activities of non-police agencies they succeed all too well in highlighting the shortfall in their own capabilities and in revealing both that there is no immutable definition of what constitutes 'policing' and that the police are not the only ones who can perform 'policing' tasks. Other agencies, communities and individuals do this work not only when the police fail to deal with a category of crime adequately, as with shoplifting or racial attacks, but also routinely as a part of everyday living (Shapland and Vagg, 1988). In other words, policing is a term which defines a set of activities, not the work of a particular group of people. This stands against the view of the police, who readily acknowledge the importance of outside groups and individuals in crime prevention and detection, but seek to do so in terms of a relationship – Newman called it a 'notional social contract' – which portrays the police as ultimately in control. So, although the government's change of direction on policing emerged from very specific political concerns, the furious debate which followed has raised the possibility of some attention being given to fundamental questions about police work. Certainly the police are trying to give the impression that the government is considering these questions. Of course, to some extent this makes dubious assumptions about the formation of criminal justice policy, but leaving that aside the problem is that the government's answers to the questions about policing are likely to come not from a dogmatic adherence to unconnected ideological objectives.

REFERENCES

BRIDGMAN, R., OLDING, G. and CROSSLAND, M. (1988) *The Private Security Industry*, mimeograph.

CLARKE, A. and TAYLOR, I. (1980) 'Vandals, Pickets and Muggers: Television Coverage of Law and Order in the 1979 Election', *Screen Education*, 36 (Autumn), pp. 99–111.

CLARKE, A., TAYLOR, I. and WREN-LEWIS, J. (1981) *Law and Order, Television and the General Election of 1979*, University of Sheffield, Centre for Criminological and Sociological Studies, Law and Order Project, paper no. 1.

CLARKE, A., TAYLOR, I. and WREN-LEWIS, J. (1982) 'Inequality of Access to Political Television: The Case of the General Election of 1979', in D. Robbins (ed.), *Rethinking Social Inequality*, Aldershot: Gower, pp. 149–83.

CONSERVATIVE CENTRAL OFFICE (1977) *The Right Approach*, London.

CONSERVATIVE CENTRAL OFFICE (1979) *Manifesto*, London.

DRUCKER, P. (1955) *The Practice of Management*, London: Heinemann.

EAST, D. A. (1988) *Annual Report 1987*, South Wales Constabulary.

EDMUND-DAVIES, LORD (1978) *Committee of Inquiry on the Police*, Cmnd 7283.

ELLIOTT, N. (1989) *Streets Ahead*, London: Adam Smith Institute.

GRAHAM, D. J. (1988) *Chief Constable's Annual Report 1987*, Cheshire Constabulary.

HALL, J. (1988) *Humberside Police Annual Report 1987*.

HALL, S. (1979) *Drifting into a Law and Order Society*, London: Cobden Trust.

HM CHIEF INSPECTOR (1987) *Report of Her Majesty's Chief Inspector of Constabulary for the year 1986*, HC 32, July 1987.

IMBERT, SIR P. (1988) 'Policing London', *Police Journal*, 61, pp. 199–208.

JOWELL, R., WITHERSPOON, S. and BROOK, L. (1988) *British Social Attitudes: The 5th Report*, Aldershot: Gower.

LOVEDAY, B. (1986) 'Central Coordination, Police Authorities and the Miners' Strike', *Political Quarterly*, 57, pp. 60–73.

LOVEDAY, B. (1989) 'Poor Prospects for Police Civilians'. *Policing*, 5, 2 (Summer) pp. 86–95.

MARK, R. (1977) *Report of the Commissioner of Police of the Metropolis for the year 1976*.

MAXFIELD, M. (1984) *Fear of Crime in England and Wales*, London: HMSO.

MORRIS, T. (1987) 'Police Force', *New Society*, 20 March, pp. 12–14

MORRIS, T. A. (1988) *Hertfordshire Constabulary Annual Report 1987*.

NEWMAN, SIR K. (1985) *Principles of Policing and Guidance for Professional Behaviour*, London: Public Information Department, Metropolitan Police.

NEWMAN, SIR K. (1986a) *A Police for the People: Report of the Commissioner of Police of the Metropolis for the year 1985*, Cmnd 9790.

NEWMAN, SIR K. (1986b) *The Strategy Report of the Commissioner of Police of the Metropolis to the Home Secretary*, London: Home Office.

NEWMAN, SIR K. (1987) *Report of the Commissioner of Police of the Metropolis for the year 1986*. Cmnd 158.

OVER, J. (1988) *Chief Constable's Annual Report 1987, Gwent.*

PENNELL, S., CURTIS, C. and HENDERSON, J. (1986) *Guardian Angels: An Assessment of Citizen Response to Crime*, US Dept. of Justice, National Institute of Justice.

RAWLINGS, P. (1985) ' "Bobbies", "Aliens" and Subversives: The Relationship between Community Policing and Coercive Policing', in J. Baxter and L. Koffman (eds), *The Police, the Constitution and the Community*, Abingdon: Professional Books.

REINER, R. (1980) 'Fuzzy Thoughts: The Police and Law-and-Order Politics', *Sociological Review*, 28, 2, pp. 377–413.

REINER, R. (1985a) *The Politics of Policing*, London: Wheatsheaf.

REINER, R. (1985b) 'A Watershed in Policing', *Political Quarterly*, 56, pp. 122–31.

SCARMAN, LORD (1981) *The Brixton Disorders, April 10–12, 1981,* Cmnd 8427.

SHAPLAND, J. and VAGG, J. (1988) *Policing by the Public*, London: Routledge.

SMITH, C. (1988) *The Annual Report of the Chief Constable to the Thames Valey Police Authority 1987.*

SPENCER, S. (1985) *Police Authorities during the Miners' Strike*, Working Paper No. 1, London: Cobden Trust.

TAYLOR, I. (1987) 'Law and Order, Moral Order: The Changing Rhetorics of the Thatcher Government', *Socialist Register*, pp. 297–331.

TUCK, M. (1989) *Drinking and Disorder: A Study of Non-Metropolitan Violence*, Home Office Research & Planning Unit, Paper 108, London: HMSO.

WADDINGTON, P. A. J. (1985) *The Effects of Police Manpower Depletion During the NUM Strike, 1984–85*, London: The Police Foundation.

WILKINSON, F. (1989) 'Forget About Oliver Twist', *Policing*, 5, 2 (Summer), pp. 96–106.

WRIGHT, P. (1988) *Annual Report of the Chief Constable of South Yorkshire Police 1987.*

3 Chief Constables in England and Wales: A Social Portrait of a Criminal Justice Elite

Robert Reiner

'The term "elite" originally meant, and in many contexts still means, the best, the excellent, the noble, or the creme de la creme' (Dunleavy and O'Leary, 1987, p. 136)

'ACPO Rules is not OK' (*New Statesman*, 23 May 1986, p. 3)

INTRODUCTION

The leadership of the police forces in this country has never been considered in analyses of elites or of the structure of power. Policing generally has largely been ignored in political sociology, figuring only in some Marxist analyses as a taken-for-granted aspect of the state, its first-line repressive apparatus whose inner functioning scarcely called for serious research or analysis.

The aim of this chapter is to establish that the leadership of police forces, the chief constables in the United Kingdom, are an elite group of increasing national importance. It will be shown, however, that their social characteristics differ significantly from other elite groups which have traditionally been considered in assessments of the structure of power. It is perhaps these sociological differences which have diverted attention away from a consideration of police chiefs in the context of elite studies. The idiosyncratic characteristics of the police elite, it will be argued, can readily be made sense of in terms of the peculiar function of the police in the social structure, especially in Britain.

THE RESEARCH PROJECT

The data on which this chapter is based derive from a research project which was aimed at discovering the demographic characteristics and the policing philosophy of contemporary chief constables. This was intended to fill what I saw as a crucial gap in our knowledge of policing. While public debate and political controversy has focused largely on chief constables, their accountability (and their divinity), the growing body of social research on the police has had the opposite tendency. While there is now a large body of data on the characteristics of policing and police officers lower down the rank structure, virtually nothing is known about routine police life at the top.

The reasons for this are various. Partly it is due to a focus on the determination of street-level policing decisions, coupled with the belief that the police department has the special property within it discretion increases as one moves down the hierarchy' (Wilson, 1968, p. 7). A lot of sociological research has emphasised the over-simplifications entailed by the hierarchical model of top-down management control implied in much of the accountability debate. But if management cannot simply impose its will on police organisations, it is an equally one-sided distortion to disregard the importance of the formal policy-making levels (Reiner, 1985, pp. 174–80).

Probably the main reasons for the research focus on the lower ranks of the police are the same as those which explain the prevailing lack of empirical research on elites throughout sociology. Access and funding are largely dependent on elite levels of organisations and thus the bulk of attention is likely to be directed to issues relevant to their problems of control, and what they need to know in order to achieve this, i.e. the activities and the culture of the lower levels. These pressures in effect often conspire to make researchers willy-nilly 'servants of power' (Baritz, 1965). It is harder to gain access for studies of elites, because this knowledge is less useful to elites, and it may even be dangerous knowledge.

Given the almost complete lack of knowledge about chief constables, the purpose of my research was quite straightforward. In brief, the study was directed at finding out who chief constables are, and how they look at the world. The basic data-gathering was by a series of interviews with as many of the chief constables in post in England and Wales in September 1986 as I could get to see. (This was financed by a Nuffield Social Science Research Fellowship in 1986/7, for which I am profoundly grateful.) The process of negotiating access was protracted, and will be detailed in a forthcoming book on chief constables (to be published by Oxford University Press). I originally thought of the project in 1981–2, but at that time was not successful in getting approval from ACPO or the Home Office. However, I was able to get the support of these bodies in late 1986, and began approaching individual chief constables for interviews from October of that year. In the event I received an impressive and gratifying positive response from chief constables. Out of the 43 chief officers in England and Wales, I completed interviews with 40, all but one on tape. This amounts to a virtual census of current chief officers. The interviews lasted for between one-and-a-half to two hours in most cases, and asked questions about personal background, career history, and views on a range of policing issues: conceptions of the police role, crime control and public order methods, internal management, general social trends, and accountability.

This chapter will concentrate on the data gathered about the social characteristics of chief constables. (The more qualitative aspects examining the ideology of chief constables are not fully analysed yet.)

CHIEF CONSTABLES AS AN ELITE

Studies of the social origins and educational experiences of those elite groups which have been the focus of previous elite research all exhibit a common pattern which has become almost monotonous in its regularity and predictability. In a comprehensive and rigorous view of the theoretical and empirical literature on elites in Britain, Stanworth concludes:

> Despite a recent broadening in the recruitment of specific elites they remain dominated by persons from privileged social backgrounds. The contribution of the upper classes to most elites has declined but remains significant. Increasingly, British elites are drawn from the upper middle classes, and, to a much lesser extent, the lower middle classes. [T]here has been little working-class penetration of these institutional elites. The public school and Oxbridge continue to play a preeminent role in elite recruitment. Conversely, the contribution of the state sector has always remained small. (Stanworth, 1984, pp. 261–2)

These conclusion are based on a synthesis of research on the elites in the Church, the armed forces, the judiciary, the civil service, Parliament, industry and finance. As my data will show, the police elite differ profoundly from all these other institutions, in every one of the above cited points. There is only one common element between chief constables and Stanworth's summary of the social characteristics of elites in general: 'British elites have been almost exclusively male' (Stanworth, 1984). It should not go without saying that chief constables are also exclusively male (and white).

Is the explanation of the social differences between chief constables and other elites in fact that chief constables should not be considered an elite group? This can only be maintained if we adopt a circular definition of elites as groups with a privileged social background. Such a usage would not be unfamiliar, and indeed I found it among some chief constables. In my letter of introduction to chief constables seeking an interview, I said I was interested in them as an elite group with considerable power and influence. One chief I interviewed questioned my use of the word elite. He could not see this word as appropriate to describe a group of people many of whom came from ordinary working-class backgrounds. While these origins distinguish chief constables from most groups traditionally thought of as elites, I would maintain the term is appropriate.

Chief constables today all rank high on the three dimensions conventionally considered in studies of social stratification: economic class, social status or prestige, and political power. In economic terms, they command large salaries, with a wide range (according to size of force) upwards of £45 000 per annum. They also command very large resources. In 1983–4 the net expenditure of police forces ranged from a low of £16.3m (Dyfed-Powys) to a high (for the Metropolitan Police) of £66.71m. (The highest provincial budget was Greater Manchester: £131.5m.)

In status terms, perhaps the clearest index of the rise in chief constables' social standing is their move up in the New Year's Honours lists. Last year, Sir Philip Knights, former chief of West Midlands, became the first chief constable to be given a peerage. The knighting of one or two chief constables has become an annual pattern. The frequently remarked decline in the standing of the police in general in public opinion polls is more symptomatic of a questioning of all public institutions than of the police in particular (though they no longer enjoy the untarnished image of the Dixonesque 'golden age' of the 1950s). Such studies as the recent British Social Attitudes survey show that the police institution and leadership remains the most trusted pillar of the state.

In terms of power, the constitutional position of chief constables enshrined in statute and case-law gives them clear primacy in determining the policies of their forces – the doctrine of 'constabulary independence' (Lustgarten 1986; Reiner, 1988). This gives them at any rate formal power of an extensive kind. They have the last word in law in determining law-enforcement policies affecting considerable numbers of subordinate officers and citizens in their force areas. Police forces range in size from 935 (Dyfed-Powys) to the largest provincial force (Greater Manchester) 6 943, and the Met. with 28 115. The populations they police range from 445 000 (Gwent) to the largest provincial force population 2 624 000 (West Midlands), and 7 237 000 for the Met.

It seems clear that the 43 chief constables in England and Wales must on any reckoning be deemed a significant part of local elite structures. Many commentators have also argued that collectively, through the pressure-group activities of the Association of Chief Police Officers (ACPO), they have become the power that effectively determines national criminal justice policy. An influential vein of radical journalism has claimed that 'Policing in this country is run by an extra-constitutional and (in theory) informal body – the Association of Chief Police Officers' (*New Statesman*, 23 May 1986, pp. 3–4). (See also, Campbell, 1987 and Northam, 1988, where this thesis is elaborated with particular reference to the controversial ACPO Public Order Manual.) I have argued on the basis of my interviews with chief constables that the primary direction of influence runs from Home Office to chief constables rather than vice versa. But my data support the basic contention of a *de facto* national police force (Reiner, 1988, 1989). In the processes of negotiating national policing strategy there can be no doubt of the significant influence of chief constables collectively (and in some cases individually), even if the conspiratorial police-state versions which attribute them with effective control are one-sided accentuations with the emphasis on the wrong pole of a complex partnership.

It is this powerful position of chief constables today,

economically, socially and politically, which makes analysis of their social position and perspectives important. As one important recent study remarked: 'The kind of policing we enjoy is determined by this small group of men whose personal attitudes are a major factor in the creation of policing styles' (McCabe, Wallington *et al.*, 1988, p. 134).

WHO ARE THE CHIEF CONSTABLES? A SOCIAL PROFILE

Until the 1964 Police Act there remained a substantial divide in legal and social status between county chief constables and their borough namesakes. A valuable recent historical study by Wall has shown that while borough chiefs were upwardly mobile career police officers from humble origins, county chiefs were firmly parts of the local social elite. In 1905, three-quarters of county chiefs were included in such contemporary elite directories as *Who's Who* (Wall, 1987, p. 87). This was because of who they were rather than what they were (unlike the 50 per cent of contemporary chiefs who find themselves in such hallowed pages). 'The county chief constableship became a popular occupation for the younger sons of the landed gentry in the same way that the army and the cloth had done.' (Wall, ibid). This same social cachet which integrated county chiefs with the local elite cut them off from their men.

By contrast only 5 per cent of the borough chiefs in office in 1905 feature in the elite directories, and these were usually the heads of the very large city forces, whose origins were more exalted than those of their subordinates (albeit usually they were recruited from professional rather than military careers). But the majority of borough chiefs were men who had worked their way up the police ranks, and came from the same working (or at most lower-middle) class backgrounds as their subordinates. A common pattern was for boroughs to recruit their chiefs from the middle ranks of larger forces – usually the Met.

This division began to be eroded after the 1919 Desborough Committee recommended that chief constables should not be appointed without previous police experience. However, a number of devices limited the effect of this recommendation in the inter-war years, even though it was incorporated into an official regulation by the Home Secretary (Wall, 1987, p. 93). In the post-war period, the after-effects of the short-lived Trenchard Scheme in the 1930s which provided for direct entry of (mainly middle-class) graduates into the Hendon Police College as 'officer material' with accelerated promotion meant that down to the end of the 1960s a substantial proportion of chief officers, especially in the Met. and the largest provincial forces, were from middle-class backgrounds. However, coincidentally with the elimination of the differences in the constitutional position of county and borough chief constables by the 1964 Police Act, there occurred a homogenisation of their social origins as all chiefs converged on a common pattern of promotion from formally equal starting positions. (The constitutional position of the Commissioners of Police in London remains different, but they are not socially distinct any longer – all recent Commissioners have worked their way through the ranks, and most have been from provincial forces.)

THE BACKGROUND OF CHIEF CONSTABLES

Table 3.1 shows that the social backgrounds of chief constables are not wildly divergent from police officers in general, nor the population at large. The majority (52.5 per cent) had fathers whose work careers were spent mainly in skilled manual jobs, with 65 per cent having fathers who were in manual jobs for most of their careers. The majority of the rest (25 per cent overall) were in routine non-manual jobs. However, nearly half (45 per cent) of their fathers experienced occupational mobility during their own careers, and by the time the chiefs were 18, only 50 per cent remained in manual work. About a third had fathers who ended up in managerial or professional positions (31.5 per cent and 2.5 per cent respectively).

This experience of upward social mobility is a characteristic of the police in general (Reiner, 1978, p. 150). But it is far more marked among chief officers. They have themselves moved up into the Registrar General's Class II, by virtue of being chief constables. In addition, their initial pre-police ocupations were predominantly non-manual (47.5 overall, with 32.5 per cent having no previous job). Their own adult children exhibit even more marked mobility (allowing for the distortions of parental

Table 3.1 Social origins and mobility of chief constables

(A)	*Father's social class*	%	
	I	–	
	II	5	
	III Non-manual	25	
	III Manual	52.5	
	IV	5	
	V	7.5	
	N.A.	5	
	Police	15	
			N = *40*
(B)	*Class of own pre-police jobs*	%	
	I	10	
	II	7.5	
	III Non-manual	30	
	III Manual	20	
	IV	–	
	V	–	
	None	32.5	
			N = *40*
(C)	*Class of adult children's jobs*	%	
	I	17.3	
	II	52	
	III Non-manual	8	
	III Manual	–	
	IV	–	
	V	–	
	None	5.3	
	Police	17.4	
			N = *75*

pride). None are in manual occupations, and nearly 70 per cent are in professional or managerial ones.

Comparing chief constables with the sample of the Federated ranks (Reiner, 1978) in terms of father's occupation at age 18, Table 3.1 shows that the chiefs differed slightly but not enormously in the direction of having higher status fathers. But the difference is not marked, and is the result of the chiefs' fathers' own occupational mobility.

The proportion of chief constables with police fathers (15 per cent) is roughly the same as in the Federated ranks (14 per cent). But 42.5 per cent mentioned some police relative as an influence on joining. Interestingly 17 per cent of their children have followed their footsteps into the police (18 per cent have at least one child in the police, and there are a few three-generation police families).

The conclusion is clear: the chief constables of today are drawn predominantly from skilled working-class backgrounds, and have a family tradition very much marked by upward social mobility, over three generations. Chief constables can fairly be characterised as a 'working-class elite'. This is reflected in their educational experiences, shown in Table 3.2. The chiefs show a remarkable level of educational achievement compared with the norm for their class of origin, and with the general police level. I found in my earlier study of the Federated ranks that:

> policemen have done rather better educationally than other children from manual or lower level backgrounds. Twenty per cent of lower grade non-manual and skilled manual children born in the late 1930s went to grammar or independent schools. (Reiner 1978, p. 152)

But 50 per cent of the lower-ranked police in that study had done so; and of current chief constables, Table 3.2 shows that it was 85 per cent. Moreover, my earlier study showed that while the Federated ranks had done better than normal for their class of origin in terms of type of school attended, they did not do well in terms of school-leaving qualifications. But this is not true of chief constables. Only 15 per cent of chief constables left school with no qualifications, compared with 28.6 per cent of the lower ranks. Most chief constables left with some 'O' levels or school certificate passes.

In the 1962 Royal Commission, anxiety was expressed that there was 'no recent instance of a university graduate entering the service' (para. 308). This has been partly rectified because 9.3 per cent of the current intake of recruits are graduates, and 6 per cent of all police are (HMI Report 1988). But the chief constables are from earlier generations, and none entered the police with a degree. However, over a quarter acquired degrees during their service. Half of these degrees were obtained through the Bramshill Scholarship scheme, whereby the most successful students on the

Table 3.2 Education of chief constables

(A)	*School*	%	
	Elementary	7.5	
	Secondary modern	5	
	Technical	5	
	Grammar	80	
	Private	5	
			N = 40
(B)	*Age left school*	%	
	14	10	
	15	7.5	
	16	45	
	17	15	
	18+	22.5	
			N = 40
(C)	*School leaving qualifications*	%	
	None	15	
	School certificate	52.5	
	'O' levels	20	
	'A' levels	13.1	
			N = 40
(D)	*Degrees*	%	
	Chief constables	26	*N = 43*
	Deputy chief constables	40	*N = 43*
	Assistant chief constables	37	*N = 89*
	Current recruits	9.3	*N = 5225*
	All police	6	*N = 124 759*
(E)	*Present Age*	%	
	46–9	7.5	
	50–54	30	
	55–59	50	
	60+	12.5	
			N = 40
(F)	*Years as chief*	%	
	–3	30	
	4–5	32.5	
	6–9	17.5	
	10+	20	
			N = 40

Special Course at Bramshill go to university on police scholarships. The majority of the other degrees were either London externals or OU degrees, with a few gained by force secondments. In addition to these degrees, several chief constables have university diplomas, usually in criminology or management.

All this confirms the image of chief constables derived from looking at their social origins. They are predominantly drawn from the upwardly mobile, meritocratically achieving, skilled working class. If all police officers are socially mobile, the chiefs are 'super-mobile'.

ORIENTATION TO WORK AND CAREER HISTORIES

Most of the chiefs were set on a police career from a relatively young age. Although 67.5 per cent had worked outside the force before joining, only 12 had worked for more than two years at anything else. Ninety per cent had experience of military service, but of these the overwhelming majority (85 per cent) had only done National Service.

Eighty-five per cent of the chiefs had joined by the age of 22, and all before the age of 25, as Table 3.3 shows. However, my earlier study showed that of the same generation in the Federated ranks, over 113 joined after the age of 25. Most of the current chief constables (70 per cent) joined before 1954, and only one later than 1960. Their reasons for joining are predominantly an attraction to the job itself: 54 per cent gave purely non-instrumental reasons, 30 per cent mixed, with only 16 per cent instrumental. This is unusual in their generation. My earlier research found that of recruits joining before 1960, 41 per cent gave non-instrumental and 30 per cent instrumental reasons. Furthermore, while the main instrumental reason mentioned by the lower ranks was security, for the chief constable it was more likely to be the attraction of a career. (Though only two thought they would end up as a chief constable.)

Most of the chiefs were overwhelmingly satisfied with their careers. All said they were, and 76 per cent said they would rejoin if starting all over again. (This is a level that compares with professionals, and is far more than the norm for police, 51 per cent: Reiner, 1978, p. 173.) Thus most of the chiefs had looked to

Table 3.3 Careers of chief constables

(A)	*Date joined police*	%	
	–1949	20	
	1950–4	50	
	1955–9	27.5	
	1960–	2.5	
			N = *40*
(B)	*Age when joined*	%	
	19	5	
	20	32.5	
	21	30	
	22	17.5	
	23	7.5	
	24	5	
	25	2.5	
			N = *40*
(C)	*Service when promoted to sergeant*	%	
	–5 years	27.5	
	6–7 years	30	
	8–9 years	35	
	10+	7.5	
			N = *40*
(D)	*Age became chief constable*	%	
	–45	12.5	
	46–50	45	
	50+	42.5	
			N = *40*
(E)	*Present age*	%	
	46–9	7.5	
	50–54	30	
	55–50	59	
	60+	12.5	
			N = *40*
(F)	*Years as chief*	%	
	–3	30	
	4–5	32.5	
	6–9	17.5	
	10+	20	
			N = *40*

policing for an intrinsically interesting career, and had clearly found what they were looking for.

EXPERIENCES IN THE JOB

Most police officers are 'locals' not 'cosmopolitans' in Robert Merton's terminology. They have spent most if not all of their lives in the force area where they work. This is decidedly not true of chief constables. Indeed this is partly due to explicit policy. Regulations prevent a person serving more than two of the three ACPO ranks in the same force.

Consequently all chiefs will have served in at least one other force during their careers. However, only 10 per cent have served in only the minimum one other force. As Table 3.4 shows, 50 per cent have served in two others, and 40 per cent in three or more others. Most will have experience of a mixture of city and county forces. Nine have only worked in city forces, and only three have purely county experience (although most forces are county ones). Interestingly, as many as 40 per cent have served in the Met. (usually as the Force they initally joined and worked most of their careers in). It still seems to be the pattern, as in the early history of provincial city policy, that the Met. provides their senior officers!

Almost all will have had experience of at least one of the command courses at the Police Staff College, Bramshill. Only two of the chiefs had not been on the Senior Command Course. Fifteen per cent have been on the Special Course for potential high-flyers amongst constables, which since it only started in 1962 is a high proportion of those chiefs young enough to be eligible for it. In addition to these national elite training courses, several (15 per cent) have been on the Royal College of Defence Studies Course, an invitation-only one-year course primarily for senior military officers, diplomats and civil servants. Almost all have served on an operational attachment to a national policing body, for example, HM Inspectorate.

In terms of careers and training, chief constables, unlike their subordinates, are decidedly (and by design) 'cosmopolitans' not 'locals'. By the time they reach ACPO rank they will have developed a network of national contacts and experiences. Most will have had a variety of work experience within their forces. It is a commonly held police myth that specialist detectives are

Table 3.4 Work experience of chief constables

(A)	*No. of previous forces worked in*	%	
	1	10	
	2	50	
	3	32.5	
	4+	7.5	
			N = *40*
(B)	*Types of previous force*	%	
	County only	7.5	
	City only	22.5	
	Mixed	70	
	Metropolitan Police	40	
			N = *40*
(C)	*Specialism*	%	
	CID more than half career	32.5	
	Uniform more than half career	57.5	
	CID = uniform	10	
			N = *40*
(D)	*National courses*	%	
	Senior command course	95	
	Other command course	85	
	Special course	15	
	Royal College of Defence Studies	15	
			N = *40*
(E)	*Previous post when appointed chief constable*	%	
	Deputy chief constable in another force	52.5	
	Deputy chief constable in same force	27.5	
	Chief constable in another force	7.5	
	ACPO rank in Metropolitan Police	7.5	
	Other	5	
			N = *40*

unlikely to reach the top. In fact, 32.5 per cent of my sample have been detectives for more than half of their careers. But the majority had a mixed bag of operational experience, albeit predominantly in uniform territorial patrol work.

For most, promotion was rapid, at any rate after the first hurdle of promotion to sergeant, which took 7 years on average. The average time for all other promotions was 2–3 years. The average age of appointment as chief constable was 50. The youngest appointment was 42, and the oldest 56. Only five were appointed chief constable before 45, and most were appointed in their late 40s. They had been chief constables for somewhere between a few months and twelve years, and on average had been in post for five years. The longevity in service of earlier generations has disappeared.

The percentage appointed chief constable while being deputy in another force was 52.5, and 27.5 per cent had been promoted from deputy in the same force. Three had been chief constables in smaller forces, three had held ACPO rank in the Met. when appointed, and two had been respectively commandant and deputy commandant at Bramshill.

What conclusions can be drawn from the demographic profile of chief constables? Their origins, education, occupational socialisation, and career patterns indicate that they constitute a unitary national elite. They overwhelmingly come from a similar background, the upwardly mobile, educationally successful, skilled working class. They have similar (though atypical) education experiences. they came with similar initial approaches to the police, and were singled out comparatively early on for rapid advancement. They will have got to know each other through moving between forces, and passing through the Police Staff College, and other shared training experiences. They will have been exposed to the same nationally designed curriculum for senior officers. If this is not enough, none will have been appointed chief constable unless they have first been approved by the Home Office as suitable to be on the short-list interviewed by the Police Authority, and after selection their appointment must be formally approved by the Home Secretary (Police Act 1964, s. 4(2)). Small wonder there are no publicly aired disputes between chief constables and central government. The chances of a rogue appointment being made are clearly minuscule.

In the interview, an orientation to central rather than local government comes through fairly consistently. Most chiefs wish to cultivate and indeed believe they enjoy good relations with their police authorities. This means at best that they would seek to persuade them to accept their views if disagreements arose, not that they would accept the authority's opinions. (Reiner, 1988, 1989). This comes out clearly, for example, in a question I asked about the use of plastic bullets. Most chief constables (76 per cent) would use them if they deemed it necessary, even in the face of police authority opposition, although they would prefer to carry them along by persuasion. The following approach is typical: 'A lot depends on the circumstances. To start with I wouldn't be concerned about the police authority. If it came down to my professional judgment. It all depends, the scenario is not always the same. If you do have your elected members at the scene, your community relations council, there is nothing like them seeing what the situation is. If not, what you're going to do is make the decision, go ahead, use it, and then provide the evidence afterwards.' This indicates that while consensus is preferred, when the buck has to stop the decisions is the chief constable's regardless of the police authority's views.

But this is not the attitude taken to the Home Office. While many rail at this, often bitterly, it is recognised that the Home Office issues many regulations which in effect have to be obeyed. Even its nominally advisory circulars can be ignored only at the chief constable's peril. While disagreements may be strongly argued, this time when the buck stops it is normally the chief who backs down. Again a typical quote: 'We would all stand and fight our corner to the death if we felt that we were right and they (the Home Office) were wrong, and they were trying to manipulate us or instruct us, but on the other hand one would wish certainly not to be too far out of step with the thinking of the Home Office, who of course are influenced by the government of the day.'

For all the pride that chief constables express in their independence, and all the testimony they pay to the value attached to good relations with local authorities, the overall sense I have is that their professional colleagues – and it is ACPO and the HMI that are seen as their peers – are the prime reference group. The Home Office is often resented, and its authority may not be respected. But at the end of the day it has power, as well as the legitimacy of an electoral mandate. The local authority is not seen in this light. Preferably it can be educated to understand the professional point of view. But if not, it is that professional judgement which counts. To an extent this picture is over-drawn and over-simplified. There are individual variations and some chiefs are more fiercely independent, and more locally oriented, than others. But in the main the prime reference group is the national professional one, and the Home Office is accepted as boss, however resentfully (Reiner, 1989).

CONCLUSION

Where do chief constables fit in the pattern of British elites? It has been established that chief constables command as much power, people, prestige, pay and other resources as most groups usually considered in elite analyses. However, they are radically different in social origins and career patterns. Uniquely for a group of their importance they come from working-class backgrounds and lack any roots in ruling or privileged circles. This has always been true of the majority of chief police officers, although until the Second World War it was not the case for county chiefs or the Metropolitan Commissioners.

The reasons for this lie in the peculiar role of the police institution in the social and political structure. The police are the front-line of the penetration by the state of civil society, and more particularly of the most marginal and least integrated sectors of society. Policing is the process whereby in modern states the 'central power exercises potentially violent supervision over the population by bureaucratic means widely diffused through civil society in small and discretionary operations that are capable of rapid concentration' (Silver, 1976, p. 8).

In all liberal democracies, but especially in England, the state and police elites have tried to achieve the objective of 'policing by consent' by constructing widespread popular legitimacy for the police. Over the long sweep of police history this legitimacy has been achieved, however tenuously, by a variety of devices (Reiner, 1985, chs 1 and 2). One part of the self-conscious strategy for legitimating the police in England was the recruitment of men who (in Robert Peel's words) 'had not the rank, habits or station of gentlemen' (cited in Gash, 1961, p. 502). As the standard text of police history puts it: 'The police was to be a homogeneous and democratic body, in tune with the people, understanding the people, belonging to the people, and drawing its strength from the people' (Critchley, 1978, p. 52).

This has been the predominant model for city forces, although throughout the nineteenth century an alternative more militaristic model prevailed in county policing (Steedman, 1984). The idea of a more militaristic model for at any rate the senior levels of police forces has continued to be influential, and was embodied in the Trenchard notion of a distinct 'officer class' to be produced by the Hendon Police College in the 1930s. This notion remains popular in some conservative circles, with *The Daily Telegraph* for example calling in recent years for a revived Trenchard Scheme and 'officer class'.

However, the weight of official thinking has supported the view that effective police leadership requires extensive experience in the operational ranks. This is particularly important in view of the perennial tendency within police organisations of alienation between 'street' and 'management' levels. The extra requirements of managerial responsibility, especially in recent years with the growing emphasis on a more 'professional' style represented by such fashions as 'policing by objectives' (Butler, 1984; Bradley *et al.*, 1986), has carried with it a growing concern for the quality of training for leadership. To date this has not meant any fundamental departure from the Desborough principle of internally recruited leadership. Training and education have been delivered in mid-career to recruits joining without higher education qualifications, at the Bramshill Police Staff College and by secondments to universities. In the last 25 years the Graduate Entry Scheme and the Special Course at Bramshill have provided limited avenues of accelerated promotion for a favoured few, but the full effects of these will only be manifest in the next generation of chief constables. The House of Commons Home Affairs Committee is currently conducting an inquiry into higher police training and the role of Bramshill, and there may be profound changes in future.

However, there is now a solid weight of tradition (as well as the voice of the Police Federation) supporting the view that legitimacy and effectiveness of policing can best be achieved by an internally generated leadership. The result of this has been the production of the socially unique elite constituted by chief constables, who may truly be regarded as a working-class aristocracy.

REFERENCES

BARITZ, L. (1965) *The Servants of Power*, New York: Wiley.

BUTLER, A. J. P. (1984) *Police Management*, Aldershot: Gower.

BRADLEY, D., WALKER, N. and WILKIE, R. (1986) *Managing the Police*, Brighton: Wheatsheaf.

CAMPBELL, D. (1987) 'Policing: A Power in the Land', *New Statesman*, 8 May, pp. 11–12.

CRITCHLEY, T. A. (1978) *A History of Police in England and Wales*, London: Constable.

DUNLEAVY, P. and O'LEARY, B. (1987) *Theories of the State*, London: Macmillan.

GASH, N. (1961) *Mr. Secretary Peel* London: Longman.

LUSTGARTEN, L. (1986), *The Governance of the Police*, London: Sweet & Maxwell.

McCABE, S., WALLINGTON, P *et al.*, (1988) *The Police, Public Order and Civil Liberties*, London: Macmillan.

NORTHAM, G. (1988) *Shooting in the Dark*, London: Faber.

REINER, R. (1978) *The Blue-Coated Worker*, Cambridge: Cambridge University Press.

REINER, R. (1985) *The Politics of the Police*, Brighton: Wheatsheaf.

REINER, R. (1988) 'In the Office of Chief Constables', *Current Legal Problems 1988*, London: Stevens.

REINER, R. (1989) 'Where the Buck Stops: Chief Constables' Views on Police Accountability', in R. Morgan and D. Smith (eds), *Coming to Terms with Policing*, London: Routledge.

SILVER, A. (1967) 'The Demand for Order in Civil Society', in D. Bordua (ed.), *The Police*, New York: Wiley.

STANWORTH, P. (1984) 'Elites and Privilege', in P. Abrams and R. Brown (eds), *UK Society*, London: Weidenfeld & Nicholson.

STEEDMAN, C. (1984) *Policing the Victorian Community*, London: Routledge.

WALL, D. (1987) 'Chief Constables: A Changing Elite', in R. Mawby (ed.), *Policing Britain*, Plymouth Polytechnic: Dept. of Social and Political Studies.

WILSON, J. Q. (1968) *Varieties of Police Behaviour*, Cambridge: Harvard University Press.

4 The Dual Role of the Royal Ulster Constabulary in Northern Ireland

Kathleen Magee

HISTORICAL BACKGROUND AND POLITICAL DEVELOPMENT OF THE ROYAL ULSTER CONSTABULARY

Under the government of Ireland Act 1920, the Royal Irish Constabulary (RIC) was to be split into two forces under the new devolved authorities in the North and South. The Northern Ireland government and the Minister for Home Affairs took on responsibility for establishing a new force in Northern Ireland. A committee was appointed and in March 1922 it recommended that the new force consist of 3000 policemen, of which one-third was to be Catholic, one third Protestant, recruited from the RIC, and the remaining third drawn from the Ulster Special Constabulary (USC). Under the Constabulary Act, the Royal Ulster Constabulary (RUC) formally came into existence in June 1922. However, the Catholic quota was never filled due to political pressures on the Unionist government, the attitudes of Catholics towards the new state, and relations between Protestants and Catholics within the new police force (Brewer *et al.* 1988, pp. 48–9).

The Civil Authorities, or Special Powers Act, which came into operation in April 1922, gave the security forces arbitrary powers of arrest and search. The act was renewed annually up until 1928 when it was renewed for a further five years. In 1933 the Special Powers Act was enacted on a permanent basis. It was eventually repealed after the imposition of Direct Rule in the North in 1972. Central to the demands of the Civil Rights Movement in the 1960s, which set out to challenge the continuance of the Protestant monopoly of political power within Northern Ireland, was the repeal of the Special Powers Act and the disbandment of the B Specials. More general dissatisfaction with the RUC has meant that several Committees of Inquiry have been set up by British governments into its operations. In 1969 the Hunt Report looked into what it saw as the dual role of the RUC: on the one hand performing 'all those duties normally associated in the public mind with police forces elsewhere in the United Kingdom' while, on the other hand, undertaking, 'security duties of a military nature' (Hunt Committee, 1969, p. 13).

The Hunt Committee recommended that the RUC be relieved of all military duties for the reason that, 'any police force, military in appearance and equipment, is less acceptable to the minority and moderate opinion than if it is clearly civilian in character' (Hunt Committee, 1969, p. 21). The Hunt report was an attempt to normalise policing in Northern Ireland, bringing it closer to practices elsewhere in the United Kingdom: 'In effect, it represented the extension to Northern Ireland of the British state's liberal-democratic mode of policing' (Brewer *et al.*, 1988, p. 51). The period of disarmament following Hunt's recommendations was short-lived. The continuing political violence, resulting in several police fatalities, led to the rearmament of the RUC at the beginning of 1971.

Direct Rule from Westminster came into operation in Northern Ireland in 1972, under which the British government assumed full responsibility for security in the North. However, the security role of the RUC remained subordinate to that of the army. The idea behind Direct Rule was to encourage the development of devolved government in Northern Ireland. Failures to establish a satisfactory form of government in Northern Ireland form the back-drop to the adoption between 1975 and 1976 of the policies of police primacy, Ulsterisation, and the criminalisation of political violence.

By 1976 the policy of police primacy put the army in a subordinate role to that of the RUC; the role of the army being to provide aid for the civil power. In the face of continuing political violence, the militarisation of policing has been the inevitable outcome of a policy of police primacy (Brewer *et al.*, 1988, p. 59). The RUC's principle role in the security field has not only meant the partial remilitarisation of the police, but the adoption of sophisticated technologies and a large-scale construction programme. Since 1970 a variety of specialist units have been set up to assist in maintaining public order and combating terrorism. Particularly important are Headquarters Mobile Support Units (HMSU) and Divisional Mobile Support Units (DMSU). established in the early 1980s to provide mobile reserve forces used both in a counter-insurgency role and in riot situations. A specialist surveillance unit trained by the SAS, known as E4A, was set up to take on an anti-terrorist role within the force. It is this unit which was central to the controversial 'shoot-to-kill' incidents in 1982.

While the army has now assumed a low profile in Northern Ireland the resurgence of police primacy has not had the effect of substantially demilitarising the overall security effort. Paramilitary-style policing has become the core feature of police work in Northern Ireland (Weitzer 1985: 48). The rationale behind the British government's policy of police primacy, which undermined the role of the army, was to fundamentally redefine the nature of the conflict – giving the impression of normality instead of crisis, and to target the security exercise provincially (Weitzer, 1985, p. 43; Brewer *et al.*, 1988, p. 65). Another contributory factor in the government's decision to give the lead in the security field over to the RUC was the decrease in the level of political violence. For example in 1972 the number of deaths resulting from 'the troubles' was 467; by 1976 this figure had fallen to 297 (Flackes and Elliott, 1989, p. 411). Using the army rather than the police to combat political violence tended to enhance the Provisional IRA's legitimacy internationally by projecting an image of the organisation as a guerrilla army fighting a war of national liberation. The strength of the British army fell from 22 000 in 1972 to 9500 in 1984 while RUC personnel increased from 4257 to 8127 (Weitzer, 1985, p. 44). Primary responsibility for riot control, counter-insurgency operations, and intelligence gathering was gradually transferred to the RUC (Hamill, 1985, chs 7, 8).

An important element of Ulsterisation is the Ulster Defence Regiment (UDR) which was established in 1970 to replace the discredited B Specials, regarded as Ulster's most blatantly biased police body. This move seemed to signal a new commitment to liberalise policing in Northern Ireland. However, although the UDR initially attracted significant numbers of Catholic recruits, Catholic disaffection grew due to the introduction of internment and intimidation by Republican paramilitaries. The UDR is now an almost wholly Protestant force with the number of Catholics falling below 3 per cent.

The Police Federation, the body which comes closest to a police trade union, has been critical of the militarisation of policing. Alan Wright, the Chairman of the Federation, has argued that the army should be responsible for border security and counter-insurgency operations as these are not functions of a civilian police force. The Federation's concern to limit the role of the police stems from the very high rate of casualties among police officers since the adoption of police force primacy – the highest in the world for a police in terms of fatalities (Murray, 1984).

The pervasiveness of security duties in RUC work is reflected in the Chief Constable's disclosure that insurgent activity consumes 80 per cent of police time (*Irish Times*, 24 January 1985). The fact that the police ride in armoured landrovers, wear bullet-proof flakjackets, patrol in combat-ready style and operate out of fortress-like police stations, is indicative of their military image (Weitzer, 1985, p. 48).

Northern Ireland's profound divisions militate against the normalisation of policing. And although significant changes have been made in certain areas of policing in the North, the force still remains overwhelmingly Protestant and is considered illegitimate by a significant proportion of the Catholic population. The introduction of the Anglo-Irish Agreement in November 1985 outlined a need for a programme of special measures in Northern Ireland to improve relations between the security forces and the community. A suggestion endorsed in the agreement was to increase the proportion of Catholics in the force.

Enloe sees unrest and disorder as characteristic of ethnically divided societies, pointing out that 'the police force's ability to maintain order in ethnically divided countries is in part determined by the ethnic composition and ethnic biases of the police' (1980, p. 86). Referring to the political situation in Northern Ireland, Enloe argues that 'any lasting resolution to the inter-ethnic conflict in Ulster will require military withdrawal and the establishment of a multi-ethnic Ulster police force accepted by both Catholics and Protestants' (1980, p. 103).

RESEARCHING THE ROYAL ULSTER CONSTABULARY

Throughout the year I spend researching the RUC, the duality of their role was a subject which tended to recur time and again, in talk about how members saw this dichotomy and how they felt it affecting other aspects of policing, such as comradeship, attitudes to transfers and the threat of attack. One constable at 'Easton', the pseudonym for the station where I was based, had this to say on the military aspect of policing in the North:

> The thing I resented when I was in Carrickmore was we had to do exactly the same work as the army, but we didn't have the same equipment or facilities. Like we've still to wear our caps; the soldiers have berets which are more practical for the sort of work you're doing. You see, that's the Chief Constable's idea; he wants the police to maintain a police image; even though we're doing a soldier's job. It's not practical so it's not.
>
> In Carrickmore the army had those ACM things. I'm sure you've seen them, they carry them on their backs, they're used to block a radio controlled bomb from going off. A policeman was blown up by one of those radio controlled bombs and the police asked for those ACMs, but they wouldn't supply the police with them. Yet we have to do the same job as the army without them.

The military aspect of policing in Northern Ireland pervades the life of the force. Even in so-called 'soft areas', where there is little or no terrorist activity, police wear flakjackets, patrol in landrovers, carry hand guns, and occasionally machine guns. In the more dangerous areas, the paramilitary mode of policing is yet more prominent. The following extract from the field-notes illustrates my awareness of the change in styles of policing from the 'soft' setting of 'Easton' to the 'hard' setting of West Belfast:

> The inspector who would be showing me around the Falls area of West Belfast prepared himself to go out in an armoured vehicle. First he put on his gun, then his flakjacket; he put his baton into his pocket; he then put on his radio, attaching a microphone from the radio to the flakjacket and putting on an ear-piece, so that messages would not be blurted out in public and only he would hear them. Finally he put on his hat and we were ready.

The RUC in West Belfast patrol under army cover: yet another feature of policing in a hard area which does not exist in softer areas. Army cover involves the police patrolling in a landrover flanked in front and behind by army landrovers – one of which will have a hatch with two soldiers poised, rifles in hands, providing cover for the vehicles.

Although the police in West Belfast work in relatively close contact with the army, the relationship between the two is best described as official rather than collegial. One of the reasons for this is that army units are only based in Northern Ireland for four-month periods at a time. The following quote from an inspector in West Belfast gives some idea of the nature of relations between the police and army in this area:

> We have a good working relationship on the ground, but our relationship with the army authorities tends to be not so good. Ach, it varies really, but like the current major that we have now is not great and it really depends on what he's like. Some units are OK, some aren't. The ones we have in at the minute are cretins and we tell them that to their faces, they're useless they really are.
>
> See, we had the Royal Marines in here and they were great, a real crack regiment . . . The Marines are also far more relaxed about things like rank and they were a better regiment . . . It was part of their whole attitude, the Marines had better things to worry about than rank. But basically the role of the army here is to stop the terrorists from killing us. To provide us with cover.

This quote illustrates how the police view the role of the army as subordinate to their own.

THE DUAL ROLE AND ASPECTS OF POLICING IN NORTHERN IRELAND

What I intend to consider in the remainder of this chapter is how the paramilitary role which the police are required to adopt influences their attitudes to such aspects of the job as transfers, the threat of attack, comradeship, informality in stations, and so on. Finally I will consider the overall implications of the increasing militarisation of policing.

Surprising as it may seem, some members of the force expressed a preference for policing in the 'harder' more dangerous areas. Of course a desire to impress a female researcher and to appear brave and macho may have influenced these accounts to some extent. Although only a minority expressed this choice, this chapter will address them in order to demonstrate that some members enjoy a paramilitary role.

There are several elements intertwined with this preference

toward policing in dangerous areas. Some constables may derive more satisfaction from policing under dangerous conditions because they feel they are getting closer to the goals of the organisation. Such feelings are conveyed by a constable in the following remark:

> I've been at Easton for two years now and you come in, do your eight hours, they [higher ranking officers] get you to do a few files, a wee bit of this, a wee bit of that. You go home, get your pay at the end of the month . . . But the thing that really gets me about here is, they kick up a big fuss over the least wee thing. This is where I feel they've lost sight of what it's all about to me. The sarg will think I've cracked, but I'm thinking of putting in for a transfer to somewhere like Andytown [Andersonstown in West Belfast]. At least there the sergeants aren't ordering you about like you're their slaves. They're down at your level, they have to be. No one in Andytown station is concerned with the shine on your boots or if you need a haircut. You're getting closer to the problem in areas like that.

Deriving a greater degree of satisfaction from tasks which are regarded as closer to the overall goals of the organisation, has been a characteristic finding of other occupational studies. For instance, Blauner's study of automobile assembly-line workers illustrates how workers experienced feelings of alienation when working on only a small part of the whole product (1964, p. 23).

In soft areas like 'Easton', where there is virtually no terrorist activity, the priority of policing is the control of ordinary crime. Many officers at 'Easton' seemed to find the daily prospect of carrying out routine police tasks unsatisfying in comparison with the daring image that defeating terrorism conjures up. This preoccupation with the more dangerous side of policing, and their dissatisfaction with the mundane tasks of the job, is a topic identified by many writers on the police (Niederhoffer, 1967; Manning, 1977; Holdaway, 1983; Reiner, 1985; Fielding, 1988). Fielding has the following to say on why, in his opinion, police regard paperwork as an unsatisfying chore:

> One ground for the cynicism officers feel about paperwork stems from their development of a detailed local knowledge . . . Paper is less and less a satisfactory index of activity as the officer becomes increasingly informed by a rich body of particularised local knowledge. (1988, p. 7)

Furthermore, the more trivial aspects of policing in softer areas undermines what Reiner calls the constable's sense of mission

(1985, p. 88). Through this sense of mission the officer sees him/herself performing an essential role in safeguarding social order, a role which police in more dangerous areas come closer to fulfilling. As Manning points out, 'paperwork, court appearances, administrative tasks, or report writing were considered *ex post facto* glosses upon the real work on the ground' (1977, p. 160). At 'Easton' the officers continually complained about the amount of paperwork required of them, and although the constables in more dangerous areas are also required to do paperwork, the authorities in softer areas are more strict about it. Such attention to detail was regarded as pettiness by the police at 'Easton':

> You'll find that if a guy's been somewhere like Crossmaglen, often people tend to prefer that sort of place. They come here ['Easton'] and they complain that we pay too much attention to the wee trivial things. And a lot of the work we do here is just that. You see at 'Easton' you come into contact with Joe Public all the time; it's not like it's enemy number one outside the station door, as in some areas where you're constantly on your guard, you know.

The high level of comradeship existing in stations in the more dangerous areas of Northern Ireland was a factor that was continually mentioned by those who preferred policing in dangerous areas:

> Ach, basically I think it's because in harder areas like this [a station in West Belfast] there's a greater sense of comradeship among the men. You take it; up here if you're out on the street your life might depend on the reaction of your colleagues so people can't afford to fall out with one another up here. That's why you don't get as much bitching and that sort of think going on here as you probably would in areas like 'Easton'.

This endorses van Maanen's suggestion that 'The danger inherent in police work is part of the centripetal force pulling patrolmen together' (Manning and van Maanen, 1978, p. 118).

In Northern Ireland the threat involved in being a member of the security forces acts to intensify feelings of *esprit de corps* and cohesiveness thoughout the RUC. Officers would frequently comment on their tendency to socialise with colleagues; something which contributes to and is a consequence of the isolation of the police from the wider society. The danger which van Maanen sees pulling officers together, engenders a dependency on colleagues in harder areas and contributes to higher levels of comradeship not only within but between ranks.

The fact that several stations in hard areas do not have an officers' mess, the norm in stations in softer areas, is indicative of the relaxation of rank distinction. The imminence of danger in hard areas gives the police a sense of 'all in it together', which naturally undermines the rank hierarchy in such areas:

> There has been talk in the past about setting up an officers' mess here, but there's never been enough support to actually get it off the ground. I certainly wouldn't use one. Like you'll find in most bad areas the authorities will adopt a more relaxed attitude. At the very least sergeants are expected to go out in vehicles and inspectors are also expected to make the occasional appearance on the ground. If an incident occurs the inspector must go out to it. You can't be aloof. Can you imagine if I had been out in the vehicle with the lads and coming back for the break I said, 'OK I'm away off to the mess here. See ya back out in the vehicle.' You just don't do things like that here.

In contrast the police at 'Easton' continually complained about the strict authoritarian outlook of senior officers. The higher level of formality and discipline at Easton operated to undermine internal solidarity between the ranks. Police who had been based in a dangerous setting would often reminisce about the more relaxed disciplinary attitude which prevails in stations in harder areas. A reason for this relaxation of discipline in dangerous areas is due to the fact that senior officers do not want to add to the pressure the constables are already under. Therefore, turning a blind eye to rule bending and easing is more commonplace in hard areas:

> Like the men will come to me and they'll say, look I had to leave my car in, can I knock off half hour or an hour earlier to collect it. And I'll say OK. Or they might ask if they can go into town for a bit of PB [personal business]. Like they're probably only going to get a card for the wife's birthday or something, so I'd let them go.

Other writers on the police have noted that police work which does not incorporate the essential elements of danger, speed and excitement get categorised as not 'real police work' (Manning, 1977). For the outsider observing the RUC and witnessing clashes between the police and rioters on television, the riot situation appears violent and terrifying. However, when questioned about how they felt when involved in a riot situation it would seem that some officers get a buzz from this action-centred style of policing:

Riots? Well, put it like this, most of the boys here enjoy them. There's not a bit of fear. It's a big game really. No one gets unduly concerned about a riot. It's a bit of crack, a bit of fun. That's how I would describe it. Like if a man's asked to go on guard duty when a riot's on he'd probably complain because he'd want to be out in it. The way I would describe it is, it's the same sort of feeling as going out to a football match.

Of course such opportunities to vent frustration at being targets for republicans and other paramilitary groups rarely occur in the softer areas. Also in the remote border areas the absence of a 'visible enemy' was a factor which those who had served in such areas were cogently aware of. They often described their feelings of vulnerability in these settings in terms of: 'You're a sitting duck up there in those stations', or 'You're a moving target'. The insecurity arising from this feeling of being a 'moving target'. nurtures prejudical attitudes among the police in any area with a high level of terrorist activity.

This is not, however, the place in which to discuss bigotry within the RUC; only to say that sectarian attitudes are present in some members of the force, and would seem to be most prominent in more dangerous areas where police awareness of the terrorist threat is heightened by the vulnerabilty of their position.

CONCLUSION

What must be considered at this juncture is the significance of the paramilitary role which the RUC adopt. As Ronald Weitzer suggests, there is the problem that 'paramilitary style [policing] will have a brutalising effect on officers, and that its institutionalisation will undermine progress toward normalisation' (1985, p. 49). Even the former Chief Constable, Sir John Hermon has acknowledged the problems facing the RUC should 'the troubles' end: 'we'd have a stupendous job of reorienting the whole force to a community style service role . . . [each officer] would have to become almost an entirely different sort of policeman' (quoted in Hart, 1980, p. 30).

There are several factors which act to deter the normalisation of policing in Northern Ireland. A major factor is the continuing political violence, a facet of which are the frequent and fatal attacks on members of the security forces. The fact that the security force's main assailants are largely drawn from, and foster support within, Catholic ghetto areas has an adverse influence on the police view of Catholics. Consequently a minority of the force tend to view any member of the Catholic community with suspicion. Coupled with this is the fact that the RUC continues to be seen as a Protestant force siding with Protestant loyalism, despite the hiatus in RUC-loyalist relations following the inception of the Anglo-Irish agreement. Furthermore, the RUC's illegitimacy, in the eyes of a significant proportion of the Catholic community, renders them an integral feature of the perennial conflict.

Current government policy would seem to be to continue along the lines of Ulsterisation and primacy of the police, with the RUC's role being strengthened while the army maintains a low profile. However, as Weitzer (1985) implies, the militarisation of policing operates to enforce prejudicial views. Training police to take on a counter-insurgency role equips them with the attitude that they should be prepared to face 'enemy number one' out on the street. 'The enemy' can be narrowly defined in terms of paramilitary organisations or more broadly in terms of certain sectors of the population; in Northern Ireland this means the Catholic community. However, doing away with sectarian factions, such as the Special Patrol Group (SPG) and the B-Specials, has meant that the RUC is no longer the 'crude old bludgeoning' force is once was (State Research, 1981, p. 18). The Anglo-Irish Agreement recognised 'a need for a programme of special measures in Northern Ireland to improve relations between the security forces and the community' (Cmnd 9657, 1985, p. 7). The Agreement recommended the setting-up of new local consultative machinery, improvements in the complaints system and action to increase the proportion of Catholics in the RUC (Brewer *et al.*, 1988, p. 53).

Throughout the United Kingdom there is currently a trend towards the militarisation of policing, with more police officers being trained in the use of firearms, riot control and counter-insurgency techniques. Government has regarded the public order disputes of the 1980s as indicative of the need for a more heavy-handed policing approach. Consequently this is changing the archetypal role of the 'British Bobby' to something more formidable, moving towards the RUC model.

Alternatives to a militarised police force have been taken on board in other countries by creating specialist units. China has an

Armed Police Division, Israel its Special Duties Division, SWAT and similar forces exist in the USA, the Special Task Force operates in the Irish Republic, and Great Britain has the specially trained and equipped Police Support Units, District Support and Territorial Support Groups, who are drawn from the ranks of the regular force and deployed in incidents of disorder. Such specialist units help to separate the regular police force from the depreciating consequences which often follow police involvement in violent public order incidents. This is part of the justification for employing the National Guard in periods of unrest in the USA, for it absolves the regular police force from association with the actions of those who police public order. In Northern Ireland the involvement of specialist units of the RUC in controversial incidents like 'shoot-to-kill' has tarnished the force's image, with certain sectors of the population, though some Ulster loyalists would support such a policy. Britain, therefore, should take a lesson from the Northern Ireland experience when considering developing such specialist units and perhaps consider establishing two completely separate forces.

A possible alternative to the current form of policing provided by the RUC might be along the lines of the French model: whereby policing in Northern Ireland would become the task of two distinct agencies – one adopting a civilian policing role, patrolling the 'soft' areas, with a separately trained counter-insurgency force used in the more dangerous areas and to control public order situations. However, the disadvantage of this proposal is that police who are responsible for riot control tend to become brutalised, especially when they perform no other policing functions. The advantage is that one of the forces would take on a consensus model of policing and may be more acceptable to the community as a whole. A further suggestion is that the present force be disbanded and re-recruitment for the two forces be along more ethnically representative lines. Such suggestions, however, cannot be considered in a political vacuum and given the historical experiences and political background of the RUC the feasibility of these remarks is highly questionable.

NOTE

The research reported in this chapter is part of a study on routine policing in Northern Ireland directed by John Brewer and funded by the ESRC on grant no. E00232246.

REFERENCES

Agreement between the Government of the United Kingdom of Great Britain and Northern Ireland and the Government of the Republic of Ireland (1985) Cmnd 9657, London: HMSO.

BLAUNER, R. (1964) *Alienation and Freedom*, Chicago: University of Chicago Press.

BREWER, J. GUELKE, A., HUME, I., MOXON-BROWN, E. and WILFORD, R. (1988) *Police, Public Order and the State*, London: Macmillan.

ENLOE, C. H. (1980) *Ethnic Soldiers: State Security in a Divided Society*, Harmondsworth: Penguin.

FIELDING, N. (1988) *Joining Forces*, London: Routledge.

FLACKES, W. D. and ELLIOTT, S. (1989) *Northern Ireland: A Political Directory 1968–1988*, Belfast: Blackstaff.

HAMILL, D. (1985) *Pig in the Middle: The Army in Northern Ireland 1964–1984*, London: Methuen.

HART, W. (1980) 'Waging Peace in Northern Ireland', *Police Magazine*, 3 (May) pp. 23–7.

HOLDAWAY, S. (1983) *Inside the British Police*, Oxford: Blackwell.

Irish Times (1985) 'Hermon Stresses Loyalist Conviction Rate', Dublin, 24 June.

HUNT COMMITTEE (1964) *Report of the Advisory Committee on Police in Northern Ireland* (Hunt Report) (1969) Cmnd 535, Belfast: HMSO.

MANNING, P. K. (1977) *Police Work: The Social Organization of Policing*, London: MIT Press.

MANNING, P. K. and VAN MAANEN, J. (1978) *Policing: A View from the Street*, New York: Random House.

MURRAY, R. (1984) 'Killing of Local Security Forces in Northern Ireland 1969–1981', *Terrorism*, 7, pp. 11–52.

NIEDERHOFFER, A. (1967) *Behind the Shield: The Police in Urban Society*, New York: Anchor.

REINER, R. (1985) *The Politics of the Police*, Brighton: Wheatsheaf.

STATE RESEARCH (1981) 'The RUC: A Sectarian Police Force', *State Research Bulletin*, 26, pp. 17–23.

WEITZER, R. (1985) 'Policing a Divided Society: Obstacles to Normalisation in Northern Ireland', *Social Problems*, 33, 1 (October) pp. 41–53.

5 Mirroring the Market? Police Reorganisation and Effectiveness Against Drug Trafficking

Nicholas Dorn, Karim Murji and Nigel South

INTRODUCTION

This chapter is concerned with debates about reorganisation of the police, particularly in respect of CID and criminal intelligence, and the way in which one particular understanding of policing of illicit drug markets fits into and advances those debates.

Of course, law enforcement is just one arm of the government's response to drug problems. The pamphlet *Tackling Drug Misuse* (Home Office, 1985) describes a five-prong approach: reducing supplies from abroad, making enforcement more effective, maintaining effective deterrents and tight domestic controls, developing prevention, and treatment and rehabilitation. Of these, however, it is law enforcement, particularly against drug traffickers, that came into the spotlight in the latter half of the 1980s. This tendency is likely to be enhanced in future by the influence upon British government of the American strategy outlined by President Bush and his advisors in the Autumn of 1989, emphasising enforcement in South American countries and in the United States (Executive Office of the President, 1989; *Financial Times*, 7 September 1989, p. 6).

The general emphasis upon law enforcement gives added force to an idea that has been current for several years in policing circles in Britain – that anti-drug law enforcement agencies need to be reorganised so as to correspond to, and hence better engage, the structure of the drug market. This 'mirroring' argument seems to make (common) sense. But it has barely been questioned, and there is a possibility that other approaches can be sidelined in the push for bigger and more technologically sophisticated organisations. Perhaps 'big is beautiful' when it comes to some levels of drug enforcement, but there is no *a priori* reason to think that the efficacy of law enforcement can best be measured in terms of size, amalgamation or centralisation.

At the outset, it is important to place the debate on reorganisation in perspective by pointing to a number of alternative propositions which have been articulated in academic circles. These alternatives include, for example, an acceleration of the process whereby some functions of the police are being hived off to a number of separate agencies each dealing with different areas of public concern; the privatisation of some or all functions of policing, with consumers of each type of service paying directly for it (South 1988); the concept of minimal policing, with the police only intervening in any particular space within the community when invited to do so (Kinsey, Lea and Young, 1986); the somewhat related concept of workplace and community self-policing (Henry, 1983); various rather idealist proposals for a society without any criminal justice system (Foucault, 1980); and analyses of the relationship between conventional policing and the crimes of the powerful (Pearce, 1976), violence perpetrated by men against women (Dunhill, 1989), and polluters of the environment and manufacturers of dangerous foodstuffs (Pallister, 1989).

Clearly, there are a variety of views on the way that policing is, could or should be organised and targeted. However, the explicit assumptions underpinning thinking in this area of policy are that terrorism and drug trafficking typify 'serious crime', that they go hand-in-hand, and that they are increasingly organised on a national or international level. The corresponding assumption is that policing should therefore be reorganised on national or international levels to meet this challenge. In this chapter we look at the emergence of this broad consensus, and at the variations within it.

CRACKING THE PROBLEM?

Much has been written about the police as 'moral entrepreneurs', responsible for re-working and generally extending definitions of criminal deviancy, their interactions with specific social and political groups ('Law and Order' politics), their relationship with mass media, their role in the popularisation of particular images of crime, and so on.

Within Britain, it is the work done by the Centre for Contemporary Cultural Studies at Birmingham University that most elaborately drew together various strands of this critical perspective, analysing the construction during the 1970s of the 'mugging' phenomenon (Hall *et al.*, 1978). To a certain extent, only, the police's relation to definitions of 1980s drug problems, and particularly to 'crack' (a smokable form of cocaine), can be thought through in a similar way. For example, the Association of Chief Police Officers (ACPO) decided that crack posed a sufficiently serious threat to warrant a two-day special seminar in August 1989. The resulting press release (ACPO 1989) called for a meeting with the Home Secretary to 'prevent the escalation of the lethal drug'. Exactly why they felt this urgent need to alert Mr Hurd is somewhat unclear considering that he had already likened the threat of crack to 'a medieval plague' and called for more joint work between EC countries (*Times*, 19 May 1989; *Daily Telegraph*, 19 May 1989).

But crack cannot be read simply as a replay of the 'mugging' crisis. In the latter, the police played a major role in setting the agenda (Hall *et al.*, 1978). Somewhat in contrast, in 1989, after a summer during which visiting US 'experts', British politicians and media had been fulminating about crack (see *Druglink*, 1989, for an overview of the issues), the police found themselves confronted by expectations that they should play a starring role in an anti-drugs war that was not of their making, and the definition of which has spun from their grasp. Beginning the decade with Prime Minister Margaret Thatcher's 'We Shall Get You' anti-trafficker statements, continuing through bi-partisan parliamentary support for life penalties and asset confiscation for convicted drug dealers, progressing through considerable panic over cocaine trafficking and 'crack' (Home Affairs Committee, 1985, 1989; *Police Review*, 4 August 1989; ACPO, 1989) and culminating in US 'Drug Czar' William Bennett's statements that tearing off the heads of convicted drug dealers and other forms of judicial slaying would be 'morally plausible' (*Independent*, 17 June 1989), increasingly tough talk against drug traffickers has become virtually *de rigueur* for people in high office.

So far advanced is this process of 'talking up' the problem and anticipating its imminent transmogrification into yet more terrifying forms, that the police, far from feeling in command of the debate in the manner in which they could in the 1970s, have often found themselves caught in the awkward position of being required to respond to a problem which the press and politicians say exists, but which figures to only a very limited extent in their daily routine. The mid-1989 debate over 'crack' illustrates this perfectly. At a time when US officials were priming the Home Office, Ministers and the national press (through non-attributable briefings) about the potential of this drug for instant addiction, inner-city violence and sexual abandon, and when Ministers were instructing puzzled civil servants to brief them on how to combat a problem before it began, the police felt themselves under pressure to 'nip the problem in the bud'. They were urged on by Robert Stutman (1989), an American Drugs Enforcement Administration (DEA) official, who told a private meeting of ACPO that in the US the 'war' against crack had already been lost:

> We have screwed up enough to write 10 000 books . . . I will personally guarantee you that in two years from now, you will have a serious crack problem . . . three years from today . . . you will be looking back on the good old days of 1989, and that won't be pleasant

The consequences were a few 'crack' raids such as the one in Wolverhampton in May 1989 hailed by an expectant press with large photographs of very small 'rocks' of crack (*Police Review*, 26 May 1989; Hyder, 1989) and further escalation in the pressure for the police to 'do something'. Throughout the 1980s, the average drug squad officer continued to deal primarily with cannabis, amphetamine (the main stimulant drug problem of the 1980s) and sometimes heroin; for most officers, cocain and crack were 'not our problem' in strictly practical terms.

The spectacular representation of a crack/crime control problem completely *out of control* – even before it was properly started – stands in contrast to the situation of the 1970s, when policing was portrayed as having problems but, conveniently, none that more resources and more public support could not solve. By the late 1980s, the general argument that the war on crime could be won if only greater resources were made available to the police had worn thin. In this new landscape, the police have discovered the classic concern of organisations which are confronted with a slowing of forward momentum – whether, and if so how, to reorganise themselves. Arguments about resources and powers remained, but as implicit corollaries in debates over organisation, methods, indicators and cost-effectiveness, rather than as claims with their own, evident validity. One of the principal signifiers of modern policing – the war on drugs – had become one for defeat.

REORGANISING THE POLICE

The argument for the reorganisation of the police has moved from unpublished internal police reports, throught the specialist policing magazines and journals, to appear as overt pressure for change, expressed through chief police officers and Members of Parliament. This movement is closely linked in policing circles with a more specific concern with drug trafficking, and here we describe the historical development of that link.

From the mid-1980s onwards, representatives of the US Drugs Enforcement Administration were urging senior British officers to press for the assets of traffickers, once confiscated under the Drug Trafficking Offences Act 1986, to be given to law enforcement agencies rather than the Treasury (personal communications with DEA and senior British police officers, 1989). This is what occurs in the US, where the DEA is the primary national anti-drugs enforcement agency. For police forces no longer assured of automatic increases in government funding and under pressure to provide more 'value for money' (Rawlings, this volume), and especially for detectives feeling a need for more resources for electronic surveillance equipment, more cars and longer paid overtime, the argument that *they* should inherit the profits of crime was an intriguing one (Saltmarsh, 1989).

At least three things, however, stood in the way. One was the Treasury, which saw assets seized by the courts as a useful and expanding source of income to the Exchequer. Second, there was a problem over division of the spoils: the fact that there is no single national British policing agency corresponding to the United States' DEA meant that there was no obvious agency available to share out the funds according to the contributions of each law enforcement agency involved in each particular case (as occurs in the US). A third, more subtle problem was perceived by a minority of officers: allowing police forces and customs to have all or some of the assets seized by the courts, in proportion to their relative successes in bringing prosecutions, would intensify existing reluctance to share intelligence with other forces (Zander, 1989, pp. 48–9). This was apparent in Mr Douglas Hogg's statement in Parliament (1989, p. 523) that 'It is undesirable to give a police force or any enforcement agency a pecuniary interest in an enquiry, and I fear that it would distort policing policies.'

The stage was therefore set for ressurection of earlier debates for and against reorganisation and centralisation of police forces (or the detective parts thereof) into a national (or regionally based) organisation in place of the present 52 separate local forces in the UK.

Before moving on to the contemporary debate, it is worth pointing to a previous occasion when the issue of reorganisation had been raised in relation to drugs. The ACPO Crime Committee's report (1985) on drug related crime (the so-called Broome Committee) stated that discussion at the 1984 ACPO National Drugs Conference had 'largely centred around the idea of creating a regional or national police structure to tackle the drug problem'. The idea of a national drug squad was described as a 'proposal [that] has been made in a number of quarters over recent years and is regarded by many, particularly those outside the service, as being an attractive option'. However, the Committee went on to say:

> This solution has one major disadvantage. Constitutionally it would be a new and radical innovation in British policy. There is considerable antipathy to a National Police Force. This would be seen by many as a step in that direction and would be likely to arouse strong opposition. In the current climate significant difficulties would be encountered if such a measure were to be favoured. (ACPO, 1985, p. 25)

In looking at the idea more closely the Committee noted four possible drawbacks to such an idea. The traditional tripartite structure of control would be broken; the Home Secretary and central government would be seen as having direct operational control; the unit would be seen to be operating without restraint or effective supervision; and Chief Constables would be unhappy about a unit operating in their area, yet outside of their control.

To glimpse aspects of the further development of the debate about reorganisation we turn to the pages of the magazine *Police Review*. In April 1989 the Chief Constable of Leicestershire (Hirst, 1989) argued for reform of the current structure and the magazine itself speculated about the idea of creating ten 'super-forces'. At the time, the Home Secretary himself had ruled out any changes but, soon afterwards, the Metropolitan Police Commissioner called first for more coordination of policing across Europe and then the creation of an FBI-style national investigative organisaton (Imbert, 1989a, 1989b; Carvel, 1989a, p. 28). Shortly after this, the Chairman of the Home Affairs Committee declared that local control of the police should be put aside in order to fight organised crime and drug traffickers more effectively (*Guardian*, 13 July 1989). Speculation that this may have been a 'straw in the wind' for the next election has been discounted by the Home Secretary. In a speech to the Police Superintendents Association in September 1989, he denied that such proposals 'formed part of a hidden Tory agenda for the next Parliament' (Carvel, 1989b, p. 4). As we have indicated, any such changes will and are being legitimised by emphasising the scale of the opposition (i.e. organised crime and international drug trafficking) and by reference to the latest in a long line of 'worse-than-ever' drugs, crack.

OPTIONS FOR REORGANISATION

As far as the general debate about restructuring of police forces in Britain is concerned, there seem to be six broad proposals, each with implications for the organisation of drugs enforcement.

1 Status Quo

Leave the situation as it is, with 52 police forces nationally (43 of which are in England and Wales). However, pressure from some senior officers has moved the debate on beyond arguments for the status quo. Partly this pressure is motivated by concern that the police are likely to lose out to HM Customs and Excise on a number of fronts in Europe, unless they move further towards a national structure for at least those crimes requiring international liaison. The Broome Committee reflected some of this concern when talking about a lack of uniformity in the approach of different police forces around the country:

> In may respects this was understandable as drug distribution was largely confined to urban and city areas. But inconsistencies there were and HM Customs and Excise being a national body, began to adopt a higher profile as regards drug trafficking and this led them into inland investigation. (ACPO, 1985, p. 16)

The historically uneasy relationship between police and Customs and the wish by each not to be up-staged by the other provides one of the dynamics in the debate on reorganisation of policing in Britain.

2 Regional Forces

The second proposal revolves around creating twelve 'super-forces'. A speculative plan for this was presented in the magazine *Police Review* (28 April 1989, p. 858) suggesting boundaries for ten forces in England and Wales. Other sources suggest that nine regional forces within England and Wales would be a more sensible figure, since it would coincide with the existing structure of Regional Crime Squads (RCS), of which there are nine (excluding Scotland and Northern Ireland). Each RCS has a Drugs Wing. To expand the RCSs would then be a relatively easy reform that would decrease the power and influence of Chief Constables by degrees. This plan has the advantage of being easily absorbable into an existing but developing structure, and the disadvantage of being seen by some officers as only a stepping-stone to a single national police force.

3 Multi-Region Forces

There has also been a rather unclear proposal for reorganisation to create about six even larger forces. This could be done by merging and expanding Regional Crime Squads. The argument for between five and ten regional forces has been put by John Wheeler MP, the Chairman of the Home Affairs Committee

(*Police Review*, 14 July 1989, 1404) but would according to *Police Review* (editorial, 14 July 1989, p. 1404) take 'at least a year to be agreed'. There is no clear rationale for this plan and that makes it the easiest option to discount. It may possibly have been put forward not as a serious option but in order to facilitate the debate by setting up a 'straw person' which all parties can agree is undesirable.

4 Joint Regional Police/Customs Operations

This proposal arises from the ACPO seminar on crack in August 1989. This conference proposed that Customs and Excise officers should be attached to each Regional Crime Squad Drugs Wing and, controversially, that the head of the joint organisation would not necessarily be a police officer. 'That went down like a lead balloon', according to one police officer at the seminar, but it remains one possible way forward, offering a degree of centralisation.

5 A National Detective Agency (NDA)

There has been a call for a single national law enforcement agency, to deal with all aspects of serious crime requiring a national response, including major trafficking, and to place this new structure alongside or, more accurately, on top of either options 1, 2 or 3 above (Imbert, 1989b). The rationale is that it would be a mobile, specialist unit which could deal with all major crime, thereby leaving local police forces to provide the service that the public expects from the police. This 'British Bureau of Investigation' (British FBI) model is chiefly associated with the Metropolitan Police Commissioner after his Police Foundation lecture (Imbert, 1989b). This has been presented to us by one senior drugs squad officer as the likeliest *ultimate* outcome, but the familiar British practice of 'muddling along' means that it may only emerge via a circuitous route. However, the Chairman of the Home Affairs Committee has said that an NDA would cause confusion due to overlapping jurisdictions between itself and local CID squads, and has been argued for more comprehensive reorganisation along the lines of option 3 above (*Police Review*, 14 July 1989, p. 1404). Eventually, at its conference in October 1989, ACPO decided to set up a working party, due to report by the end of 1989, to consider the case for a national detective agency (Tendler, 1989, p. 8). According to Mr Peter Wright, the Chairman of ACPO:

> Our association is reviewing current and developing trends in national and international crime and how, if necessary, we should restructure our operational response . . . Basic changes in the structure and legislation governing the police will remain an issue and pressure for change will intensify rather than recede. (quoted in Tendler, 1989, p. 8)

6 National Criminal Intelligence Unit (NCIU)

This option lies midway between the present National Drugs Intelligence Unit and the idea of a national detective agency. Unlike the latter, it would involve no operational staff and would not therefore take any business (or any arrests) away from regional or local detectives. It would simply centralise intelligence databases on, for example, drug trafficking, terrorism, immigration, football hooliganism, and perhaps fraud and other crime. The evolution of intelligence coordination is reflected in the work of the Baumber Committee (which created collators and force and regional intelligence officers – ACPO, 1975), the establishment of the NDIU and, most recently, the National Football Intelligence Unit (NFIU) (see *Police Review*, 15 September 1989). This proposal has received clear support from the Home Secretary in his call for such a unit to 'spearhead the fight against increasingly sophisticated organised crime' (Carvel, 1989b, p. 4; Hurd, 1989). In his speech to the Superintendents' Association, the Home Secretary emphasised the progress that has been made in improving drugs intelligence, but went on to argue that:

> We must ask ourselves whether the increasing sophistication of major crime, and clear links between drugs and other crimes, make it necessary to bring all criminal intelligence together in a national unit . . . The NDIU provides a model for how this might be done and the benefits to be gained.

Looking further ahead, Mr Hurd went on to observe that, 'a facility of this kind may also be necessary to co-operate effectively with enforcement agencies abroad' (Hurd, 1989). Already in Europe, following Hurd's exhortatons, the EC has established a coordinating secretariat to combat serious crime (*Daily Telegraph*, 13 May 1989). The Schengen group (the three Benelux countries and France and West Germany) are building joint information systems, providing a European focus for the sharing of criminal intelligence and immigration control (for a description, see Birch, 1989; on the dangers, see Jenkins, 1989a, 1989b). Similarly, the TREVI group (Ministers from EC countries set up to combat terrorism) has also been looking a greater cooperation against drug trafficking (Birch, 1989; see also Pallister, 1989).

The proposal for a National Criminal Intelligence Unit seems to have drawn relatively little opposition within enforcement circles, and has avoided raising the hackles of HM Customs and Excise in the way that proposals for an *operational* national detective agency might do. For this reason and because of the Home Secretary's support, the NCIU emerged in late 1989 as the leading contender. However, in practice, the NCIU may be seen as a stalking-horse for a national detective agency. Sir Peter Imbert has welcomed the setting-up of the ACPO working party to elaborate the form of a national detective agency and said that one could be established in Britain within three years (see *The Times*, 6 October 1989, p. 7). Similarly, the Home Secretary described a NCIU as a 'first step' (Carvel, 1989b, p. 4) towards the British FBI advocated by Imbert (1989b).

MATCHING LIKE WITH LIKE?

In the debate on reorganisation of drugs policing, the most important reference point for the 'mirror' approach is the report of the Broome Committee. The Committee argued for regional and national policing, but also stated that it was

> *not necessary* to go as far as to create a national unit. While major drug operations are geographically extensive, there are a few examples of major drug distributors operating on a truly national scale. What really happens is that there is a criminal conspiracy with tentacles of that conspiracy stretching to other areas but not throughout the entire country. (ACPO, 1985, p. 26; see also *The Times*, 28 May 1985)

Advocating a 'three tier approach' to act as 'a series of checks against drug misuse', the Committee stated that:

> When examining the drug problem it became apparent to the Working Party that the effort against drug abuse can effectively be structured on three levels.

> In many respects this already occurs, but in our view a clear strategy needs to be identified. (ACPO, 1985, p. 19)

According to the Committee, the three levels should be

> First . . . a strategy of preventing importation and distribution and this must be done in conjunction with HM Customs. Secondly Force Drug Squads must tackle drug distribution where it has evaded the first level of control. Finally all officers at Divisional level should seek to remove drugs that reach street level. (ibid, p. 19)

This influential outline of the three-tier approach to the drugs market – through national, regional and local levels – created the structure of drugs enforcement which exists today. As a model of the drug market it is based largely on the idea that there are five levels within the market (cf. Wagstaff and Maynard, 1988) – importer (national level), distributor and wholesaler (regional level), retailer and user-dealer (local level). The operational assumption is that these are identifiable levels of the market that can be matched and neutralised by corresponding structures of law enforcement. Underlying this is a conception of the structure of drug markets as fixed, static and hierarchical. Recent research and the practical experience of many police officers calls this view into question (Dorn and South, 1990; Wright and Waymont, forthcoming). Nevertheless, the five-tier market model and three-tier response have the merits of simplicity, of correspondence to 'common sense' (e.g. the 'big traffickers' at the top) and of giving apparent justification for the reorganisation of anti-drug policing.

The most common arguments for a national or reorganised police force (c.f. Bond, 1988) are that it is necessary to fight highly organised crime syndicates (see *Police Review*, 23 June 1989); that police effectiveness is undermined by bureaucratic and other barriers (see *Police Review*, 9 June 1989); and that there is a need to direct police policy from a central, national organisation (Cozens, 1989; *Guardian*, 13 July 1989). A typical example is the following editorial in the *Observer* (9 July 1989) newspaper following Imbert's (1989b) speech:

> A national agency to deal with organised crime is attractive, if only because it would match like with like. If criminals can work on a national, and even a supra-national, scale, it makes sense for the police to do likewise.

According to Imbert (1989b), a national investigative agency would 'provide a really effective operational detective unit across the whole country', because it could ensure an appropriate response to serious, as distinct from general, crime. Yet, crucially, what has not been explained is *why* restructuring law enforcement so as to match or 'mirror' the presumed structure of crime will lead to greater efficiency. It has been argued that the advantage of a national organisation would be its increased command of resources to mount intensive and expensive operations (e.g. surveillance) but this has not been substantiated. Indeed, as was demonstrated in the policing of the coal dispute for example, the 52 nominally separate police forces are already capable of operating with a high degree of cohesion, maintained formally through the Police National Computer and the National Reporting Centre and informally through ACPO. Furthermore, the existence of the nine RCS' in England and Wales already provides a regional level of policing surpassing the county-based police forces.

However, if the momentum for change continues to gather pace, the question posed in the 1990s may be 'why stop at a *national* police force?' Since 1992 and increased economic cooperation are widely held to presage increased political cooperation, too, is not a European police force the logical conclusion? And if drug trafficking is truly a trans-continental enterprise, why stop there? One implication of the 'mirroring' concept of policing would be the expansion of international enforcement agencies, operating from Bogota to London, and directed by a few international specialists. Already, many drug squad and other detective officers outside London are somewhat suspicious of what they see as the ambitions of the Metropolitan police in any national set-up. Presumably they would not feel much happier about being run from Washington.

What might follow from national reorganisation? It is quite broadly accepted in British law enforcement circles that there is a reciprocal relationship between policing and crime, with criminal entrepreneurs re-shaping their operations so as to exploit those spaces less rigorously policed (Grieve, 1987; Hobbs, 1988; Dorn and South, 1990). Since it would take years to get a national or international operational anti-trafficking agency into full working order, the opposition would have ample opportunity to re-jig their operations to fall between the interstices of control. Indeed, it is arguable that recent developments such as bilateral extradition, asset seizures and the possible development of 'Fortress Europe' have *already* made large-scale cross-national criminal operations more difficult and therefore more dangerous in terms of risks of apprehension, and that smaller and more flexible criminal organisations which can 'bob and weave' around large-scale control structures are already at a relative advantage.

It would be ironic if Britain and Europe were to spend years setting up strucures targeting national and international Mafia-style organisations, only to find the market had for some time 'gone local'. Larger organisations are generally less flexible, and a national or international anti-drugs agency may make it easier for criminals to 'predict' or understand what the police response to their operations might look like, thereby, ultimately, making policing less effective (cf. Reuter *et al.*, 1988, pp. 120–1). Certainly, the development of the drug problem in the United States under the care of the DEA does not provide a compelling illustration of the efficiency of a national enforcement agency.

CONCLUSION

In Britain a single national force covering all branches of policing, uniform and detective, seems unlikely in the foreseeable future, but a national detective agency is a possibility and a national criminal intelligence unit seemed imminent in late 1989.

However, the argument for any general national reorganisation of policing to mirror the supposed national organisation of drug traffickers or other criminal organisations is very poorly developed. It has a superficial appeal, but lacks detail, and can only be sustained by rhetorical gestures in the direction of 'big traffickers', 'evil men' and 'medieval plagues'. The argument itself is not new, but the debate now has a new momentum. Clearly, any substantial reorganisation along national (or even regional) lines involves major gains for a few, select police officers. The downside is that there must be some losers in this game too and that a number of Chief Constables and other senior police officers may prefer futures as big fish in local ponds, rather than as small fish in a bigger pond.

Meanwhile, the 'out of control' rhetoric of the 'war on drugs' positions the police in a posture of retreat, if not defeat. The police, like other professions since the 1980s, have come to be perceived as fallible. Any national reorganisation, when and if it comes, will hardly compensate for this fall from grace.

REFERENCES

ACPO (1975) 'Report of the Sub-Committee on Criminal Intelligence' (Chairman, G. H. Baumber) unpublished.
ACPO (1985) 'Final Report of the Working Party on Drug Related Crime' (Chairman, R. F. Broome) unpublished.
ACPO (1989) 'Police Call for Summit to Tackle Crack Menace', press release, 1 September.
BIRCH, R. (1989) 'Policing Europe in 1992', *Police Review*, 5 May.
BOND, K. (1988) 'The Case for a National Police Force', *Policing*, 4, pp. 293–308.
CARVEL, J. (1989a) 'Imbert Calls for National Crime Agency', *The Guardian*, 7 July.
CARVEL, J. (1989b) 'Hurd Signals Move Towards Central Intelligence Unit', *The Guardian*, 27 September.
COZENS, R. (1989) 'Forming a Force for the Future', *Police Review*, 7 July.
DORN, N. and SOUTH, N. (1990) 'Drug Markets and Law Enforcement', *British Journal of Criminology*, pp. 171–88.
Druglink (1989) (special issue on crack), September/October.
DUNHILL, C. (ed.) (1989) *Boys in Blue*, London: Virago.
EXECUTIVE OFFICE OF THE PRESIDENT (1989) *National Drug Control Strategy*, Washington DC: Office of National Drug Control Policy.
FOUCAULT, M. (1980) 'On Popular Justice: A Discussion With Maoists', in C. Gordon (ed.), *Michel Foucault Power/Knowledge: Selected Interviews and Other Writings 1972–1977,* Brighton: Harvester.
GRIEVE, J. (1987) 'Comparative Police Strategies – Drug Related Crime', unpublished M. Phil. thesis, Cranfield Institute of Technology.
HALL, S. et al. (1978) *Policing the Crisis: Mugging, the State and Law and Order,* London: Macmillan.
HENRY, S. (1983) *Private Justice: Towards Integrated Theorising in the Sociology of Law*, London: Routledge.
HIRST, M. (1989) '1989 – Year of the Superforces?', *Police Review*, 28 April.
HOBBS, D. (1988) *Doing the Business: Entrepreneurship, the Working Class and Detectives in the East End of London*, Oxford: Clarendon.
HOGG, D. (1989) 'Drug Abuse', Hansard, 9 June.
HOME AFFAIRS COMMITTEE (1985) *Misuse of Hard Drugs* (interim report) HC66, London: HMSO.
HOME AFFAIRS COMMITTEE (1989) *Crack: The Threat of Hard Drugs in the Next Decade* (interim report) HC536, London: HMSO.
HOME OFFICE (1985) *Tackling Drug Misuse: A Summary of the Government's Strategy*, London: Home Office.

HURD, D. (1989) 'Speech by the Home Secretary to the Superintendents' Association's Annual Conference: 26 September'.

HYDER, K. (1989) 'The Real Danger Behind Crack', *Police Review*, 2 (June).

IMBERT, P. (1989a) 'Crimes Without Frontiers', *Police Review*, 9 (June).

IMBERT, P. (1989b) 'Do We Need a British FBI?', *Police Review*, 14 (July).

JENKINS, J. (1989a) 'Foreign Exchange', *New Statesman and Society*, 28 July.

JENKINS, J. (1989b) 'The Return of "Sus" ', *New Statesman and Society*, 4 August.

KINSEY, R., LEA, J. and YOUNG, J. (1986) *Losing the Fight Against Crime*, Oxford: Blackwell.

PALLISTER, D. (1989) 'Hot Pursuit Urged for Euro-Police', *The Guardian*, 28 September.

PEARCE, F. (1976) *Crimes of the Powerful*, London: Pluto.

RAWLINGS, P. (1989) ' "Creeping Privatisation"? The Police, the Conservative Government and Policing in the Late 1980s', chapter in this volume.

REUTER, P., CRAWFORD, G. and CAVE, J. (1988) *Sealing the Borders: The Effects of Increased Military Participation in Drug Interdiction*, California: RAND Corporation.

SALTMARSH, G. (1989) 'Cleaning Up With Dirty Money', *Police Review*, 24 February.

SOUTH, N. (1988) *Policing for Profit*, London: Sage.

STUTMAN, R. (1989) 'Crack Stories from the States', *Druglink*, 4 (5) (September/October).

TENDLER, S. (1989) 'Police Chiefs Study FBI-Style National Force for Detectives', *The Times*, 5 October.

WAGSTAFF, A. and MAYNARD, A. (1988) *Economic Aspects of the Illicit Drugs Market and Drug Enforcement Policies in the U.K.*, Home Office Research study no. 95, London: HMSO.

WRIGHT, A. and WAYMONT, A. (forthcoming) *Drug Enforcement Strategies and Intelligence Needs*, ACPO/Police Foundation.

ZANDER, M. (1989) *Confiscation and Forfeiture Law: English and American Comparisons*, London: Police Foundation.

6 Investigating Tax and Supplementary Benefit Fraud

Dee Cook

The slogan that 'there is one law for the rich and another for the poor' is often used, in commonsense terms, to explain unequal responses to those who fiddle personal taxes and those who fiddle welfare benefits. Both tax and benefit fraudsters engage in similar economic crimes – defrauding the public purse by making false statements to government departments – but social responses to these activities differ widely. Through research, conducted between 1984 and 1988, I explored the 'rich law, poor law' slogan by analysing, first, the precise nature of the activities engaged in by the relatively 'rich' who evade income tax and the 'poor' who fiddle supplementary benefit;[1] second, the ways in which these illegal activities were regulated by the Inland Revenue and DHSS,[2] both in official 'theory' and in investigatory practice; and third, the different social and judicial responses to tax and benefit fraud. Although tax fraud is clearly more costly than benefit fraud (Keith Committee, 1983; Board of Inland Revenue, 1983/4, 1988), social security 'scroungers' are represented as posing a greater social threat than tax evaders in political, popular and official discourses (Golding and Middleton, 1982).

This chapter summarises some of the principle themes of my research by analysing Revenue and DSS enforcement policies, the consequences that these (inconsistent) policies have for claimants and taxpayers (in terms of their interactions with DSS and Revenue staff), and the different modes of punishing tax and benefit fraudsters, focusing in particular on the contrasting uses of private and criminal justice.

JUSTIFYING DIFFERENT ENFORCEMENT POLICIES

The primary function of the Inland Revenue, according to officials I spoke to, is 'the care and management of the Taxes

Acts', administering them efficiently and equitably so as to ensure the *compliance* of the taxpayer. (The term 'compliance' signifies the Revenue's equanimity in regulating activities which the DHSS would simply term 'fraud and abuse'.) A crucial factor in securing taxpayers' compliance to the tax laws is an unspoken agreement that financial settlement, not punishment, will be sought if the Revenue discover an 'omission' from returns of income. In practice this often means any offences discovered are 'underclassified' so as to 'spare the taxpayer's feelings' and 'secure a reasonable settlement by agreement' (Keith Committee, 1983). Put simply the Revenue's primary aim is to recoup taxes.

Revenue enforcement policy therefore aims to ensure *compliance* to the tax laws through negotiation, bargaining and private settlement where tax is found to be due. But if there is evidence of 'fraud, wilful default or neglect' on the part of a taxpayer, additional financial penalties (as well as interest on back taxes) *may* be imposed. Penalties are calculated as a percentage of tax unpaid and, although the Revenue can seek penalties of 100 per cent, in practice this figure is invariably reduced according to the gravity of the offence, the taxpayer's cooperation in any investigation and fullness of the voluntary disclosures s/he makes (Inland Revenue, 1987).

Although the *official* rationale for enforcement policy is therefore the desire to collect taxes by the most effective means, the relatively lenient treatment of tax evaders cannot be justified solely in terms of administrative pragmatism: ultimately, policy is also shaped by popular perceptions of the relationship between the taxpayer and the state. The British have a traditional distaste for paying personal taxes, as exemplified in Disraeli's comment that there are only two inevitabilities in life – death and taxation. It is not surprising that subsequent commentators draw on similar historical notions in representing the tax evader as *victim* of repressive state taxation, someone who merely 'prefers to keep' a larger slice of *their* income than the coercive taxman allows (Myddleton, 1979, p. 47). Moreover, the over-burdened taxpayer is also represented as a victim of the welfare drones (or 'tax consumers'), whom s/he is forced to 'subsidise' through hard-earned taxes (Burton, 1985, p. 75; Boyson, 1971). In this respect taxation and welfare policy have always been inextricably linked, both ideologically and practically, though the nature of that link can be perceived very differently: where enforcement policy is concerned, inconsistencies inevitably arise.

Beneath the official rhetoric of Revenue enforcement policy lies the unresolved contradiction between the principles of *collectivism* and *individualism*, and ultimately the competing ideologies of social justice and the free market. According to the former, citizens willingly contribute to the state through taxation in order to finance collective state welfare provision. By contrast free-market individualism is realised through wealth creation and the unfettered exercise of the entrepreneurial spirit. According to this latter view progressive taxation is seen as anathema to the spirit of individualism and the 'enterprise culture'.

Whichever perspective is adopted, the taxpayer is invariably constituted as 'giver' to the state, so enabling enforcement policies which justify compliance through 'sparing the taxpayer's feelings'. But benefit claimants are bound to be constituted as 'takers' from the state, whether this is seen to derive from the positive 'gift relationship' effected through social policy, or from the allegedly negative effects of a cosseting welfare state which fosters idle dependency. Both perspectives uneasily co-exist within DSS enforcement policy because, as The National Association for the Care and Resettlement of Offenders (NACRO) has argued:

> there is an unavoidable tension between the Department's first duty – prompt payment of benefit and relief of need with due consideration for people's dignity and welfare – and the highly important but secondary function of combatting fraud and abuse. (NACRO, 1986, p. 16)

Official policy statements may emphasise the former (the efficient payment of benefit for the relief of need), but effectively DSS practice stresses the latter (rigorous means and work-testing to demonstrate the genuineness, desert and need of individual claimants). Any notion of 'rights' is inevitably subverted by policies which concentrate on the prevention of *abuse* rather than on the efficient and courteous payment of benefit *entitlement*.

Staff–claimant relations have been further damaged by other specific policies geared to departmental cost-cutting: for instance through reductions in the home visiting of claimants; through (impersonal) postal claiming; *cutbacks* in routine local office staff concurrent with *increases* in anti-fraud staff through initiatives such as Special Claims Control (SCC)[3] and, more recently, the activities of 'dolebusters' (Beltram, 1984; Ward 1985; Coetzee, 1983; Mandla, 1987). It could be argued that the hidden agenda behind DSS enforcement policy has been to reduce expenditure by deterring benefit claims either through the effects of bureaucratic welfare-rationing or through the spectre (or suspicion) of 'fraud and abuse' (Laurence, 1987). The effect of such deterrence can (arguably) be seen in DSS figures indicating that 6 million supplementary benefit claims were made in 1986/7, yet only 3.9 million income support claims were projected for 1988/9 (*Guardian*, 31 October 1988).

Bearing this argument in mind, it is notable that John Moore told the 1988 Conservative Party conference that it was time to correct the balance between rights and responsibilities in the 'citizenship equation', and went on to ask:

> Is it right that an able-bodied adult can draw unemployment benefit simply by signing on once a fortnight without any real effort to find work? (*Guardian*, 13 October 1988)

He also questioned, 'Is the hope of a council flat and a guaranteed income a factor in unmarried teenage pregnancy?' (*Times*, 13 October 1988). Clearly the historical distinction between the *deserving* (the elderly, sick and handicapped) and the *undeserving* poor (dating from the 1834 Poor Law) was re-emphasised in the 1980s (Fraser, 1973; Deacon and Bradshaw, 1983; Minford, 1987). It is no coincidence that the able-bodied unemployed and lone mothers have in recent years been designated targets for the most coercive anti-fraud investigation methods – for instance, those used by SCC units and 'dolebusters' (Cook, 1989a).

Significantly, at the same conference Employment Secretary Norman Fowler declared that 'we are not prepared to see taxpayers' money being used to finance the fraudulent' and he announced the creation of 500 more investigation posts to combat dole fraud (*Times*, 13 October 1988). However, these resources would have been more productively directed at non-compliant taxpayers: Mr Fowler had alleged that £54.6 million in benefits was 'saved' in the previous year as the result of investigating 'dole fraud', yet this was clearly dwarfed by the £741 million *actually* yielded by tax investigations in that year (Board of Inland Revenue, 1987). Ironically, the Revenue had been promised an extra 850 staff for counter-evasion work in 1984, but in 1987 only 380 had been deployed, the deficiency being blamed on 'staff shortages' (ibid). Clearly staff shortages (and lack of political will?) hinders the regulation of the rich who defraud the state, but there seems to be no similar hindrance to the ever-increasing policing of the poor.

THE CONSEQUENCES OF INVESTIGATION POLICIES FOR TAXPAYERS AND CLAIMANTS

Rationales for Revenue and DHSS enforcement policies are therefore both unequal and contradictory. They also give rise to entirely different relations between the individual taxpayer/claimant and departmental staff. For example, when speaking about tax investigations a former Revenue Enquiry Branch official commented that the policy of seeking financial settlement was 'the only sensible way to carry on – after all, we have all sinned!' By contrast, according to Cooper (1985, p. 13) the manager of an urban DHSS office had a very different attitude towards 'fiddling':

> I run a tight ship here, and I know how to do that because I've been in the business since the NAB [National Assistance Board] days. In those days we didn't give anything out unless it was really needed and unless it was a really deserving claim. Now it's easy for claimants; too easy. I can tell you that it takes a lot of pride out of the job when you know that nine out of ten of your customers are fiddling you . . . I tell all my staff to be on their watch and get all the information they can on people. There's just too much abuse.

The double standards evident in these reactions to claimants and taxpayers suspected of fraud are not only a reflection of different enforcement policies. They also indicate historical and ideological differences in perceptions of taxpayers as 'givers' and benefit claimants as 'takers' from the state. These differences are accentuated in the New Right's polarised visions of the 'enterprise culture' on the one hand and the 'benefit cultures' on the other. (The very real consequences for those who succeed in the former and for those who are relegated to the latter are evident in the contradictory provisions of the 1988 Budget and Social Security Reforms, briefly discussed later, which enable and encourage the rich to become richer still, yet penalise the poor.) This is the ideological and political context within which the investigation of taxpayer and claimant takes place.

Some Revenue investigations do involve the same techniques as used by DSS investigators: for instance, the targeting of particular occupations or locations and officers' use of their experience to pursue 'hunches' (*Network*, July 1985 and January 1986). But Revenue compliance officers must ensure they have adequate evidence before confronting and interviewing suspected fraudsters, and their interviews are conducted on a formal and professional basis. The same could not be said of many DHSS investigations, as was evident in the activities of notorious SCC units whose methods were said to involve 'questionable interrogation techniques . . . in an atmosphere overcharged with the desire to meet targeted savings and root out fraud' (Smith, 1985, p. 118).

Trades unions representing DHSS staff protested at these methods, which included the coercion and intimidation of the most vulnerable claimant groups – lone mothers and the unemployed. Research indicated the use of techniques such as interviewing women in locked rooms (sometimes by two male SCC officers), 'late afternon . . . with mothers pre-occupied about their children at school, home or in wating rooms', false allegations that claimants have been followed and found to be working, the presentation of false evidence of fraud, threats to lone mothers that their children will be taken into care unless they handed over their order books, all of which were undertaken under the guise of the 'non-prosecution interview' which was geared to achieving 'benefit savings' through the cessation of claims (Cook, 1989a).

The DHSS's non-prosecution policy was initially presented as a more 'humane' way of dealing with fraud and abuse as it sought to avoid criminal prosecution (Hansard, 7 February 1983, col. 811). But more recently the BBC *40 Minutes* programme 'Dolebusters' (October 1988) confirmed many earlier doubts about the 'humanity' of this approach when put into practice. The investigations of the unemployed which it screened were based on anonymous tip-offs (often unsubstantiated), and the targeting of fraud-prone jobs (in, for instance, the building trade and taxi firms). But claimants who merely parked outside local offices were also under camera surveillance for signs of 'working on the side' (such as a tool-box, a bucket, a ladder). When inside the dole offices claimants were physically under surveillance for 'dirty hands' or other subjective indications of paid work. Imagine the outcry if taxpayers were investigated on the basis of being too well-dressed for their declared salary level, or if taxpayers were photographed by Revenue officials as they parked 'expensive' vehicles in tax office car parks!

A high degree of intrusive regulation is evidently justifiable for those who are seen as *takers* from the state, are without the knowledge or power to exercise their 'rights' and who may be coerced into withdrawing their claim to benefit by dubious 'evidence' (or merely suspicion) of fraud. By contrast the productive and *giving* taxpayer has both the knowledge and the economic powers to insist on rights which are, in any case, formally acknowledged by the Revenue in the form of the 'Taxpayers Charter' (1986). Perhaps as a consequence of this, relations between taxpayer and Revenue staff may be tense, but usually display (sometimes grudgingly!) a mutual respect.

Nonetheless, the Revenue's relatively lenient approach to compliance and investigation is still regarded, in some quarters, as draconian: for example, during the trial of Ken Dodd, the Revenue Inspectors who investigated his tax affairs were likened to the Gestapo and the KGB (*Guardian*, 23 June 1989). But I would argue (on the basis of the discussion of DHSS investigation methods above), that such epithets would more aptly describe the policing of benefit claimants than taxpayers.

MODES OF PUNISHMENT

It could be argued that claimants who are 'persuaded' to relinquish their benefit entitlement following non-prosecution interviews are in fact *paying* for alleged crimes without being convicted. One magistrate commented to me that this approach had 'elements of blackmail'. But despite the (officially) pragmatic and 'humane' rationale behind the non-prosecution policy, the DHSS still prosecuted over nine thousand supplementary benefit claimants in 1987/8.

The outcome of a non-prosecution strategy is very different for taxpayers who have failed to declare income: for them non-prosecution, repayment of tax and perhaps (in serious cases) the imposition of additional financial penalties, all have the positive advantage of avoiding adverse publicity and the stigma of criminal proceedings. However, one Revenue official commented to me that although *lack* of publicity may be helpful in gaining compliance in a handful of cases, the *use* of publicity was probably of far greater value as a general deterrent. This view appears to be supported by recent research indicating that a sample of executives would fear national media publicity of their frauds more than they would fear a suspended prison sentence (Levi, 1987).

It is often argued that the relatively rich taxpayer can afford to 'pay' for his or her crimes, whereas the poor benefit claimant cannot, and that this explains the use of private justice for the former and criminal justice for the latter. But this argument fails to take into account that benefit fraudsters *do* repay to the DHSS the benefits they have fiddled. Current regulations enable up to £7 per week to be deducted from (poverty line) income support payments where claimants have admitted fraud (CPAG, 1989). Moreover, if criminal proceedings are then taken, a fine may be imposed too. It is difficult to see how claimants are deterred from fiddling the state by deepening the very poverty that generated their economic crimes in the first place (Cook, 1989a).

In 1987/8 the total figure yielded by the Inland Revenue's compliance initiatives was £2013 million (Board of Inland Revenue, 1988). In that year only 322 criminal prosecutions were mounted by the Revenue as compared with 9847 prosecutions for supplementary benefit fraud. Moreover, the DHSS prosecutions may involve only trivial amounts: for example, I found (during the period of my research, in one magistrates' court in the Midlands) immediate custodial sentences imposed for giro fiddles, one of which was for £67.10. Three suspended prison sentences were imposed for giro frauds worth £63, £94 and £129 (Cook, 1989b).

Analysis of judicial discourses on tax and benefit fraud demonstrates a further dimension of inequality. When sentencing supplementary benefit fraudsters, magistrates I observed made comments such as 'the country's fed up to the teeth with people like you scrounging from fellow citizens'. They also referred to supplementary benefit fraud as 'deceiving society', 'taking from the state', 'one of the worst forms of stealing there is'. Also, patronising comments – such as 'you are old enough to know better' and 'you need to be taught a lesson' – contrast sharply with judicial responses to tax fraudsters, which frequently stress that the offender has 'suffered enough' through loss of standing within the community. Other factors often accepted as mitigation for tax fraudsters include 'anxiety, disgrace, modest standard of living, good background and character, and shattered careers' (Cook, 1989b). But it must be emphasised that the Revenue's policy of financial settlement keeps all but the most 'heinous' of tax evaders out of court in the first place! Moreover, what is regarded as a 'heinous' case is often determined by a taxpayer's lack of *compliance*: for instance, it is significant that Lester Piggot not only fiddled over £3 million but had been investigated before and had lied to the Revenue in previous statements of 'full disclosure' (*New Law Journal*, 30 October 1987).

To summarise, the consequences of the Revenue's selective prosecution policy (leading to 322 prosecutions in 1987/8) contrasts sharply with the outcome of the DHSS's ostensibly *non-prosecution* policy, which led to over 9000 prosecutions for supplementary benefit fraud in the same year. The ideological roots of enforcement policies (described above) also have consequences in terms of the sentences passed on tax and benefit fraudsters. Although only 'heinous' cases of tax evasion are prosecuted, sentences are frequently non-custodial, often involving a fine. (Once more, a key factor is the offender's ability *to pay* for their crime.) Sentencing inequities also derive from notions of *whose* money is seen to be at stake when taxes and benefits are defrauded – the taxpayer's own hard-earned income, or the taxpayer's taxes, handed out to the feckless poor.

CONCLUSION

Several important issues, both theoretical and practical, are raised by a comparative analysis of responses to tax and benefit fraud. Theoretically it is extremely difficult to use conventional terms (such as 'white-collar crime') to cover fiddling and welfare benefits. Although both involve essentially the same illegal activity (knowingly or dishonestly making false statements to state officials), there are other significant differences: notably in the likely social status of tax and benefit fraudsters themselves, and in the very different historical construction of taxpayers and claimants as, respectively, 'givers to' and 'takers from' the state.

Terminology which concentrates on the technicality of offences also fails to give due weight to the way in which meaning is imputed to both offences and offenders. For example, the crimes of tax and benefit fraud are both economically motivated – tax evasion by the desire for further gain, benefit fraud by poverty and need – yet entirely contradictory motives are attributed to the offenders involved. For instance, within popular and political discourses 'scroungers' are seen to be selfish, idle and greedy, but those who fiddle taxes are seen as merely acting within the logic of a society geared to entrepreneurialism, risk and wealth. By ideological sleight of hand the motives of 'need' and 'greed' have thus been reversed (Cook, 1989a).

As Levi (1987) succinctly noted, white-collar criminals have committed *offences* of high gravity' but are perceived as '*offenders* of low "essential' badness'. This would apply to tax fraudsters, but the reverse seems to apply to official treatment of those who fiddle at the meagre level of social security payments! A comparative approach to these two levels of offending therefore broadens the scope of enquiry from 'white-collar crime' *per se*, to issues of social justice.

In practical terms, how can we move towards greater parity in the way the state regulates the lives of the rich and the poor? This question poses fundamental problems, not least because New Right social and economic policy currently advocates the *de-regulation* of the lives of the rich through the economics of 'choice', lower taxes and less 'red tape' for business. This is justified because of the need for administrative simplification and the maintenance of incentives. At the same time the Thatcher government justifies *more* regulation of the poor (through work tests, stringent means-testing and, for young people, compulsory training schemes) on identical grounds – the need for administrative simplification and work-incentives! The 1988 Budget and Social Security reforms both allegedly promoted effort-incentives, though by very different means: for high-earners such as Burtons stores' Sir Ralph Halpern the Budget meant (in the words of *The Sun*) a 'bonking great boost of £5097 a week'. But social security changes promoted effort-incentives for the young unemployed through reductions in benefit. It would seem that while the state polices the poor more avidly than it polices the rich, the injustices I have described are likely to continue. But change is possible.

First, the stated administrative goals of 'cost-effectiveness' can be used to good effect to press for change: it is hardly cost-effective for government to direct more staff and resources in pursuit of frauds which are limited in scale to the level of income support payments, whilst at the same time failing to adequately staff counter-evasion initiatives which could, potentially, raise hundreds of millions of pounds! Awareness of the economic absurdity of current investigation priorities therefore needs to be heightened.

Second, increased advice and representation for those accused of benefit fraud may prevent some of the abuses described here. For instance, many claimants who admit fraud are unaware that criminal proceedings may still follow and so do not take legal advice. Once proceedings start, many remain unrepresented: of 206 cases of supplementary benefit fraud heard in one magistrates court in the Midlands (from 1981 to 1987) 43 per cent were not represented, and this despite a duty solicitor scheme (Cook, 1989a). Efforts need to be made to shift the balance of information and power in favour of welfare recipients, as claimants, unlike taxpayers, have no 'Charter'.

Third, possibilities for change in policy and practice may also be opened up by departmental staff themselves: for instance, the Revenue staff (through the Inland Revenue Staff Federation – IRSF) are campaigning for more manpower for counter-evasion work, and have been vociferous in their condemnation of DSS anti-fraud drives. In so doing they draw attention to the injustice of 'rich law, poor law': for example, IRSF Assistant Secretary Bob Hawkes persuasively argued that:

> Every successful challenge or investigation which recovered tax means that someone has lied to the Revenue – not just made a mistake. When the white middle classes lie it is seen as part of the game. If black working people lie to the DHSS, the morality of it is seen quite differently. (*Assessment*, March 1988)

Similarly, DHSS staff unions actively campaigned for the abolition of SCC units (Ward, 1985), and continue to press for more staff and resources to enable efficient service delivery to claimants, surely a first step in combating abuse.

Fourth, the ideological conditions which enable differential response should be challenged. This is no easy task. The manufacture of post-Budget euphoria in 1988 indicated the extent to which the ideology of liberalism (re-packaged as 'the enterprise culture') dominates popular discourse. For instance, media reactions included 'Lotsa Lovely Lolly!' (*The Sun*), 'We're all in the money' (*Daily Express*). *The Times* saw the Budget as putting the values of 'incentive and opportunity in place of old fashioned egalitarianism'. But the values of 'old fashioned egalitarianism' need to be reasserted: if administrative systems are to be judged on the grounds of equity and efficiency then current Revenue and DSS enforcement policies fail on *both* grounds. It is not enough to argue only that the Treasury can recoup more money more cost-effectively from the fraudlent taxpayer than the fraudulent benefit claimant – the injustsice of current policy needs to be exposed and challenged. Disparity in departmental, political and judicial responses to tax and welfare fraud does constitute, in commonsense terms, 'one law for the rich and another for the poor'. But the political, judicial and popular discourses which enable and sustain this injustice remain open to deconstruction and to challenge.

NOTES

1. The research upon which this article was based was conducted between 1984 and 1988, but changes in terminology accompanied the April 1988 reforms of social security. The terms 'income support' and 'DSS' will appear where current regulations are at issue, although the terms 'supplementary benefit' and 'DHSS', which were in use during the time of my research, will also be used where appropriate.
2. To maintain a reasonable basis for comparison with the experiences of individual supplementary benefit claimants, my research focused on the frauds of individual taxpayers (PAYE taxpayers, traders, the self-employed), but not those of larger corporations.
3. The abolition of SCC units was announced in May 1986. However, their legacy, in terms of coercive investigation techniques and damaged relations with claimants is still evident in the regulation of the homeless poor, the unemployed and single mothers.

REFERENCES

BELTRAM, G. (1984) *Testing the Safety Net*, London: NCVO.

BOARD OF INLAND REVENUE (1983/4) *Committee of Public Accounts: Control of Investigation Work*, Board of Inland Revenue, HC 102, London: HMSO.

BOARD OF INLAND REVENUE (1987) *129th Annual Report*, London: HMSO.

BOARD OF INLAND REVENUE (1988) *130th Annual Report*, London: HMSO.

BOYSON, R. (1971) *Down With the Poor*, London: Churchill Press.

BOYSON, R. (1978) *Centre Foreward*, London: Maurice Temple Smith.

BURTON, J. (1985) *Why No Cuts?*, London: IEA.

COETZEE, S. (1983) *Flat Broke: How the Welfare State Collapsed in Birmingham*, Birmingham Welfare Rights Group.
COOK, D. :1989a) *Rich Law, Poor Law: Different Responses to Tax and Supplementary Benefit Fraud*, Milton Keynes: Open University Press.
COOK, D. (1989b) 'Fiddling Tax and Benefits: Inculpating the Poor and Exculpating the Rich', in P. Carlen and D. Cook (eds), *Paying for Crime*, Milton Keynes: Open University Press.
COOPER, S. (1985) *Observatons in Supplementary Benefit Offices. The Reform of Supplementary Benefit: Working Paper C*, London: PSI.
CPAG (1989) *National Welfare Benefits Handbook*, London: Child Poverty Action Group.
DEACON, A. and BRADSHAW, J. (1983) *Reserved for the Poor*, Oxford: Basil Blackwell.
FRASER, D. (1983) *The Evolution of the British Welfare State*, London: Macmillan.
GOLDING, P. and MIDDLETON, S. (1982) *Images of Welfare*, Oxford: Martin Robertson.
HOUGHTON, LORD (1977) 'Adminstration, Politics and Equity', in *The State of Taxation*, London: IEA.
INLAND REVENUE (1987) *How Settlements are Negotiated*, Leaflet no. 73, London: HMSO.
KEITH COMMITTEE (1983) *Keith Committee Report on the Enforcement Powers of the Revenue Departments*, Cmnd 8822, London: HMSO.
LAURENCE, J. (1987) 'Avoidance Tactics?' *New Society*, 29 May.
LEVI, M. (1987) *Regulating Fraud*, London: Tavistock.
MANDLA, D. (1987) 'War on the Dole', *New Society*, 26 June.
MINFORD, P. (1987) 'The Role of the Social Services: A View from the New Right', in M. Loney (ed.), *The State or the Market*, Milton Keynes: Open University Press.
MOORE, P. (1981) 'Scroungermania Again at the DHSS', *New Society*, 22 January.
MYDDLETON, D. R. (1979) 'Tax Avoision – its Costs and Benefits' in Seldon, A. (ed.) *Tax Avoision*, London: IEA.
NACRO (1986) *Enforcement of the Law Relating to Social Security*, London. NACRO.
NCASSC (National Campaign Against Social Security Cuts) (1985) Bulletin 3.
PARKER, H. (1985) *The Moral Hazards of Social Benefits*, London: IEA.
RENTOUL J. (1988) 'The New Idle Rich', *New Statesman Society*, 25 March.
SHENFIELD, A. A. (1968) *The Political Economy of Tax Avoidance*, IEA Occasional Paper 24.
SMITH, R. (1985) 'Who's Fiddling?' in S. Ward (ed.) *DHSS in Crisis*, London: CPAG.
Taxpayers Charter (1986) Board of Inland Revenue/Customs and Excise.
WARD, S. (ed.) (1985) *DHSS in Crisis*, London: CPAG.

7 Community Involvement in Criminal Justice: The Representativeness of Volunteers

R. I. Mawby

INTRODUCTION

When I first conceived of a research project on community involvement in the criminal justice system, there was little literature from within the criminal justice system on which to draw, and indeed, little interest among criminologists. Instead, I was drawn to the socialy policy literature for an analysis of the key issues surrounding community, and especially voluntary sector, involvement in the provision of welfare services. Such issues included attempts to categorise different forms of voluntary agency, concerns over the political independence and financial viability of voluntary organisations, professional/volunteer relationships, and in particular the characteristics of those who, as volunteers, become involved in the provision of services (Aves, 1969; Hatch, 1980; Johnson, 1981; Wolfenden, 1978).

Today, government enthusiasm for the mixed economy principle has extended from welfare to penal policies, and has incorporated both commitment to private sector developments and a pledge of faith for voluntary agencies and volunteers. Within the police, for example, renewed interest in the special constabulary (Home Office, 1987) parallels near-fundamentalist conversion to the principles of neighbourhood watch (Bennett, 1987) and public involvement in the search for accountability and legitimacy is reflected in consultative groups (Morgan, 1987) and lay visitor schemes (Walklate, 1987). At the same time, the traditional role of the public within the criminal justice system is more readily acknowledged, both informally as reporters of crime and potential 'good Samaritans' (Mawby, 1985) and in a more formal capacity.

In considering the role of the voluntary sector, and specifically volunteers, in the criminal justice system it is instructive to assess the social policy literature. This suggests that we can make three initial distinctions: between the voluntary sector and other 'providers' of services; between different types of voluntary agency; and between voluntary organisations and volunteers.

On the first level, the 'mixed economy of welfare' is a term used to identify the various contributions made to service provision by the state, the voluntary sector, the private sector, and an informal level of family and neighbourhood (Wolfenden, 1978). Whilst a concern to roll back the boundaries of state involvement has been late arriving in the criminal justice field, it is clearly now to the forefront of government policy. That is, too great an involvement of the state is seen as ideologically wrong and practically inefficient. The community, voluntary sector and private sector are thus seen as alternative service providers, to be valued precisely because they minimise the role of the state. In this sense, we might argue that the community and voluntary sector are doubly important. On the one hand they encompass the prospects of greater public involvement in the provision of services, a constraint on political control and a greater responsiveness of services to public demands. On the other hand, we might see them as more desirable alternatives to an increased private sector. Unfortunately both points are misplaced. First, as will be discussed below, the equating of voluntary involvement with public accountability depends on both the power accredited to the community and the representativeness of the 'public' who become involved. Second, as has been argued in more detail elsewhere (Gill and Mawby, 1990a; Mawby, 1989), the boundaries between community and voluntary sector involvement on the one hand, and private and voluntary provision on the other, are blurred. In the latter case, for example, North Americans tend to use the term 'private' to incorporate what we might call 'voluntary', a tempting alternative when one considers that there is no hard and fast distinction between the two, especially when, as in many facets of the criminal justice system, consumer choice is inoperative (Mawby, 1989).

On the second level, authors such as Hatch (1980) have stressed the considerable variation between different agencies which fall within the voluntary sector category. Hatch draws a distinction based on three criteria: whether the service depends on volunteers; whether or not such volunteers are distinct from consumers of the service; and how funding is provided. Elsewhere, specifically for the criminal justice system my colleague Martin Gill and I have used a somewhat different categorisation (Gill and Mawby, 1990a, Mawby, 1989). We compared voluntary agencies according to their rating on four criteria: the relationship between the voluntary agency and state organisations; dependence on government funding; the goals of the agency; and the relationship between helper and helped. This fourfold distinction allows us to contrast a number of voluntary organisations. It also suggests that where relationships with government can influence funding, certain voluntary agencies may be more acceptable to government, and thus receive greater funding, while others – which are critical of state services, prioritise political goals, and identify with deviant clients – may find it very difficult to attract government grants. The fact that the present government is highly supportive of all initiatives within the sector, is a point of considerable relevance for the criminal justice system.

On the third level, a distinction must be drawn between voluntary agencies and volunteers. Many voluntary organisations utilise volunteers, but not all do and many do so only in a subsidiary capacity. For example, many of the large funded charities (like NSPCC and National Childrens Homes) are highly dependent on government funds and professional paid staff. Equally, organisations that Hatch (1980) terms 'special agencies', like nightshelters, survive on short-term grants with low-paid staff and a dearth of volunteers. On the other hand, state agencies and indeed some private bodies deploy volunteers. Examples of the former, to be covered in more detail here, include the police and the probation service.

The distinction between voluntary organisations and volunteers is important because the advantages of an expanded voluntary sector and an increased use of volunteers are not always identical, and equally the disadvantages of each are distinctive. For example, dependence on voluntary agencies may not, in fact, be less expensive than state services, except where salaries are lower, but a shift from paid workers to volunteers may be cost-effective, at least as long as the administration and training of volunteers is not excessively expensive. On the other hand, government control of services may be tightened by a greater emphasis upon the direct funding of voluntary agencies but lessened by greater reliance on volunteers within any agency.

The use of volunteers does, moreover, have a number of additional advantages, centred around the notion of community involvement, and for this reason the remainder of this chapter is focused upon *volunteers*. Of course, the role of the public in the provision of services has a long tradition within the criminal justice system. The jury system, stretching back to Norman England, is a case in point, illustrating a concern to make the law answerable to public opinion. Ironically the jury system is the one example where 'volunteer' is a misnomer since the public often participate against their wishes! Rather differently, the lay magistracy is historically a voluntary role encompassing considerable status and power, where willingess to volunteer one's services is less important than acceptance that an applicant (or potential applicant) is the 'right sort of person'. Similar concerns are reflected in more recent examples of posts at the apex of volunteer statuses, such as membership of the Parole Board or Prison Boards of Visitors.

Yet the precise nature of volunteers to the criminal justice system is a key feature of critiques of an expanding role of the community, as developed by Cohen (1985), following Foucault (1977). The key question becomes: is power being devolved to the community, or merely transferred from professional to voluntary elites? In this repect findings within social policy that volunteers are predominantly middle-aged, middle-class (and middle-minded?) are reflected in critiques of the traditional middle-class base for the special constabulary (Gill and Mawby, 1990b; Mather, 1959) as well as more recent concern over, for example, representation of lay visitors (Walklate, 1987), consultative groups (Morgan, 1987) and neighbourhood watch (Kinsey *et al.*, 1986).

One key aspect of the research conducted by my colleague Martin Gill and myself in Devon and Cornwall, then, was a concern to identify the social characteristics of different groups of volunteers. Initially, we concentrated on three groups of volunteers: two groups, special constables and probation volunteers, based within state agencies; the third, victim support volunteers, from a voluntary organisation. Our choice of these three groups was also geared towards tapping possibly different emphases *vis-à-vis* the aims of the service: probation volunteers, we hypothesised, would reflect a concern to help offenders; victim support scheme volunteers might evidence a concern to meet the needs, and indeed rights, of crime victims; and police specials, we hypothesised, would be oriented towards an emphasis on 'law and order' in the community. In each case we considered agency and professional perspectives, as well as those of the volunteers themselves. This chapter, however, focuses on one aspect of our interest in the three groups of volunteers, namely their social characteristics. Here we collected data on the age, gender, social class, and marital statuses of volunteers; and additionally considered their perspectives on a range of relevant issues. For example, we asked why they had become involved as volunteers, their views on the agency and professionals with whom they worked, their attitudes towards a range of 'law and order' issues, and their political preferences.

THE VOLUNTEERS

Elsewhere, we have detailed the stages through which potential volunteers might pass before becoming involved in voluntary work. Essentially, we can distinguish two levels of decisions with regard to these stages – those made by the individual and those made by the agency. Individuals may be involved in decisions to opt for voluntary work, on the nature of the work and agency with which to work, and ultimately on whether or not to continue with this work. Agencies make decisions on how to attract volunteers, whether or not applicants are suitable, and on the means whereby volunteers are trained, deployed, and ultimately integrated into the agency. These stages are illustrated dramatically in Figure 7.1, which is taken from our more detailed analysis elsewhere (Gill and Mawby, 1990b) where we have also indicated differences at each level between volunteers to the three different agencies included in the research.

What, then, of the outcome of this process? Overall our findings reflect earlier studies of welfare volunteers, with a predominance of female, middle-aged to elderly, middle-class volunteers. There were, however, differences between the three groups, suggesting that the nature of the agency and/or its work may appeal to different types of potential volunteers. Thus, police specials

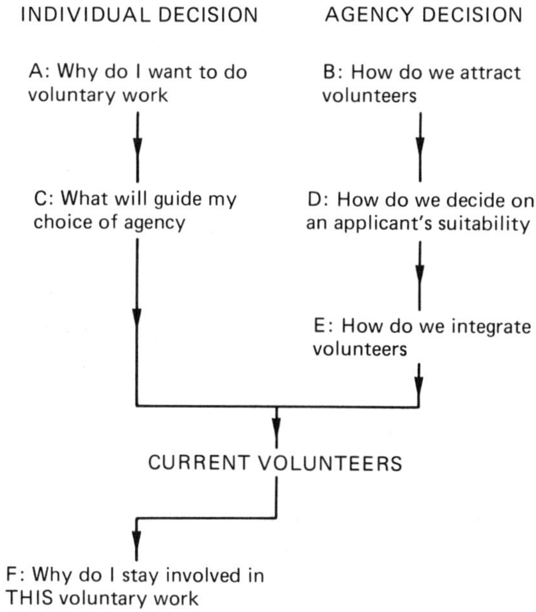

Figure 7.1 The volunteering process: a decision-making model

tended to be relatively younger, predominantly male, and lower middle-class; victim support volunteers were considerably older and commonly upper middle-class. In terms of most of these variables, probation volunteers were not too dissimilar to victim support volunteers, suggesting that welfare work might attract a different pool of applicants to police work.

However, when we considered the attitudes of volunteers, a different picture emerged. True, a question on the appropriateness of different sentencing alternatives elicited a similar pattern, with police specials distinct from the other two groups in evidencing more punitive views. In other respects, though, we found probation volunteers distinctive from the other two groups which espoused traditionally right-wing views. This was reflected in past voting behaviour and current voting intentions. It was also evident from the attitude scales included in the questionnaire.

ATTITUDES TOWARDS CRIME-RELATED ISSUES

The attitude scales used had been developed in the mid-1970s as part of a survey of public perceptions and experiences of crime in Sheffield. Given widespread findings that the public hold more negative views of crime in general than of crime which is 'closer to home', the scales were then used as one of a number of means of comparing the views of residents of different neighbourhoods in the city (Mawby, 1986). Results from Sheffield also indicated marked variations by age and gender (Mawby, 1983).

Three of the scales used in Sheffield were modified for incorporation in our research in the South West, measuring perspectives on the crime problem, attitudes towards the police, and perceptions of offenders. As in Sheffield, we found respondents' scores to be skewed towards the top of each scale; that is, volunteers typically evidenced positive views of the police, were unsympathetic towards and distanced themselves from offenders, and agreed that there was a serious crime problem. As anticipated, individual scores on the three scales were significantly related to one another.

The relationship between political allegiance and scale scores was also as expected. Those scoring above the sample mean on the police and crime problems scales in particular were significantly more likely than lower scorers to be conservative voters, either at the preceding election or by intention (see Figure 7.2). However, differences on the offender scale were less marked and did not attain statistical significance.

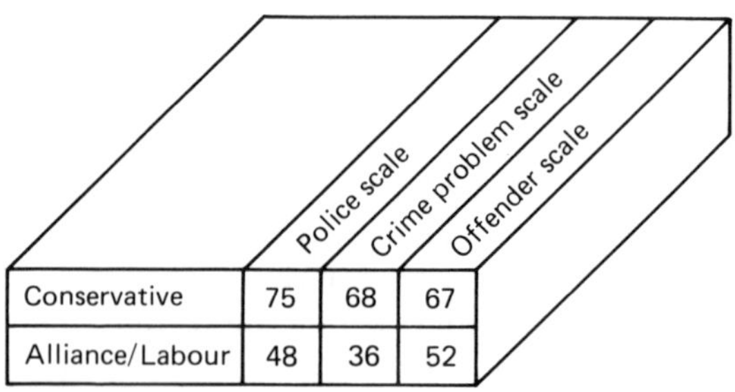

Figure 7.2 For three volunteer groups combined percentage of high scores on each scale among those intending to vote Conservative or Alliance/Labour

	Prob. vol.	V.S.S.	Specials
Police scale	18.74	21.06	22.18
Crime problem scale	16.84	18.55	19.1
Offender scale	16.25	20.32	20.65

Figure 7.3 Comparison of mean scale scores for three groups of volunteers

A comparison of scale scores for the three groups of volunteers produced two interesting findings. First, there were differences between the three groups, as in voting behaviour/intentions, with probation volunteers scoring lower than victim support volunteers and especially police specials (see Figure 7.3). Thus mean scores for the three groups were significantly different. Second, and following this, analysis of the relationship between volunteer group, scale scores and voting patterns demonstrated that volunteer group membership was more closely associated with scale scores than were voting patterns. In other words, *if we wished to predict the scale scores of volunteers, voting patterns were less valid indicators than information on what voluntary activity the individual was undertaking.*

Clearly, there is no barrier between the three groups of volunteers. This is well illustrated in Figure 7.4 where the three groups are compared on the offender scale. Thus while the median scores of police specials and victim support volunteers fall in the high (21–25) category, and those of probation volunteers fall in the medium (16–20) category with a skew to the low end of the scale, in three of the five categories there are representatives of all three groups of volunteers.

The results do, however, indicate significant differences between those involved in voluntary work with different agencies, differences which have both practical and theoretical implications. On a practical level, clearly agencies might consider the desirability of widening the representation of their volunteers and the implications of their policies on volunteer characteristics. On a theoretical level, the following section focuses on the extent to which volunteers might ascribe to some form of volunteer culture.

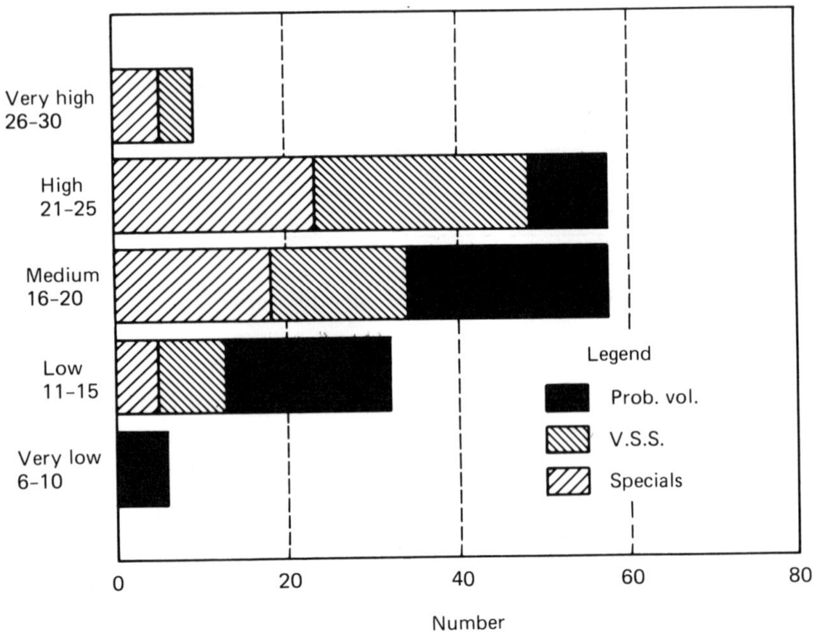

Figure 7.4 Comparison of offender scale scores for three groups of volunteers

VOLUNTEER CULTURES

Occupational cultures have been identified by researchers as incorporating a number of features. Essentially, adherence to such a culture involves sharing a group of core values which include commitment to the organisation and solidarity with colleagues as well as shared perspectives on a range of job-related issues. Police researchers, for example, have identified as central to the occupational culture an adherence to values of excitement and action, with an emphasis on macho elements, to the detriment of service or welfare aims (Holdaway, 1983; 1986).

With regard to the three agencies in our research, a number of questions might be posed. First, we can ask whether an equivalent culture can be discerned. Second, if the answer is in the affirmative, we can ask about the membership of such a culture. Third, we might consider its origins, and finally its consequences.

On the first level, the discussion so far suggests that shared characteristics and values provide the ingredients on which a volunteer culture might be formed. Whether or not it develops, however, depends on whether individual volunteers recognise themselves to be part of that culture. This brings us to the second question, concerning group boundaries.

Two points are crucial here. First, it is clear that the differences between our samples of volunteers are such that we cannot talk of a combined volunteer culture; if a culture exists, it is at the very least specific to a particular agency. In this case, the second point is pertinent: namely, who within the agency is included?

An adequate answer to this question presumes a degree of detail on the role of volunteers within the three agencies which cannot be incorporated here but which is available elsewhere (Gill and Mawby, 1990a; 1990b). Briefly, though, it seems that for the special constabulary and probation volunteers, volunteers closely identified themselves with the agency and its employees. Within the police, this was reflected in an identification with the values expressed by police officers themselves. That is, police specials were committed to values associated with policework as defined by the police occupational culture. Despite the rejection of *specials in general* by many police officers, *individual* volunteers sought acceptance and approval on an individual basis by the officers with whom they came into contact. Identification at this level was facilitated by the training process, the nature of the voluntary work – which brought specials into close contact with regular officers on patrol or in the policing of special events – and the opportunity for shared time 'out of work', primarily in the police bars.

In contrast, probation volunteers had less opportunity for close involvement with probation officers on each of these levels; training was minimal, work was more commonly on an individual basis with contact with one or two probation officers, and shared leisure activities were less common. Moreover, for the same reasons, probation volunteers had less contact with their fellow volunteers. As a result, probation volunteers, whilst strongly associating themselves with probation officers, moulded their values on those of the agency rather than probation officers in general. They thus shared, to some extent, a set of values on, for example, the nature of offenders. *However*, minimal interaction with other volunteers and probation officers was such as to limit the extent to which such shared identifications might be said to result in a volunteer culture.

In contrast, victim support volunteers had no directly equivalent professionals with whom to identify, although they clearly saw the police as demonstrating rather more appropriate attitudes towards crime than did other agencies. Again, like probation, the nature of the work and the lack of shared leisure activities meant that volunteers were relatively isolated from the agency and other volunteers. However, training was emphasised rather more, and initial training and regular volunteer meetings provided a forum for the development of a group identity, further emphasised by the recency of the victims' movement. Thus volunteer culture tended to be based around a *cause*, where the objective was to restore the victim to his/her appropriate place within the criminal justice system.

This is clearly relevant to a consideration of the origins of volunteer cultures. Referring back to Figure 7.1, different work with different agencies appeals to different people. However, we would not wish to overemphasise the importance of this level, partly because we found no evidence that those who were most definite in their choice of agency were any more committed to the values of its volunteers than were others who, for example, drifted into work with an agency. The extent to which agencies choose volunteers who are considered appropriate, and the ways in which volunteers are integrated, are thus of at least parallel importance. This latter point is significant since it reflects similar conclusions among those who have assessed police cultures (see, for a discussion, Brogden *et al*., 1988).

Finally, however, we can briefly consider the consequences of the development of volunteer cultures. Essentially, and on a practical level, these fall into two camps. On the one hand, there are considerable advantages to the development of strong identification among volunteers with each other, the agency and its paid staff. Volunteer morale is improved, teamwork and cooperation may be made possible, turnover minimised and the overall management of the agency improved. On the other hand, over-identification may bring with it certain dangers. For example, the advantages of incorporating volunteers with distinctly different outlooks and approaches, and the possibility of using volunteers to make agencies more responsive to the community may be threatened. If this is no tidy conclusion, it at least illustrates one of the problems shared by theoretically oriented and policy-guided research.

SUMMARY

The discussion of different groups of volunteers, their social characteristics, their attitudes and values, and ultimately the emergence of a subculture among volunteers, is important for a number of reasons. First, it allows us to focus on the differences, not merely the similarities, between volunteers, and associate such differences with the ideologies of agencies and their staff. Second, it provides a more theoretical orientation than a traditional, social administration based discussion of the characteristics of volunteers and their motives for getting involved. Third, however, it provides a basis for considering other forms of community involvement and assessing in the same way the extent to which involvement is truly community based, and the orientations which underpin the decision to volunteer and to continue one's involvement. It is in this context that I am currently researching neighbourhood watch in the South West.

Ironically, in a sense, we have been led to conclude that where volunteers are well organised and morale among volunteers is high, then volunteers may, in association closely with the staff and aims of the agency, lose their community roots. In this case, it may be that the distinctive advantages of deploying volunteers are lost. Indeed, it appears that boundaries between volunteers working for different agencies may be deep-rooted, as are boundaries between the agencies themselves – for example, between police and probation.

It is easier to spell out aims than to offer solutions. However, accepting that the use of volunteers does bring with it a number of potential benefits in narrowing the gap between professional organisation and community, it seems appropriate to conclude by stressing three priorities for good practice. First, it is imperative that volunteers are drawn from as broad a base as possible so as to reflect the interests and views of the local community. What is currently of relevance here, in the debate over the use of (Red) Guardian Angels or police-led Blue Angels, is that the evidence from the United States shows that Guardian Angles have succeeded in attracting a very different type of person compared with more traditional police volunteers (Gill and Mawby, 1990b). Second, it is crucial that volunteers are effectively deployed by agencies, which involves both proper training and a well-organised management structure *vis-à-vis* volunteer roles and responsibilities. Third, however, it is important that identification with the agency should not replace outside loyalties. Volunteers should maintain responsibilities within the communities from which they are drawn and maintain contacts with volunteers in other agencies. To implement this, priority should be given to using volunteers in community-based initiatives and in contexts where inter-agency cooperation is important, and thought might be given to inter-agency training initiatives.

Essentially, I have argued that while one may dispute the motives behind current government initiatives, a greater involvement of the community in the criminal justice system is desirable. It is, however, also a double-edged sword. We should not assume that current services which deploy volunteers necessarily result in greater community involvement than where services are provided by paid staff. Just as occupational cultures bring the attendant dangers of organisational conservatism and a lack of response to outside initiatives for change, so volunteer cultures, where they develop, may limit the accountability of the agency to the community. Crucial to this issue is the question of how far volunteers are, in fact, representative of their communities.

REFERENCES

AVES, G. (1969) *Voluntary Workers in the Social Services*, London: Allen & Unwin/BASW.

BENNETT, T. (1987) 'Neighbourhood Watch: Principles and Practices' in R. I. Mawby (ed.), *Policing Britain*, Plymouth: Plymouth Polytechnic.

BROGDEN, M., JEFFERSON, T. and WALKLATE, S. (1988) *Introducing Policework*, London: Unwin Hyman.

COHEN, S. (1985) *Visions of Social Control*, Cambridge: Polity Press.

FOUCAULT, M. (1977) *Discipline and Punish: The Birth of the Prison*, London: Allen Lane.

GILL, M. L. and MAWBY, R. I. (199a) *Volunteers in the Criminal Justice System*, Milton Keynes: Open University Press.

GILL, M. L. and MAWBY, R. I. (1990b) *A Special Constable?*, Aldershot: Avebury.

HATCH, S. (1980) *Outside the State*, London: Bedford Square Press.

HOLDAWAY, S. (1983) *Inside the British Police Force: A Force At Work*, Oxford: Blackwell.
HOLDAWAY, S. (1986) 'Police and Social Work Relations – Problems and Possibilities', *British Journal of Social Work*, 16, pp. 137–60.
HOME OFFICE (1987) *Report of the Conference on Special Constables on 7th December 1987*, London: HMSO (mimeo).
JOHNSON, N. (1981) *Voluntary Social Services*, Oxford: Blackwell/Robertson.
KINSEY, R., LEA, J. and YOUNG, J. (1986) *Losing the Fight against Crime*, Oxford: Blackwell.
MATHER, F. C. (1959) *Public Order in the Age of the Chartists*, Manchester: Manchester University Press.
MAWBY, R. I. (1983) 'Crime and the Elderly: Experiences and Perceptions', in D. Jerrome (ed.), *Ageing in Modern Society*, London: Croom-Helm.
MAWBY, R. I. (1985) 'Bystander Responses to the Victims of Crime: Is the Good Samaritan Alive and Well?', *Victimology*, 10, pp. 461–75.
MAWBY, R. I. (1986) 'Contrasting Measures of Area Crime Rates: The Use of Official Records and Victim Studies in Seven Residential Areas', in K. Miyazawak and M. Ohya (eds), *Victimology in Comparative Perspective*, Tokyo: Sidbundo.
MAWBY, R. I. (1989) 'The Voluntary Sector's Role in a Mixed Economy of Criminal Justice', in R. Matthews (ed.), *Privatising Criminal Justice*, London: Sage, pp. 135–54.
MORGAN, R. (1987) 'Consultation and Police Accountability', in R. I. Mawby (ed.), *Policing Britain*, Plymouth: Plymouth Polytechnic.
WALKLATE, S. (1987) 'Public Monitoring and Police Accountability', Paper to British Criminology Conference, Sheffield.
WOLFENDEN, J. (1978) *The Future of Voluntary Organisations*, London: Croom Helm.

8 A Fresh Start: Managing the Prison Service

Roy D. King and Kathleen McDermott

On 13 May 1986, the Home Secretary Mr Douglas Hurd announced the publication of the Report of the joint study by Prison Department and PA Management Consultants on the complementing and shift systems worked by prison officers (Prison Service, 1986). In a written answer the Home Secretary claimed that the report presented 'a telling indictment of the present shift and complementing systems in the Prison Service and the working practices which surround them'. The Report, he went on to say, made 'recommendations for new systems which would release large amounts of now unproductive capacity which ought to be used for other purposes'. The recommendations represented a 'major programme of reform' for which he set a target date for implementation, after appropriate discussions, of April 1987. Thus was ushered in the package which has come to be called 'Fresh Start'. It represented the government's attempt to bring the prison system into line with its general pursuit of 'economy, efficiency and effectiveness' in the public services.

The name is symbolic, becauses it was the culmination of nearly a decade of industrial unrest, in a poorly managed service which had been allowed to become dependent on extremely high manning levels, on top of which were piled extraordinary amounts of overtime. This was not merely expensive, it also proved to be a powerful weapon in industrial disputes. Prison officers with low basic wages were able to achieve high take-home pay by manipulating overtime. Shift, pay and allowance systems were of such labyrinthine complexity that many prison governors frankly could not understand them. Restrictive, and what became known in the course of bitter negotiations as 'Spanish', practices prevailed in relation to a variety of tasks throughout the working day which resulted, for example, in staff being allocated to supervise areas where there were no prisoners to be supervised and the dropping of tasks from the 'essential task list' for the alleged want of staff to carry them out in safety (see Morgan, 1983).

Under all of this it was hoped to draw a line, and begin again with a salaried staff whose overtime would be progressively 'bought out'. Prison governors were given the task of reclaiming their right to manage: but prison officers perceived in all this a barely concealed agenda of breaking the power of the Prison Officers' Association.

After protracted negotiations, which went on against a backdrop of carefully managed public relations, including video presentations and elaborately produced information bulletins, Fresh Start was eventually introduced into sixteen establishments on 5 July 1987, and thereafter into other establishments on a rolling programme. it was to be more than a year later, in August 1988, that the last prison (Chelmsford) was scheduled to be 'Fresh Started'.

The amount of unproductive capacity identified by the joint study was estimated to be of the order of 15–20 per cent, and this, argued the Home Office press release, echoing the conclusions of the Report itself, could be translated into a combination of:

- enhanced regimes for prisoners
- reduced hours of work and less overtime for prison staff
- reduced manning levels
- reduced forward recruitment
- reduced costs to the taxpayer

Other benefits could include:

- greater job satisfaction for prison staff
- improved management control and accountability
- better working practices and more efficient manpower utilisation
- improved industrial relations in the prison service.

(Home Office, 13 May 1986)

In an earlier paper (McDermott and King, 1989) we explored the initial impact of Fresh Start in five representative prisons in Midland Region, with respect to the first of these hoped-for benefits: *enhanced regimes for prisoners*. Here we address some of the other issues, particularly *greater job satisfaction*, *improved management control and accountability*, *better working practices* and *improved industrial relations*.

THE FRESH START PACKAGE

The package of changes introduced under Fresh Start was inordinately complex. On 3 April 1987 the Prison Service published a special 28-page bulletin to help prison officers in deciding how to vote on the Fresh Start offer. At some risk of oversimplification Bulletin 8 (Prison Service, 1987a) addressed three central themes: (i) new working arrangements and management structures; (ii) the unification of the previously separate governor grades and uniformed officers into a single continuous structure: and (iii) the introduction of new pay scales and conditions of service. For uniformed staff this last involved the ending of hourly pay and overtime working in favour of basic monthly salaries conditioned to a 39-hour week, with the option of an additional contracted hours allowance, initally for an extra nine hours but reducing on an annual basis over a period of five years, until April 1992 by which time all officers would work a 39-hour week. As the hours were gradually reduced so a proportionate amount of the contracted hours allowance would be incorporated into basic pay. But in return staff would be expected to maintain existing workloads with increases in staffing equivalent to only half the number of hours lost each year. The other half would constitute the net efficiency savings, part of which might be returned to the Exchequer and part used to finance regime enhancement. Unfortunately, proposals for putting the complementing of the Prison Service on a sounder basis, which constituted a fourth major theme, were still being prepared.

Complementing

The fact that proposals for complementing were still in preparation at the launch left open to some question just what was to be the starting-point of the exercise. According to the document prepared by the National Executive Committee of the Prison Officers' Association (POA, no date), Prison Department had committed itself in writing to the provision of 1800 extra staff during the currency of the five-year framework agreement (leaving aside those needed to deal with expansion of the system through the opening of new establishments). This amounted to just one-third of the full-time equivalent staff needed to eliminate the 11 million hours of overtime then worked annually. From the POA standpoint, if members were not to be called upon to make still greater efficiency savings, especially if regimes were to be enhanced and not just maintained, then a further 1800 officers needed to be recruited *before* Fresh Start was introduced so that each establishment began with adequate staffing to meet existing task lists. From a management point of view, however, the removal of those very task lists from centre stage was vital if the new working arrangements and management structures were to be implemented.

On 15 April 1987 it was reported in *The Guardian* that a 'furious row' had broken out among senior officials from Prison Department over the 'no cost' basis of Fresh Start. The Home Secretary, it was said, had conceded that more officers would be needed to implement the reforms but the exact figure would not be known until September. In spite of its reservations, and in the face of a threat to introduce many of the Fresh Start proposals but without the enhanced pay scales, the NEC recommended its members to accept the package whilst pointing out that any local branch which commenced Fresh Start with inadequate complement would be doing itself considerable disservice. The membership overwhelmingly voted in favour of acceptance.

In May 1987 the Prison Service published Bulletin 9 announcing a timetable for the introduction of Fresh Start with a target completion date of October (Prison Service, 1987b). The same bulletin noted that two of the three architects of the Fresh Start package had already left the Prison Department and the third, Caines, was about to go, thereby leaving much of the most difficult negotiations, those concerning manning levels and working practices, to a completely new team. It was probably always intended that those members of the original team who had come to the Home Office from the Treasury via the Department of Health would quickly move on. But their departure was greeted with some scepticism on the ground. As Caines (1988) noted subsequently, although Fresh Start had been sold as a broad programme of reform, the major preoccupation throughout the national negotiations was with the most abstruse and specific points of detail relating to terms and conditions of employment. On working practices the decision had been taken at a very early stage to leave as much as possible to be settled locally. But it was ironic that a full year after initial implementation Caines was able to write of the need – as a matter of extreme urgency – to conclude an agreement with the POA about staffing levels.

The implementation of the new working arrangements and management structures in individual prisons was negotiated locally between governors, on the basis of varying degrees of advice from, and consultation with, their own managers and the local POA on the one hand, and Regional Directors and their support staffs on the other. We shall say more of this in a moment. But it was clearly impossible to separate these elements of Fresh Start from the thorny issue of complementing, or indeed from some niggling doubts about the seriousness of Prison Department's intentions about the unification of the staff structure. Some indication of the way in which these matters intertwined can be gained from a consideration of the discussions at the POA special delegate conference in October 1987. First, delegates were reminded of the way in which Bulletin 9 announced that 'management grades' would go on to Fresh Start immediately whilst the 'working grades' would have to wait. This was perceived not merely as an attempt to pressurise the POA into agreeing to go on to Fresh Start in advance of full complementing – which presumably is just what it was – but also a deeper indication of a lack of real commitment on the part of the Department to the principle of unification. The 'myth of unification' was also demonstrated, according to the POA, in the Minister's refusal to accept the firmly expressed wishes of the governor grades to go into uniform, and exacerbated by the fact that former chief officers who did not take the tempting retirement packages were effectively *taken out of uniform*. Indeed anyone doubting the powerful residue of class divisions in the Fresh Start package only has to look at the use of upper and lower case in some of the most crucial Fresh Start measures, thus: 'The existing Prison Governor and prison officer classes will be absorbed into the unified structure as follows . . .' (Bulletin 8).

The special delegate conference had been called amid increasing confusion as to the numbers of staff required fully to complement the prisons at the beginning of Fresh Start. Some 72 prisons were already on Fresh Start, though not without difficulties, but in many others there were serious disagreements about complementing, and in several there were limited forms of industrial action. Wandsworth had been on industrial action since July 1987, restricting the intake of prisoners to the level of certified normal accommodation and the Home Secretary had voiced his concern about the part this played in the continuing need to keep remand prisoners in police cells. Many different figures were given by different sources as to the numbers of new staff required and the numbers of new staff being recruited and trained to bridge the gaps, and since they used different base lines and different time periods, it is not surprising that confusion was widespread. What is clear is that, recognising both that there would be at least a temporary shortfall and the need to get the scheme fully launched without inordinate delay, the Department agreed that Fresh Start should effectively begin in the remaining establishments by 1 November 1987 under locally agreed transitional arrangements, with a promise that full complementing would be achieved by 28 February 1988.

By then, though, the expected savings from Fresh Start, at least for the first year, had been scaled down from 15 per cent to 10 per cent. The Department had been vigorously recruiting new officers and expanding its training course capacity to cope with the increase. But it was also taking steps to meet a substantial part of the shortfall (240 out of 400) by recruiting civilian staff. The POA saw this as an attempt to make further economies by civilianising various posts that previously had been within the domain of prison officers – not just car-park attendants but canteen, control rooms, kitchens and the like. Since these posts were seen somewhat as periodic rewards by prison officers, ways of taking respites from the unremitting grind of working the landings, this prompted new anxieties about the unity of the prison service. 'When did you last see an administration officer or civilain respond to an alarm bell?' one speaker asked the conference.

When the POA voted in a national ballot on 5 January 1988 to take industrial action they had learned to hit their bureaucratic masters with their own weapons by declining to cooperate with some of the essential paperwork for monitoring Fresh Start. Some branches, however, continued to restrict the receptions of prisoners. Even as the most recent ramifications of the continuing battle over numbers worked its way through at Wandsworth in February 1989, where for the first time in seventy years police officers were used to run a prison, it was clear that the scale of the differences which separated the two sides was no longer large.

One is left with the feeling that the numbers problems might more easily have been solved if the other matters relating to divisiveness had been more sensitively handled.

Working Arrangements and Management Structures

Bulletin 8 set out a statement of agreed principles to provide a framework within which new working arrangements were to be developed. The general aim was to replace existing management structures, systems and methods with working arrangements that:

i match more closely the work requirements of the establishment
ii are responsive to changing pressures and demands
iii enable managers to manage more effectively
iv promote the unification of the service
v improve the efficiency, effectiveness and economy of the service
vi provide the basis for enhanced regimes
vii bring increased job satisfaction
viii provide greater predictability of attendance
ix provide clear lines of operational accountability
x provide clear definitions of roles and responsibilities

Although, as Bulletin 8 made clear, the details of the working arrangements were to be agreed on a local basis with local review teams, a series of principles of approach and subsidiary objectives were outlined with which local agreements were expected to be congruent. Once again it is necessary to simplify to achieve any kind of clarity.

Most important for the new working arrangements was the principle of group working, with group managers responsible for 'detailing' their staff to duties within their area of responsibility. Hitherto detailing had been done centrally for the whole prison and its alleged inflexibility had been at the heart of a system that lost sight of the real objectives behind arcane 'Spanish' practices which dictated who could do what, when and where in covering the activities on the essential task list. It was for group managers to find ways of rostering the various grades of staff allocated to their group that would secure predictable hours of duty and time off, allow holidays to be planned ahead, provide proper facilities for staff training and so on, and still cover the activities of their group without the need to call back staff who were not on duty except in dire emergencies. If managers did have to call back staff in excess of weekly rostered hours, time off in lieu (TOIL) was to be given back as soon as possible. The staffing complements suggested by the manpower teams ostensibly built in provision for enhanced training and sick leave, as well as holidays, and still left enough to cover normal duties. Where it was necessary for staff to be called in, or for one grade to act up for another, this was to be done within the group, thereby fostering a sense of group loyalty and commitment. Continuity of allocation to a group was expected to play a major part – along with better pay, hours, training and promotion – in enhancing the job satisfaction of prison officers. The question of the actual role of the prison officer, however, was not *directly* addressed.

Group working was taken to be the 'cornerstone' of the new management structures, which were designed to help make 'everybody accountable to somebody'. At the top the role of governor was defined as the 'overall manager of all management operations and ultimate operational commander in emergencies'. This meant that many of the traditional executive duties discharged by the governor were to be delegated and a new structure of responsibilities was devised which sought to bring work activities together into coherent functional blocks. Seven such blocks were identified:

Operations	– activities in support of security, control and operational working
Residential	– activities centred on units of inmate accommodation
Inmate Services	– residentially related services which have to be organised centrally – kit, bathing, canteen, etc.
Medical Services	– activities linked to medical specialisms
Inmate Activities	– components normally understood as regime functions – education, workshops, etc.
Management Support Services	– financial, budgetary control and records
Works Services	– support services delivered by works grades.

There was some scope for discussion and negotiation as to precisely which grouping should be responsible for particular activities, so that significant variations could emerge between prisons, and in practice there were a number of boundary disputes. These could be exacerbated by the fact that, in spite of the pretensions to a unified service, professional, administratives, clerical and industrial staff were incorporated into the management structure and subjected to line accountability, but got none of the financial benefits of Fresh Start. Indeed they got precious little from Fresh Start Two when that was announced either.

Generally speaking, though, it was agreed that there should be as few management levels, with as much delegation as possible, consistent with clear definitions of individual roles and clear lines of accountability. In the absence of the chief officer role the suggested model involved the forging of a new and greatly enhanced role for the deputy governor now known as head of custody, covering operations, residential and inmate services. The head of custody, together with the heads of medical services, inmate activities, management support services, and works services would constitute the second line of management responsible to the governor. Below them at smaller establishments there might be only the group managers, at grade VI the former principal officer grade, though at larger establishments there would most likely be an intermediate level of management – at least for the larger and more complex activity groups.

On the successful implementation of such changes was the future of the prison service predicated.

THE RESEARCH

The five prisons from which our data are drawn are Gartree, a dispersal prison for high security risk prisoners; Nottingham, a Category B closed training prison; Featherstone, a Category C closed training prison; Ashwell, at the time of our main study a Category D open training prison; and Birmingham, a large urban local prison. All of the prisons are in the Midland Region. The prisons were chosen as representative institutions catering for adult male prisoners, in the course of a project on Security, Control and Humane Containment in the prison system of England and Wales.

It had been clear since before the research began that Prison Department was becoming increasingly concerned about what it delivered and how it could account for that delivery of service – and our research was soon to show that such concern was justified (see King and McDermott, 1989). Circular Instruction 55 of 1984 set out a statement of the tasks of the Prison Service and the functions of Prison Department establishments, which was clearly linked to a new framework of management accountability (Train, 1985). The success of this was soon seen to depend upon the development of information systems that could serve to monitor performance in the delivery of planned activities which together would give the service 'a sense of direction' (Dunbar, 1985; Evans, 1987).

The announcement of Fresh Start came during the very early stages of our fieldwork, and the difficult negotiations between Prison Department and the Prison Officers' Association formed part of the permanent context within which our research was actually conducted. Knowing the importance of Fresh Start and the concern that it had caused particularly to uniformed officers, we subsequently returned to each prison in an attempt to get some sense of its impact and how it was evaluated by staff. We went back to each of our study prisons, for about one week, between three and six months after its Fresh Start date, by which time, we hoped, the worst of the teething might be over, and the new management structures and working arrangements might have bedded down.

In each prison we were able to speak to governors about the implementation of Fresh Start and their 'action plans' for the coming year. We distributed a short questionnaire to staff who were on duty at the time (and, in the case of Birmingham, who were not involved that day in the court commitment), about two-thirds of whom replied. We also visited the major departments to talk to those responsible for them, and from whom we gathered material on how they and their departments had been affected by Fresh Start. Finally we managed to talk to many staff, both civilian and uniformed, and from all levels in the organisation, as well as some prisoners while we were there. These included some of our key respondents from the main study, who were often able to flesh out the account for us in greater detail. It was never part of our original intention that we should carry out a before-and-after study of Fresh Start: and this account should be taken as a rather preliminary look at some immediate consequences of Fresh Start as they appeared to staff, and to us, in prisons that we knew well. Nevertheless, this is likely to be the only independent and disinterested account by outsiders of these unique events.

THE IMPLEMENTATION OF FRESH START IN FIVE PRISONS

It is fitting to begin our discussion of the implementation of Fresh Start with a consideration of the way the five prisons were complemented.

Staff Complementing

Before Fresh Start each prison had an approved staff list (ASL) agreed between the institution and the region. The ASL comprised the number of staff required to cover the essential task list (ETL) without recourse to overtime, though it took no real account of sickness, holidays and training. Few, if any, prisons actually had these numbers of staff in post (SIP) and the difference between SIP and ASL was bridged either by staff working overtime or by shrinkage in the workload through the dropping of tasks, or some combination of the two. Generally speaking the difference between the SIP and the ASL was greater in local prisons than in training prisons, and in higher security establishments than lower security establishments. The negotiations as to the proper complement for prisons under Fresh Start was carried out locally and on a different basis. Tasks were amalgamated into coherent blocks of activity and assigned to groups responsible for those activities. There then followed a process of negotiation between the prison and the Fresh Start manpower team based in the Region, to produce an effective pattern of complementing for those groupings which took account of holidays, sickness and training as well as the rhythm and distribution of work.

Because of the changed approach it is probably inappropriate simply to compare numbers of staff before and after Fresh Start. Nevertheless it is clear that the Joint Report on Complementing and Shift Systems concluded that 'the work of the Prison Service can be undertaken within a substantially reduced number of man hours' (Prison Service, 1986, p. 94) and it was always inevitable that prison officers would make such comparisons at least in the early stages. We found it hard to establish just what should be the proper basis for making comparisons although it was clear that savings were proportionately greater in specialist grades than non-specialist uniformed staff. The savings were most marked among works staff, and to some extent catering and hospital officers, but not physical education instructors whose numbers were actually increased.

Governors, uneasily placed between the conflicting demands of prison officers and treasury bureaucrats, were concerned that they had not got as many staff as they wanted in their negotiations over complementing, and that Headquarters had then shifted the goalposts midway through the exercise, leaving them to implement the reforms too quickly and with too few resources. One of them told us: 'The shortfall in the complement has adversely affected the implementation and development of Fresh Start . . . I had such high hopes . . . now I'm just keeping my head above water.' Another, explained that people had 'lost faith in Headquarters who promised that we would get the staff after the interim period of Fresh Start' and that this had had a 'profound effect on morale'.

At the time of our return visits Birmingham was still operating well below its new complement, and Gartree and Nottingham very slightly below theirs. In Ashwell and Featherstone the new complements were in fact met at the time of our visits.

Group Detailing

A central feature of Fresh Start was that group managers should do their own detailing of officers to tasks to produce the most effective pattern of working from within the resources allocated to them. How well did this work in practice?

As far as most non-specialist uniformed staff were concerned the significant functional blocks were operations and residential, although in the nature of things the residential grouping was further subdivided according to the 'natural' breakdown of accommodation within each prison. The most obvious change in detailing, therefore, was that whereas in the past there had been a central detail office for the whole prison with a small group of staff headed by a principal officer, or sometimes a senior officer, now there were several group managers (grade VI, former principal officers) engaged in this activity, each acting independently. While in theory it was true that for each manager the detail was now a relatively small job, at the time of our visits most of them claimed that, along with other clerical tasks, it took a large amount of their time. As one of them told us: 'I figured out with the HQ's evaluation team that I spend 27 hours a week in the office, doing the detail and filling in forms. I've been turned into a clerk. I don't manage men, just paper.' One former detail officer suggested to us that group managers simply did not understand the process: 'This is a totally uneconomic way of doing it. Before there used to be one man doing the detail, now there are four. Mistakes are being made because there are too many fingers in the pie.'

Most group managers claimed that they could run their groups adequately provided they did not have to give up their staff to other groups. The move to group management, of course, was intended to foster continuity of duties within a spectrum of related activities, and so change between groups was not envisaged. Each group was supposed to be self-sufficient, with enough staff to provide cover for sickness, training and so on. Any necessary acting up was also to be done from within the group.

Fresh Start was intended to give staff greater predictability about rest days and holidays, and although the attendance systems took account of this, in most cases they were designed around the basic 39-hour week. It was always known that the additional contracted hours would be worked at management's discretion. Nevertheless, many group managers found it very hard to move away from the old methods of detailing whereby staff were given considerable choice over holidays, and when they might take time off in lieu (TOIL). Indeed whereas the overtime-led system placed the central detail officer under pressure from the overtime 'bandits' who spent as much time as possible *inside* the prison, the new group managers found themselves under pressure from a salaried staff who now sought to manipulate their working schedules to spend as much time as possible *outside* the prison. One senior officer, who was working an attendance system which required him to work four long shifts with three days off, told us: 'The new fiddle is not trying to see how much overtime you can get but how much time off you can get.' In his case it was possible to contrive, with a little help, six consecutive rest days a fortnight – though he acknowledged that this 'was bad for the job because you lose contact with what is happening on the wing. And when you do come back you find yourself just looking to get home again.'

At the time of our study there was considerable concern over sickness rates, which had doubled in some instances since before Fresh Start. There was no doubt that some sick absences resulted from the fact that staff were now able to seek medical attention for hernias and other conditions that had hitherto been put off for fear of losing money. But as well as such cold surgery there were very real fears about malingering. Bulletin 15 drew particular attention to this, and governors were encouraged to be vigilant. In the course of our visits two governors told us they had personally followed up some cases by making housecalls to staff who reported sick. We found that some group managers spoke of sickness being used as a weapon, rather as overtime had once been used. Although there was undoubtedly peer group pressures to prevent the worst abuses, for as Bulletin 15 pointed out unwarranted sick absence meant that 'the rest of the group have to work even harder than usual' (Prison Service, 1988), some group managers regretted that the move to a salaried service had not held back some element of pay in the form of attendance allowances.

There was even greater concern about training. In Midland Region a notional allowance of ten days training per man per year was built into the staffing complement. Group managers were expected to distribute the total training hours available to ensure 'that the skills to cover the work of the group are spread as widely as is practicable across the members of his team' (Annex A, Bulletin 8). In practice local training priorities and the availability of opportunities for places on regional or national courses sometimes meant that large numbers of training hours were consumed by a few individuals. As a result there was often little scope to satisfy the raised expectations of uniformed staff. Training officers complained that even when group managers were able to assign training hours four days in advance by the time it was due, sickness, or extra escorts, had often intervened leading to a cancellation. On the other hand it sometimes happened that spare staff were thrown up at short notice and were then sent home on TOIL because there was no time to organise training. In fact training departments, with the exception of Ashwell, had generally lost staff under the reorganisation. Some training officers who had carefully nurtured fragile resources before Fresh Start now felt frustrated, even betrayed, as they saw their programmes decimated. Group managers could only look on with a sense of despair: 'the staff have so much to learn about Fresh Start but we can't give them the time or the training'. When we asked staff how they felt about training, 81 per cent said that they were worse off under Fresh Start than they had been before.

During our study we were told it was often necessary in the training prisons for the residential group to borrow staff from the operations group. Inevitably these persistent, if marginal, redistributions had some impact on regimes as well as continuity and morale. But in Birmingham where the 'ordinary' problems of group detailing were combined with overcrowding and the need to meet the court commitment, borrowings were a daily occurrence and operated both ways with severe consequences. Thus if more staff were needed for external escorts then officers were taken from internal 'ops' to fill the breach, though this might result in the curtailment of visits. When more staff were required to cover internal ops then staff were borrowed from residential though that might lead to a cut in association or some other deterioration in the regime.

In such circumstances group managers tended to become 'protective' of their group, hiding any surplus where they could: 'Everyone is in the game of protecting what they've got . . . if you make the valiant effort and get your tasks done even though you are short, you're afraid someone is going to say "well you've shown you can do it with less men so we'll take some away".' In every establishment we found strong advocates of a return to central detailing. In Gartree and Birmingham a new, and somewhat unofficial, role of coordinator was created to look at surpluses and shortfalls and to effect redistribution between groups, whilst still leaving the assignment of tasks and TOIL to group managers.

It was clear that group detailing had created problems that had not been foreseen and which management sought to overcome. In extreme circumstances this could result in management calling or threatening to call limited alerts, thereby effectively putting staff on compulsory attendance, albeit at some further cost to good industrial relations.

Management Structure and Accountability

None of the prisons in our study elected to include a functional block known as 'Inmate Services', and the activities identified in Bulletin 8 as falling within that block were redistributed – either under 'Residential' or 'Inmate Actitivities'. There were some minor variations between our prisons as to where particular specialists, and the responsibility for particular activities, were located but in general clear lines of accountability were established. That is not to say, of course, that everyone was happy with their place in the management structure.

At the top of the pyramid the new chief administrator role for the governing governor took him away from many traditional duties, including the 'hands on' activities of adjudications and the daily tour of the prison with the old chief. Whilst all of our governing governors seemed to shoulder their new burdens gladly enough, four out of the five expressed varying degrees of regret that they no longer had their fingers directly on the pulse. In fact they still continued to do some adjudications and contrived to find some opportunities to 'manage by walkabout'. As one said: 'I know the staff feel that I am more remote which is why I still insist on going about the prison. But not having my chief I feel I no longer have that direct connection to the staff whereby I can feel the pulse of the place. I even had a prisoner ask me who I was. I did not come into the prison service for that! To be honest I feel isolated and I don't know how to overcome that.'

Under the new structure much of the daily command of the prison fell to the head of custody, a role which combined elements formerly carried out by the governor, the chief officer and the deputy governor. In the study prisons it was the incumbents of this role that spoke most favourably about Fresh Start generally, and about their own job satisfaction in particular. Those chief officers who did not take early retirement were absorbed into the G4 grade and given other important managerial tasks from which they might reasonably advance further, or else put out to grass. In either case they felt they had done well by Fresh Start, though some had come to terms with the charge of having sold out.

Other governor grades were less happy, particularly G5s (the former assistant governors and chief officers class 2). In some cases these were incorporated along with G4s as second-level managers, where they experienced flak from discipline officers and group managers who felt distanced from the governor: more usually they were incorporated into residential or operations where they sometimes felt and were indeed regarded as supernumary. On the whole this tier of intermediate managers felt, probably correctly in view of the glut at this level, that they were now less likely to get promotion. They also tended to feel that their relationships with uniformed staff had worsened, and not surprisingly, given the frequency with which they had to deal with the low morale of others, experienced low morale themselves. Former chief 2s additionally felt betrayed, denied the proper crowning of their careers: 'I gave my all to this job and now I'm just serving out my time until retirement' was one of the least bitter comments we received.

It was not just governors, and the chiefs themselves, who missed the old role. Many career-minded officers felt that they had lost their most realistic promotion target, and many others spoke about the loss of a father figure or a voice in the power structure for the uniformed staff. This sometimes sounded hollow, bearing in mind the undoubted loss of authority of chiefs in recent years; but there were also as many cases of genuine respect for their current performance as wing managers – particularly in crisis situations – when compared with former assistant governors fulfilling that role.

Under Fresh Start there was a concern to push the responsibilty for decisions down to group manager level. Group managers knew well enough the lines of accountability, but tended to feel beseiged by paper and to see intermediate management as involving often unnecessary duplication of effort as well as a means of restricting access to the governor. For their part senior and intermediate managers often regarded group managers as being reluctant to take real responsibility. As one governor insisted: 'We are no longer a cosy little family. We must learn to be efficient, to delegate and work though line management.'

In general it seemed to be the case that the gains made in terms of vertical accountability within each block of activity had been achieved somewhat at the expense of communication and integration between blocks. Since what ultimately has to be accounted for is a service delivered by the combined activities of the various functional blocks, to and for prisoners who move from one functional block to another, most people told us of the felt need for this to be given urgent attention. For example the traditional difficulties which have always existed between the workshops, now grouped under inmate activities with labour allocation, and the wings grouped under residential, remained without any apparent means for resolving them.

The tension between vertical accountability and horizontal integration of activity is, of course, hardly new to organisation theory, where the need for coordinating mechanisms to overcome it is widely recognised – see for example, Mooney and Riley (1939) for an early discussion. Indeed the management charts for each of our prisons delineated a task of 'regime coordination' but in practice it was a task that was assigned to no particular role. Although it was possible for these issues to be raised at senior management meetings there seemed to be no satisfactory structures at intermediate or group management level where coordination could be made to happen. As a result, even in Featherstone which before Fresh Start had the most integrated regime of any of our prisons, there was a widespread feeling that integration had fallen by the wayside.

These problems were in many respects exacerbated by group working.

Group Working and Job Satisfaction

Group working was intended both to provide a more economic method of detailing officers to duties and to give them increased job satisfaction. According to Appendix 1 of Bulletin 8 increased job satisfaction would result from the 'reduction in hours of attendance and a closer identification and involvement with their work by increased continuity'. Although the details of the role of prison officers is not directly addressed there was clearly some implication that the role would be enhanced – they would for example be part of teams 'having shared responsibility for meeting group objectives'.

In fact we found that morale on these issues was remarkably low in all of our study prisons. There was certainly a sense of identification with the group, but this was widely perceived to have been achieved at the cost of a loss of identification with the prison as a whole. Group identity forged around narrow sectional interests was said to be replacing any more general 'esprit de corps' which might have united staff behind the objectives of the institution as a whole. Variations on this theme provided the common refrain to most of our conversations with staff. As one officer said: 'Since Fresh Start each wing has become almost a prison within a prison, making all wings very insular and the lack of information now is very noticeable.' Or another: 'it's become difficult to maintain close working relationships with officers on other wings or groups'. And another: 'I see a divisiveness creeping in between functional groups due to the differing strengths and attitudes of group managers.' In this situation we were told that responsibilities, tasks and people get lost between groups as staff 'slope their shoulders' and say 'it's not our responsibility'.

Moreover the group identification seemed to result from cooperative arrangements within groups over detailing, holidays, TOIL and so on, rather than any sense of involvement arising out of greater continuity or enhanced responsibility in the work itself. Under group working the increased continuity is one that relates to *tasks* rather than to the *people* doing those tasks. Particular jobs such as, for example, induction may no longer be the responsibility of the 'induction officer' but may be assigned by the group manager on the basis of availability. Many such specialists jobs require additional training, though as we have already seen the training was difficult to provide. When the task was assigned to someone not yet trained for it we were told there could be a tendency to let things slide: 'If you're doing the job centre today you might be doing the shop tomorrow, so why bother about problems, just put it off on the other bloke who'll be there tomorrow.' In these circumstances prisoners may experience a succession of different staff, who may be perceived to make inconsistent decisions, and the job satisfaction that used to accrue under the old system has been lost. Many staff told us: 'We're just tasks now, not people.'

In other respects, though, group working has brought continuity, albeit at the cost of the increased boredom, particularly for staff assigned to residential groups: 'Fresh Start has made the job more boring because you are doing the same mundane job day in day out. At least before we had a variety of mundane jobs.'

In neither case were staff happy with their lot, though for different reasons. But it must also be apparent that in neither case could the job itself be seriously described as enhanced or more fulfilling. To the extent that more and more staff do become trained that situation could change, but meanwhile it was not surprising that staff expressed very little job satisfaction. As we went around asking people what they thought of Fresh Start we got these typical replies: 'Fresh Start is great but the job is rubbish'; or 'The job is flat: it's like a bottle of pop with the fizz taken out.'

Only with respect to hours of attendance (83 per cent) and pensions (75 per cent) did the great majority of staff (rightly) believe they were better off under Fresh Start. With regard to pay, most staff (61 per cent) believed that they were better off or about the same; but those who had worked excessive levels of overtime in the past were worse off, although even they traded this off against the improvements in hours. A good many people told us that they, or others, or their wives and families, had difficulty adjusting to the increase in leisure time. But hardly any uniformed staff reported favourably on other aspects of Fresh Start. Indeed there was substantial agreement that things had got worse. Job satisfaction (62 per cent), job consistency (59 per cent), promotion prospects (77 per cent), the regime for inmates (70 per cent), even, to a degree, relations with other uniformed staff (41 per cent), had all deteriorated under Fresh Start. While there were a few relatively minor differences between prisons on one or two of these matters, by and large this was the universal and overwhelming verdict of the uniformed staff.

CONCLUSION

The introduction of Fresh Start has involved some of the most far-reaching changes to the prison system since it was nationalised in 1878. Albeit in a limited way, we have examined its implementation in five prisons and explored the preliminary responses of staff to the changes which affected them. What conclusions may be drawn?

First, we could find little evidence that the staff derived greater job satisfaction from their work. Some senior managerial roles were enhanced but group managers felt themselves to be sinking under a sea of paper whilst more often than not uniformed staff felt that they had been reduced to an amalgam of tasks. Neither they, nor prisoners, they claimed, were treated as people. As far as prison officers were concerned it would seem that the Fresh Start package paid too much attention to the allocation and distribution of staff and not enough to the *content* of their jobs. That situation might improve if and when the level of training increases to the point where all staff within each group could take on any of the available roles in a professional manner. But the assumption that job satisfaction would be enhanced, without direct attention to the content of what prison officers actually do, seems to have been mistaken. It may be going too far to follow the logic of the POA official who argued that: 'Many times it looks like the officer is doing nothing but he's there and able to feel the temperature of the place and what's going on with individuals.' But there is no doubt that a major part of the staff role is concerned with developing relationships with prisoners and, as the same official argued, it is 'legitimating this relationship that will bring professionalism into the job, not a list of tasks'. In our view Fresh Start needs to take a fresh look at the professional content of the work of prison officers if a sense of purpose and improved job satisfaction and morale is to be achieved.

Second, the new management structures whereby everyone should be accountable to someone, and managers could be seen to be managing, seemed to be working well, give or take some anomalies and minor teething troubles. There were, however, real problems of horizontal communication and coordination of activities which in some degree were the inevitable consequence of any grouping of activities into functional blocks, but which had been sharpened to the extent that group identities had been achieved at the expense of wider loyalties. We believe there to be a pressing need for close attention to be paid to problems of communication, both in the form of meetings between staff in different functional blocks and in new procedures for the transmission of routine information to ensure greater continuity between shifts.

Third, the achievement of more efficient personpower utilisation, which in part relied upon consistency of tasks rather than people, had consequences both for the job satisfaction of staff and the experience of prisoners. Group detailing already showed some scope for the development of new 'Spanish' practices designed to maximise time off which the senior management sought to overcome through additional levels of oversight to the detail. There were real concerns about levels of sickness, and real problems in providing training. We take the view that the allocation and training of staff must be systematically related to the content of what prison officers are required to do if varied and professionally satisfying roles are to be developed for prison officers.

Fourth, and perhaps most significant, the introduction of Fresh Start has not led in any obvious way to improved industrial relations – although it has greatly weakened the power of the POA through the removal of overtime as a potential weapon. Although there are powerful reasons for thinking that Fresh Start might have been long overdue, perhaps even too late, to save a service long characterised by weak management and a lack of purpose, there are also grounds for thinking that in the event it was finally introduced in too hurried a fashion. Any changes of the magnitude of Fresh Start were bound to carry with them uncertainties. But the announcements at the outset that the package could be introduced without additional staff and still make savings of the order of 15–20 per cent out of which regimes could be enhanced all turned out to be seriously flawed. Additional staff were needed, savings of a lower order were achieved, and such modest improvements as may have been achieved in some areas of regimes have been more than offset by deteriorations elsewhere (see McDermott and King, 1989).

The way in which these miscalculations were handled seemed almost designed to maximise suspicion and cynicism about the real intentions and good faith of the Prison Department. At the end of the day, prisons were required to implement the package often without full complements and found it necessary to fall back on a variety of interim measures to 'make do'. At the time of our visits the overriding impression we were left with was the profound mistrust of Prison Department expressed by staff, which frequently amounted to a feeling of betrayal. Prison officers did not believe that the Home Office really wanted a unified service and did not believe that the Home Office placed any value on their opinions or goodwill. It was perhaps not surprising that some officers in exasperation took the view: 'Spanish practices? Don't blame us, we're from Barcelona.' Another, more regretfully, explained: 'If only they had levelled with us from the start we could have worked together to overcome the problems . . but they missed that opportunity of our giving them credibility.' Nor was this kind of view limited to prison officers, for managers too recognised that 'people have lost faith with headquarters who promise things and then fail to deliver'. It will, in our view, take time and a great deal of effort to overcome these deep-seated feelings of mistrust.

Yet, in spite of all, most staff at all levels recognised the necessity of Fresh Start or something like it. While many had unrealistically expected it to remove their problems at a stroke, some were beginning to settle down to the longer-term objectives of making it work. There is no doubt that a very great deal of hard work and thought has gone into the development of management structures and information systems. Whether these will be sufficient to overcome the legacy of suspicion, or the historical tendency of bureaucracies to revert to type after a process of reform, and yet bring about real improvements, remains to be seen. At the time of writing we understand that the new nomenclature – Grades VI, VII and VIII – for uniformed staff, which no one could get used to during our research, has already been formally abandoned in favour of the more comfortable titles of old – principal officer and so on. And no one is yet reporting any systematic enhancements to the regimes in our study prisons. But time will tell. What is clear is that without some such changes the path would have continued inexorably downhill.

NOTE

The data reported here are based on research carried out under Economic and Social Research Council (ESRC) grant no E06 25 0020, as part of the Crime and Criminal Justice System research initiative. We should like to record our gratitude to the officials at Midland Regional Office, and especially the governors and staff in each of our study prisons, as well as the prisoners in these establishments, for their cooperation throughout the research.

REFERENCES

CAINES, E. (1988) 'A View from One of the Architects', *Prison Service Journal*, 1–4 (July).

DUNBAR, I. (1985) *A Sense of Direction*, London: Home Office.

EVANS, R. (1987) 'Management Performance and Information', *Prison Service Journal*, April, pp. 9–12.

KING, R. D. and McDERMOTT, K. (1989) 'British Prisons 1970–87: The Ever-Deepening Crisis', *British Journal of Criminology*, 29, 2, pp. 107–28.

McDERMOTT, K, and KING, R. D. (1989) 'The Enhancement of Regimes', *Howard Journal of Criminal Justice*, 28, 3, pp. 161–76.
MOONEY, J. D. and REILEY, A. C. (1939) *The Principles of Organisation*, New York: Harper.
MORGAN, R. (1983) 'How Resources Are Used in the Prison System', in *A Prison System for the 80s and Beyond*, The Noel Buxton Lectures, 1982–83, London: NACRO.
POA (No Date) *A Fresh Start: The View of the NEC*, Cronin House, London: Prisons Officers' Association.
PRISON SERVICE (1986) *HM Prison Service, Study of Prison Officers' Complementing and Shift Systems*, Joint Study by Prison Department and PA Management Consultants, Volume I: Report, London: HM Prison Service.
PRISON SERVICE (1987a) *A Fresh Start: Bulletin 8*, London: HM Prison Service, 3 April.
PRISON SERVICE (1987b) *A Fresh Start: Bulletin 9*, London: HM Prison Service, 18 May.
PRISON SERVICE (1988) *A Fresh Start: Bulletin 15*, London: HM Prison Service, 29 April.
TRAIN, C. (1985) 'Management Accountability in the Prison Service', in M.
Maguire, J. Vagg and R. Morgan (eds), *Accountability and Prisons*, London and New York: Tavistock.

9 Under Siege: Probation in a Changing Environment

Tim May

> 'Offence after offence appears to be the inevitable lot of him whose foot has once slipped' (Rainer's letter to the English Temperance Society, quoted in Jarvis, 1972, p. 2).

> 'any set of social and economic arrangements which is not founded on the acceptance of individual responsibility will do nothing but harm. We are all responsible for our own actions. We cannot blame society if we break the law. *We simply cannot delegate the exercise of mercy and generosity to others*' (Margaret Thatcher speaking to the General Assembly of the Church of Scotland, May 1988. Italics added).

The 1980s has been characterised by rapid change: increased unemployment, the unleashing of market forces and a government ideology motivated by the sanctity of individual liberty and responsibility. Opinions vary on the reasons for this change in government thinking, but it is undoubtedly having an effect on economic, political and cultural life (see King, 1987). By the 'rolling back' of the state, individual initiative is no longer stifled. This freedom to choose has as its concomitant theme, increasing individual responsibility in choices of action. However, as commentators have noted, a renewal of *laissez-faire* in the economic sphere has apparently resulted in an increasing authoritarianism in the social sphere (see Hall and Jacques, 1983; Leys, 1984). Thus, the criminal justice system has not escaped the impact of these changes. Rehabilitation of the criminal is no longer the primary aim it once was. There is now a focus on punishment predicated upon individual responsibility in the undertaking of criminal acts.

It is such changes in penal thinking and political rhetoric that define the climate in which the probation service operates.

Therefore, the object of this chapter is to examine some of these changes in relation to the rise of the probation service and changes in its organisation and ethos. This results from a three-year research project in which the author was engaged, conducted in collaboration with a probation area. However, while it is intended to reflect on the changing nature of the service and its effects on the professional status of its members, its purpose is not to replicate several detailed histories of the service which already exist (King, 1969; Jarvis, 1972; Bochel, 1976; and Haxby, 1978).

THE EMERGENCE OF 'MISSION'

In order to understand the particular pressures the probation service is currently facing, it is important to locate its emergence and changing nature within the wider environment. This historical method, which draws upon Foucault's (1969, 1977) genealogical analysis, enables a greater understanding of the formation of the service and sharpens insight into contemporary changes; it does not assert a 'master reality' or posit the notion of a 'unilinear development'.

The probation service was born in a time of rising concern at the level of moral degeneration of a particular section of the population: those who were not only working class but also habitual, drunken and petty offenders whose patterns of offending were thought to be linked to their drinking habits. For these offenders incarceration, at the centre of penal sanctioning at the time, was not thought appropriate. The practices which resulted from this change in thinking are regarded as forming the beginnings of the probation system.

During the same period, criminology was preoccupied with the identification of causal factors leading to criminal behaviour. Yet this 'causal determinism' seemed incompatible with the concept of a 'responsible subject' which underpinned Victorian penality. This tension resulted in a compromise: to introduce a measure whose logic underlies and gave impetus to the formation of the probation service and the claims to professionalism of its members. Individual action becomes the result of choice which may, on occasion, be placed in doubt. A 'soft determinism' prevailed:

> *Responsibility thus became a presumption which was always put in doubt.* It replaces a philosophical principle (all men are free and responsible) with a positive psychology (each man must be investigated, his personality assessed). (Garland, 1985, p. 187. Original italics)

The criminal subject – as defined by the prevailing moral and political ideology – became an object for the *experts'* assessment: the 'age of *treatment*' had apparently begun. 'Normalisation' was the goal, diagnosis its method and probation the means. This resulting 'individualisation' of the crime problem remains to this day one of the core justifications probation officers use in their work. The movement was middle-class, charity-based in its organisation and moral in its ethos; operating in a society where the philosophy of self-help and entrepreneurial spirit were paramount:

> The solution for these Victorian pundits was therefore to define these miscreant individuals as being a social problem on account of their moral laxity or failing. (Young, 1976, p. 52)

However, the success of this strategy required greater provision than that allowed for by charitable organisation alone. Legislation provided the framework, but the *public* organisation for its effective implementation was to come later, thereby consolidating the service's vulnerability to political climates.

In the first book on probation (Leeson, 1914) the author raised the issue of central and local control of a growing service. He suggested the special training of probation officers and the formation of a Home Office department:

> there exists no body whose business it is to develop and co-ordinate probation work in a national basis. (Quoted in Jarvis, 1972, p. 32)

To add to this debate the Howard Association's Annual Report (1916), which noted the unsuitability of many officers and probationees, the short length of orders and an inadequacy in the areas of organisation and control of probation work. One year later, a deputation from the State Children's Association met the Home Secretary also disturbed at the lack of training in 'reformative methods' of many police court missionaries. Educated workers, they felt, were being asked to work with those whose outlook was 'in the past'. Probation officials were reported to be overworked and lacking in adequate coordination and supervision.

The 1920 Departmental Committee was appointed to enquire into the pay, training and appointment of probation officers. It recommended government should pay half the cost of providing probation officers, further noting the 'saving to the Exchequer' if probation were successful in its aims. Governments, spurred on by these arguments, then assumed more responsibility in the planning of probation provision to courts (despite the fact that the Geddes Committee on National Expenditure (1922) had recommended a reduction in government grants and opposed percentage grants on the basis they were determined by local authorities over whom central government exercised no control!). In particular, the 1925 Criminal Justice Act made it mandatory for every criminal court to have a probation officer attached to it. Sidney Edridge, the Chair of the National Association of Probation Officers (NAPO – formed in 1912), found cause to comment:

> At last our new Probation Act is on the Statute Book, and we may claim our rights and privileges as an integral part of the criminal justice administration of this country. (Quoted in Jarvis, 1972, p. 40)

This 'state facilitation' of the service was accompanied by the replacement of the 'evangelical spirit' of the police court missionaries, by the 'therapeutic' approach of the diagnosticians. A resulting change of discourses surrounding the 'normalisation' of the 'client' required a different approach:

> The gradual movement from the religious, missionary ideal to the scientific, diagnostic ideal, depending in part, on notions of professionalism, required that probation work should be something for which people were *trained* to enter rather than *called* to follow. (Bill McWilliams, 1985, p. 261. Italics added)

THE POST-WAR PERIOD

The 1948 Criminal Justice Act repealed all past legislation with respect to probation and provided for an increase in Home Office control of local administration – with an Exchequer grant to be paid at a rate not exceeding 50 per cent. The Home Secretary, during this period, used powers of combination, justified by the presumed increased efficiency which would result from larger areas of administration. By 1959 there were 104 probation areas in England and Wales – reduced from 292 in 1947. The changes in organisation and training of personnel led one observer of the criminal justice system to write in 1958:

> If I were asked what is the most significant contribution made by this country to the new penological theory and practice which struck root in the twentieth century – the measure which would endure, while so many other methods of treatment might well fall into limbo, or be altered beyond recognition – my answer would be probation. (Radzinowicz, 1958, 'Preface')

With the 'casework method' the offender became the subject of professional diagnostic appraisal (all drawing upon a phase in criminological thought providing for the treatment of the offender who was in some way 'maladjusted'; see Jones, 1986). This provided social workers with their prime justification for professional status which in various forms remains to this day: the skills required in one-to-one intensive casework. Mary Richmond's (1917) book *Social Diagnosis* was symptomatic of this trend. It was reprinted sixteen times up to 1964, when Monger's *Casework in Probation* was published. However, Bill McWilliams argues that underlying this 'scientism' is a disguised moral goal and in summarising this period he is led to the prophetic conclusion that 'the edifice of diagnostic and treatment thinking in the probation service is beginning to crumble' (1986, p. 258). Indeed, the probation service was about to enter a period of rapid change in its nature and function.

A Major Review

Increased pressure on probation officers, due to an absolute rise in reported crime and resulting probation orders, led to a demand for their work which was not being met by supply (numbers of full-time probation officers had increased from 1006 in 1950 to 2034 in 1963; there were no ancillaries and very few volunteers). This led to demands for increased salaries on the basis of officers requiring greater expertise and managing increasing workloads. While the Home Office was initially reluctant to launch a large-scale enquiry, a Committee was convened in May 1959 under the direction of a QC, Ronal Morison. Reporting in March 1962, the Commitee endorsed the central aim of probation as the use of 'social casework':

> To-day the probation officer must be seen, essentially, as a professional caseworker, employing, in a specialised field, skills which he [sic] holds in common with other social workers; skills which, if it opens up to him hopes of constructive work which were not enjoyed by his predecessors of twenty years ago, also make complex and subtle demands upon him, reflecting, as it does, growing awareness of the difficulty of his task. (Home Office, 1962, p. 23, para. 54)

While treatment of the individual remained a central pivot of the work of the probation officer, the Committee also invested the officer with the responsibility of protecting society and regulating the probationer's behaviour by the inculcation of society's norms. This included persuading offenders that their 'interests and those of society are identical' (1962, para. 54). Further, while a 'prime concern' is with the offenders' well-being the probation officer:

> is also the agent of a system concerned with the protection of society and as such must, to a degree which varies from case to case, and during the course of supervision, seek to regulate the probationer's behaviour. (1962, para. 54)

The Committee also noted that the functions of probation officers had increased considerably, which made additional demands on the service; even so, they considered such demands should increase (1962, paras 26 and 282). A year before, the Streatfield Committee, whose 'cardinal aim' was the provision of reliable information upon which courts could base a sentence, offered the following guidelines for the content of social enquiry reports:

> Essential details of the offender's home surroundings, and family background; his attitude to his family and their responses to him; his school and work record and spare-time activities; his attitude to his employment; his attitude to the present offence; his attitude and responses to previous forms of treatment following any previous convictions; detailed histories about relevant physical and mental conditions; an assessment of personality and character. (Home Office, 1961, para. 336)

Duties of probation officers and the service's administrative responsibilities increased rapidly over the next two decades and working practices were bolstered by the findings of official reports.

As a result, this provided arguments for the Probation Division of the Home Office (becoming the Probation and After-Care Department in 1964) for increased expenditure by governments on the service.

While probation officers had a 'long standing antipathy' (Haxby, 1978, p. 242) towards prisons, the service assumed responsibility for welfare work in prisons in 1966. A Home Office Circular (130/1967), which listed twenty-one functions of seconded prison probation officers, included nine which were related to prison management, as opposed to helping offenders as such. The 1967 Criminal Justice Act further incorporated probation officers into the prison system by the introduction of parole, giving not only additional responsibilities to seconded probation officers, but also to field officers for supervision of parolees on licence. Their presence in prisons brought them into the sharpest end of the penal system. Whilst, in practice, the 'smooth' running of the prisons was thought to be enabled by a 'welfare' presence, it also meant a blurring of probation tasks. Using Garland's (1985) terms – 'normalisation', 'correction' and 'segregation' – the former characterise the usual duties of probation personnel. However, they were now identified with another sector of the penal system: the 'segregative'. The resulting debates within the service have not been resolved and peaked when a motion on the withdrawal of seconded probation officers was put to a NAPO conference in 1981 (see NAPO, 1987).

Following the Wootton Report's (Home Office, 1970) recommendation for 'guidance or help' for those on suspended sentences, the power of courts to make supervision by a probation officer part of such a sentence was introduced in the 1972 Criminal Justice Act. Section 14 of the same Act introduced the Community Service Order (also following the recommendation of the Wootton Report). This new sentence, to be administered by the probation service, empowered courts to order offenders to undertake unpaid work for the community for not less than 40, or more than 240, hours. This also led to further changes. While a 'rehabilitative' element may exist in such a sentence, it is also designed to contain elements of 'restitution' and 'punishment' (see Pease, 1981).

In response to increasing demands, Home Office reports and allocation of resources, the service grew considerably in the period between 1960 and 1978. The number of full-time officers of all grades had increased by 3553 to a total of 5186, while the number of supervisory to non-supervisory posts increased from 13.7 to 22.9 per cent of all officers. However, these were not the only posts to proliferate. The ancillary grade was introduced by the Home Office in 1971. This post was intended to fill a gap 'between that of the probation officer and that of the clerical assistant' (Home Office, 1972, para. 39); by 1974 there were 373 ancillaries in post. Further, Mathieson (1979) stated that the service had as many accredited volunteers as probation officers. Thus, levels, types and numbers of probation personnel increased considerably over a relatively short period.

In December 1971, a House of Commons Expenditure Committee supported the continuing independence of the service from central control. A year later the Home Secretary reaffirmed this, adding the following:

> After consulting the national probation organisations and other interested organisations, I have decided to use my existing powers to establish a probation area for each new county, subject to the possibility of combination of those where the service would otherwise be very small. (Quoted in Haxby, 1978, p. 24)

The Committee noted that the maintenance of law and order was the Home Secretary's responsibility and therefore the service should also be part of the responsibilities of this Office holder. Additionally, the government grant for the administration of local services increased from 50 to 80 per cent, thereby enabling greater central control over local area decisions. In 1971 there were 79 probation areas. Following local government reorganisation in 1974 there are now 55.

PROBATION INTO THE 1980s

> 'The first priority (of the service) should be to ensure that, wherever possible, offenders can be dealt with by non-custodial measures and that standards of supervision are set and maintained at the level required for this purpose' (1984 Home Office 'Statement of National Objectives and Priorities', Section D, Part VI [a]).

The 1960s and 70s saw rapid change in the nature of the probation service, but the 1980s were not to provide a respite. The election of a Conservative government in 1979, committed to a campaign of 'law and order', continued to alter the service's tasks. Punishment is now emphasised as as core component of alternatives to custody which, again, are introduced to alleviate prison overcrowding and reduce costs; the 'justice' model prevails. As many in the service believe, these were, and are, anathema to its traditional function in the criminal justice system. Relentlessly, this continues. The impact and ramifications of such measures have been felt – organisationally and professionally – while the nature and future of the service remains uncertain; particularly with the spectre of privatisation looming large and electronic gadgets offering seemingly simple solutions to complex problems. Schisms within the service have occurred and the professional autonomy of its members is perceived to be under threat. Geographical variations in courts' sentencing practices and an expansion of prison places frustrate its attempts in providing alternatives to custody; even when research demonstrates the ineffectiveness of custodial penalties in preventing crime (see Brody, 1976). The organisation is more hierarchical and bureaucratic – more concerned with monitoring and evaluating its members' work and performing a controlling rather than enabling function (the latter being the stated aim during the expansion of the service's hierarchy). At the same time, the recent history of criminology charts the demise and ineffectiveness of the 'rehabilitative ideal' – the value underpinning its members' work.

By the mid-1970s discussions centred on the changing nature of the service. Martin Davies posed the question of a 'defensive or developmental' service for the future. He considered its commitment to development in the face of change 'true' to its heritage, but also noted the effect of these changes on its personnel:

> There is now a feeling in some quarters that the changes affecting probation officers now are so fundamental that they may be undermining the morale of employees who came into the Service *to do one job only to find themselves required to undertake another*. (1976, p. 86. Italics added)

The same research to which he alludes found job satisfaction among long-serving officers variable and, in particular, the authors noted the officers felt a lack of recognition of their work on the part of the organisation's hierarchy. However, the price for such recognition was not to be paid for by a further erosion of their autonomy (see Keynon, and Rhodes, undated). Historically, the service had appeared to accommodate to administrative change by the development of professional supervision, without an alteration in the feeling of autonomy among its officers. But, all this was to come under increasing scrutiny.

The Ethos Under Question

Fullwood (1987) notes three changes of importance that occurred during the 1970s and into the 1980s, which had a profound effect on the organisation: first, the increased role of non-professional staff in day centres, community service and other areas (47 per cent (679) of ancillaries are employed in community service – see Vass, 1984, 1988); second, the establishment of a Unit at the Home Office, which included a seconded Probation Inspector; and third, there was the 'constant search for answers', which led towards 'monitoring' and 'targeting' of probation officers' work.

While these changes are important, they cannot be considered in isolation from the environment in which the Service finds itself. They were a response to external, or what I shall call 'exogenous' conditions: changes in the criminal justice system as a result of a shift in thinking on the 'crime problem'. Thus, in order to understand organisational changes within the probation service and alterations in the professional status of its members and composition of its personnel, it is necessary to examine these in relation to 'endogeneous', or internal factors. This stands as a corrective to an organisational analysis which fails to consider the environment in which probation work is enacted. I would therefore agree with Stuart Clegg and David Dunkerley, who have argued

> for an organisational analysis that is open-ended, and which recognizes the societal nature of organizational functioning, and which is sensitive enough to respond to on-going debates outside organizational analysis but within a wider framework of social theory. (1977, p. 6)

The opposite of this approach characterises the responses of probation personnel in terms of a social-psychological adjustment to their situation – that is, how they adjust to change as opposed to examining the reasons for these changes. The psychological knowledge base upon which probation personnel draw will therefore be found wanting if applied to an analysis of changes in probation work. At the organisational policy level – whether intended or otherwise – the consequences are that control is emphasised over enabling personnel, and procedural accountability is pursued at the cost of substantive accountability. This approach necessitates turning to the political realm.

Box (1987) acknowledges that the 'lurch into prominence' of the service is difficult to explain, but two considerations deserve attention: first, the proliferation of alternatives to custody, and second, the concept of 'individualised justice'. This latter concept (as noted, with a long tradition) requires background information on the individual:

> much of the decision-making in the lower courts soon came to be centred on question concerning the type of person who committed the crime, rather than on questions of guilt or innocence. (Carlen and Powell, 1979, p. 97)

The emphasis on one-to-one casework methods with offenders was bolstered by this focus on individualised justice. The method and rationale concentrated on the offender who, it was hoped, became empowered (self-determined) to overcome his or her problems and thus lead a law-abiding way of life. Despite the fact that this was more of an expedient, subject to the whims of government, as opposed to a theoretically adequate programme, this focus carried with it the implication that the individual was in some way 'maladjusted'. In essence, the ethos of the probation service was and is predicated upon this method. Ideologically speaking, individualisation was a convenient method of bracketing a complex crime phenomenon. However, this also provided a base for the growth of an organisation and profession which sought solutions using this method. In the process a tension develops: governments look to *expedient* solutions to the 'ever present' penal crisis, while a growing organisation and profession bases its *principles* upon it – one dynamic, the other static.

Part of the above process involves the development of a whole discourse which takes on a life of its own, defining the task, its object and the method. It becomes self-fulfilling and self-perpetuating: 'needs', 'objective assessment', 'diagnosis', 'therapy', 'rehabilitation' and 'reform' (of the individual). Adherents then only need to refine their methods and therefore, by default, not question the underlying philosophy. Social problems are individualised and welfare professionals become responsible for the diagnosis and treatment of the 'client'. During this process they are given discretionary powers which themselves lead to enormous disparity and injustice outside of the courtroom. This discretion, which is 'the essence of rehabilitation' (Bean, 1976, p. 144), simply leads to demands for more discretion and better methods of diagnosis in the pursuit of effectiveness. 'Objectivity' is pursued, despite its obvious problematic nature in any area of human service work – although it has not gone uncriticised by some practitioners (Walker and Beaumont, 1981), and others have argued that social diagnosis is not neutral, but in fact contains a disguised moral goal (McWilliams, 1986). Despite the subsuming of political and value questions in the 'science of diagnosis' this had organisational consequences: the nature of the task is not amenable to standardisation (a Weberian characteristic of bureaucratic functionaries) due to its reliance on the professional skills of the individual worker and his or her assessment of the personality of the offender; a method which is, by definition, unique and non-quantifiable.

The proliferation of research within the fields of sociology, social policy, deviance and criminology, began to question the implicit assumptions of this ethos, in particular the 'neutrality' of professional assessments. No longer could it be assumed that those who worked within the criminal justice system were simply responding to deviant acts; instead they were central to the definition of deviance itself. Nevertheless, the lure of individualisation was, and is, a powerful one and the effects of such criticisms on probation practice were not profound. Nevertheless, some practitioners sought to remedy the gap between a radical analysis and action within the realm of social work (Corrigan and Leonard, 1978) and probation work (Walker and Beaumont, 1981 and 1985). Despite this, the increased monitoring of probation officers' work could always be justified by alluding to this widening body of research on the value-basis of probation officers' decisions.

These critiques were to gain their influence through actual practice and the process of training social workers and probation officers (see Epstein, 1970). However, two further influences were to arise. First, due to an emerging body of research alluding to the crime problem, governments then looked to alternative methods for its control. The probation service was to be the main means for the execution of such a policy. Organisationally, the service reacted, under Home Office pressure, by increasing the monitoring of its officers' work and the targeting of those offenders who were at the higher-risk (to society) end of offending and, therefore, 'at risk' of custody. As a result the 'professional optimism' of the 1960s gave way to a 'professional pessimism' (Pitts, 1988). Radzinowicz, who, as noted, had considered probation *the* major development in penal theory and practice, was now thinking differently regarding its impact on the crime problem:

> how can you expect an officer, with other duties to attend to and with something like fifty people under his supervision, seeing them perhaps once a week to start with, once a fortnight or less thereafter, to have time to get to know and influence more than a handful of them, or to make much of real impact on their outlook and circumstances? Must not 'supervision' in the sense of knowing what people are doing, keeping them out of trouble, be largely a fiction? (Radzinowicz and King, 1979, p. 330)

Changes in the nature of the tasks, working environment and expectations of what could be achieved, led probation practice to become reflexive and look to new innovations. Some moved to community work, emphasising the political dimension of crime control. Bottoms and McWilliams (1979), on the other hand, suggested 'A Non-Treatment Paradigm for Probation Practice', adding to a growing body of opinion on the negligible reformative effects of penal innovations. Crime was a social and not pathological phenomenon. The ethos of the service had been predicated upon a theoretically and empirically flawed model, and in such a changing climate the reaction has been to search for the 'heart of probation' (Mathieson, 1987). However, while the effectiveness of the ethos appeared to be under increasing question, it was the political response – the original impetus to the creation of the service – which was to provide the most effective challenge to the service's long tradition: welfare had failed, punishment was demanded.

FROM THERAPY TO PUNISHMENT: CHALLENGING THE PROBATION CONSENSUS

Crime out of Control?

The criminal statistics for England and Wales are 'grim and relentless in their ascending monotony'. Radzinowicz was commenting in 1959 on the rise in reported crime from a half to three-quarters of a million offences in the previous decade. During 1988 the police recorded 3 716 000 indictable crimes (Home Office Criminal Statistics 1989). The Howard League estimates that on current trends this figure will have reached 7 400 000 by the turn of the century and the number of people found guilty in magistrates courts will have nearly doubled to 4 000 000. Despite violent offences only accounting for 5 per cent of recorded crime, woundings and assaults have doubled and robberies trebled since 1974 (Howard League, 1987). Sentencing practices have responded. During 1986 magistrates committed 44 000 people to prison (including fine defaulters). Geographical variation in the courts' use of custody is between 8 per cent and 39 per cent for adults males, 4 per cent and 15 per cent for adult females, and 4 per cent and 22 per cent for males between 17 and 21 (NAPO Newsletter 1988, no. 275). Despite the government urging the use of custody as a 'last resort' in 'protecting the public' and a wide range of alternatives to custody existing, information from the Council of Europe shows the United Kingdom had a prison population of 95 per cent 100 000 on the 1st of February 1987 (Collier and Tarling, 1987). Of nineteen member states only Turkey and Austria had higher prison populations measured on this basis. In England and Wales on the 3rd of July 1987, the highest prison population in history was recorded at 50 969; the National Association for the Care and Resettlement of Offenders (NACRO) calculated a new prison the size of Dartmoor would have to open every three weeks to accommodate this increase (*Howard Journal*, May 1988, p. 146).

The government's response to the crime problem has been to increase expenditure on the prison service by 34 per cent in real terms since 1979 and nearly double the capital budget. While proposals vary, some twenty new prisons are being built and together with the refurbishment of existing prisons, approximately 20 000 new places will have been created by 1995. From 1979 to

1983 the expenditure on the police force increased by 5 per cent per annum – compared with overall government expenditure rising at 2 per cent – with, it should be added, little impact on detection rates. In millions of pounds, the law-and-order budget increased from 3179 in 1980–1 to 5388 in 1985–6 (King, 1987, p. 122). In real terms the percentage increase in expenditure from 1981–2 and the estimate for 1987–8 is 22.9 per cent for the police service, 30.8 per cent for the probation service, and 23.0 per cent for the prison service (reported in NAPO Newsletter 1988), no. 278).

The Thatcherite Response

It is clear the government's commitment to the reduction in public expenditure does not so easily extend to law and order. While the public are not so retributive as is commonly believed (see Wright, 1987), Willis, admitting this to be somewhat cynical, notes:

> Although there are no votes in prison, I suspect there are votes to be won by endorsing crime-control strategies which would send ever-increasing numbers there. (1986, p. 23)

The evidence from a survey conducted before the polls closed in the 1979 election, substantiates Willis's assertion: of those whose allegiance changed in the Tories' favour, 23 per cent had done so on their 'law and order' platform (Downes, 1983, p. 2). With a breakdown in a post-war consensus on the management of the economy (through Keynesian economic principles) and a consensus on the Welfare State, the economy is given a free-market reign to find its 'natural level'. This has meant:

> In the arena of Law and Order, Thatcherism has effectively exploited a traditional space in popular ideologies: the moralism endemic in conservative philosophies . . . traditional and uncorrected common sense is a massively conservative force, penetrated thoroughly – as it has been – by religious notions of Good and Evil, by fixed conceptions of the unchanging and unchangeable character of human nature, and by ideas of retributive justice. (Hall, 1980, pp. 177–8)

This 'authoritarian populism' (Hall, 1979) began before Thatcher came to power. However, the phenomenon of

'Thatcherism' has not only rejuvenated but added considerably to its popularity. It combines, as Hall notes, 'organic Toryism' – with its emphasis on nation, standards, authority and discipline – with the self-interest and anti-statism of 'neo-liberalism'. The homogeneity of this project is not to be over-emphasised, for these elements are contradictory. However, this is the essence of authoritarian populism. People's fear of rising crime is real enough, but the answer has been to increase the law-and-order industry whilst sentencing practices have become more retributive. The 'acquisitive individualism' of the market, increasing unemployment, homelessness, and a social security system increasingly under threat are seen as unconnected with rising crime: there is, we are told, 'no such thing as society. There are individual men and women and there are families' (Margaret Thatcher, 1 November 1987). The link between social and economic conditions and crime is irrelevant to a morality which views right and wrong in terms of personal responsibility – regardless of the circumstances in which individuals find themselves. As well as the fallacious thinking involved in such a position, a paradox arises:

> That paradox is the ease with which the law can be subverted to counterfeit justice and wrenched into the shape required by 'order' . . . The order that results is a regimented and repressive variety, not what people have in mind when they demand law and order. (Downes, 1983, p. 31)

The justice model now prevails and results in an abstraction of crime from its social context:

> the justice model thus inextricably allies itself with the use of the legal system as an important part of the apparatus of repression. (Hudson, 1987, p. 166)

Superficially, it would appear the traditional image of the probation service aligns itself with such beliefs, although by different means. By concentrating on individual pathology, the 'science of diagnosis' gives this morality its justification. However, not only is this a gross simplification, it is not mirrored in the traditional 'liberal' views of probation officers. The philosophy emphasises 'justice through punishment', the tradition, 'rehabilitation through therapy'. The means and ends are incompatible and ideologically opposed.

The implementation of the government's philosophy of

punishment requires an increase in the centralisation of the state's penal activities (Christie, 1982). Home Office Circulars, Statute and Probation Rules have become the instruments for expanding the 'alternatives to custody industry'. Locally autonomous probation committees, who are statutory bodies in their own right, are composed of magistrates, the judiciary and co-opted members. Therefore, many of the directions have been aimed at full-time professional personnel (given the traditional independence of the judiciary from the executive), in particular the Chief Probation Officer. She or he then operates with the same constraints as the criminal justice system and social work in general: these are politically bounded and cannot therefore be ignored (see Day, 1987). Jordan, in his work *Invitation to Social Work*, states:

> the probation service cannot wholly escape from political controversy, debate and conflict, because its work is constantly under political review in an era when 'law and order' is a major topic of public concern. (1984, p. 129)

As a result of these changes schisms have developed within the service. During one probation team meeting I attended, someone remarked: 'the Home Office are creating "Chiefs" in their own image more successfully than God on Man'. While the Association of Chief Probation Officers (ACOP), the Central Council of Probation Committees (CCPC) and the National Association of Probation Officers (NAPO) produced collectively, a document entitled 'Probation: The Next Five Years' (1987), controversy arose due to the subsequent publication of ACOP's (1988) document 'More Demanding than Prison' – designed to anticipate the government's Green Paper *Punishment in the Community* (1988). In the latter document the message is clear. Prisons are seen as 'colleges of crime' (Hurd, 1988, p. 10), but the alternative should not be perceived as a 'soft option'; credibility with the punitive culture of magistrates courts being an important consideration. A 'politicisation of punishment' accompanies these changes: 'So the aim is punishment and no Conservative should veer away from the notion of punishment' (Hurd, 1988, p. 11). The government, therefore, following their announcements of National Standards for Community Service, allude to public confidence in their rationale. The vandal, for instance, should be doing: 'demanding work. Clearing up his neighbourhood.

Scrubbing those graffiti off the walls, putting right the damage he has caused. That's what we want to see' (Hurd, 1988, p. 11).

A 'new realism' has found its mark. It is acknowledged that custodial sentences are ineffective and inappropriate in many cases, and the same objectives, according to the Green Paper, can 'often best be met by supervising and punishing the offender in the community' (Home Office, 1988, para. 1.6):

> For many offenders a demanding sentence carried out in the community, may be more effective in turning them from crime. For some, punishment in the community may be better than punishment in prison. (Patten, quoted in NACRO Annual Report, 1988, p. 3)

For the service, its choice is limited in colluding with these changes. The Green Paper indicates the possibilities should the probation service be reluctant to implement its programme; it 'would welcome views on the possibility of setting up a new organisation to take responsibility for the arrangements for punishment in the community' (Home Office, 1988, para. 4.5).

DISCUSSION

Management in the service is increasingly criticised, by probation officers, for the lack of any social work input into policy initiatives. It appears senior management (ACOP and above) are reacting to Home Office directives which – with increasing central control and the use of Probation Inspectors – it is difficult to resist. Despite this, area responses to directives have themselves been variable, particularly in the case of the 1984 Home Office 'Statement of National Objectives and Priorities' (see Lloyd, 1986). Even so, the senior management/front-line disparity remains wide. For instance, the increased 'selling point' of alternatives to custody is their ability to protect the public and prevent recidivism during the course of a probation order. NAPO, on the other hand, in a paper entitled *The Provision of Alternatives to Custody and the use of the Probation Order*, notes that supervision should not be based on surveillance, containment or deterrence:

> For the PS to attempt to impose such control on individual offenders would involve an unacceptable change in the principles and ethos of our work. (1981, p. 8)

NAPO has also experienced its schisms. In 1981 it passed a resolution urging withdrawal of probation officers from prisons; this has yet to come to fruition and has more recently received attention (see NAPO, 1987). The year before, breakaway organisations were formed representing different factions of the service; part of the reason being the perceived change in NAPO's function, from a professional association towards a trade union – even though the two are not as incompatible as is commonly supposed (see Alexander, 1980). However, the justice model itself mitigates against professionalism and allows for an increase in 'non-qualified' staff in the service, particularly in the administration of Community Service. This is believed to further undermine professionalism – as popularly conceived – and has created internal divisions: 'Inasmuch as the justice model seeks limitations on probation officer discretion, this suspicion is understandable (Thomson, 1987, p. 110).

Thomson makes a central point. Punishment does not require a component of professionalism – based as it is on casework methods which are still the most popular method of working with offenders (see Davies and Wright, 1989). Punishment only requires *administration*. This entails no component of discretion which is increasingly being removed from probation officers. The National CS (Community Service) Standards (1989) are designed specifically to remove elements of discretion. For instance, paragraph 3.2.3. gives the 'only acceptable reasons for a failure to attend' and paragraph 3.4 then gives instructions as to when breech proceedings 'must be started'. Even if CS were an alternative to custody (which it is not in most cases), the likely resulting increases in breech will do little to increase its 'credibility' in magistrates' eyes – the very people whom the government wished to pander to in the first place! Consider the logic of the situation in the courts – it goes something like this: 'We have sentenced this person to a community alternative to custody; they have not conformed to the requirements of their order and, being an alternative to prison, the next step is incarceration. Given the government are expanding prison places, there is therefore a place for this person, so we will sentence them to a term of imprisonment' (the government's argument that they are simply 'refurbishing' and not 'expanding' prison places is rendered even more nonsensical in the 'logic' of the courtroom). The result is that CS is presumed ineffective; the latitude of probation personnel to assist the individual with practical and emotional difficulties is rendered very limited and, in some cases, non-existent, and the task changes. As one probation officer said to me: 'I'm not trained as a prosecutor'. The 'credibility' (that all-important word) of CS deteriorates and the prison population increases. The Home Office's 'statistical conclusions' then regard the organisation as 'ineffective' and discretionary work inputs are further limited as the punishment component is increased in reaction. This cyclical process is screened by the increased use of 'monitoring' and 'targeting' by simple and yet mainly ineffective indices. An internal technical solution (more monitoring) is then offered to an external problem (the punitive decisions of magistrates). This results in what could be termed a 'quantitative politics' within the service.

As the public sector has become more politicised and private sector styles of management have been introduced, divisions within the service are not surprising. Further, individualised justice permitted probation officers an autonomy in the conception and execution of their tasks and, therefore, a degree of control. Punishment *per se* requires little discretion, and, as the above suggests, is in this sense de-skilling. However, how many people would be admitted to social work courses if, when asked 'why do you want to be a probation officer?' they then replied 'because I want to punish people'! Yet, increasingly, the Green Paper occupies interviewers of new probation officers to test how comfortable they feel with the idea of 'punishment'. The manifestations of these changes in thinking are not dramatic; they are gradual and affect those whose philosophy is 'malleable'. The results can be 'a heavy price in confusion and demoralisation' (Raynor, 1985, p. 39). Even within the profession, probation officers, who may have once been united in their therapeutic ideology, have called for changes in thinking about 'helping' and not 'treating' clients: a symptom of the realisation of the social and not individual–pathological nature of crime. In addition, the service was always vulnerable to political whim, whether in the form of government reactions to a 'penal crisis' or for the purposes of implementing alternatives to custody in order to reduce costs (see Scull, 1977). This expansion of alternatives to custody was in the professional self-interest of probation officers, but the tradition of humanitarianism renders their punishment component problematic for the service to implement. Therefore, even allusions to the lower costs of alternatives to custody do not suffice:

> The 'humanity' of community corrections is thus its Achilles' heel, precisely the feature most likely to alienate (fiscal) conservatives and indeed the public at large, who might otherwise be attracted by the idea. (Scull, 1983, p. 158)

Officers may use a collapsed dichotomy of 'care' and 'control' (Fielding, 1984). However, as the expectations and legislation surrounding the task change, so too does the equation. Peter Raynor identifies a 'silent majority':

> who simply get on with the job on a commonsense eclectic basis, supported by a healthy scepticism, and a pragmatic intolerance of abstract ideas. (1985, p. 41)

Nevertheless, pragmatism can rapidly become 'instrumentalism' and 'realism' in a climate where an occupation's ethos fluctuates and tasks change. The organisation and profession then suffers what may be called, following Bill McWilliams (1986), a 'crisis of ontology'. Administratively, one is told what to do and how to do it, but the question of 'why' remains unanswered. Within the organisation, conflicts then arise around changes which themselves result from alterations in the organisation's environment.

The government introduced the Financial Management Initiative in May 1982, led by one of the Prime Minister's first appointments, Sir (now Lord) Rayner, Chairman of Marks & Spencer. 'Economy', 'efficiency' and 'effectiveness' became important aims of the Civil Service: the 'high street' mentality becomes applicable to the public sector. Early in 1986, management consultants Deloitte, Haskins and Sells were appointed to advise and produce a Financial Management Information System for the service. Subsequently, reports by the Home Office (Grimsey Report, 1987) have suggested further 'performance indicators' and the Audit Commission (1989) reported on the service under the sub-title 'Promoting Value for Money'. Many are sceptical about 'efficiency', 'effectiveness' and 'economy' and reactions to this range from suspicion to optimism depending on the vantage point from which the service is viewed. However, senior management have reacted by increasing the use of 'hard' quantitative data as a measure of probation officers' performance. But, as Humphrey notes:

> In an area as complex as the probation service it would be foolhardy to expect to find easy answers to the question of improving performance. (1987, p. 186)

Most current research within the probation service is concerned with this very topic; few areas have escaped from evaluating or monitoring their own performance. As a result senior management is viewed with scepticism by probation officers who perceive them to be out of touch with the 'realities' of probation work – compounded further by an increasing hierarchy in the service with the creation of statuses, like those of Assistant Chief Probation Officers, who had not clearly defined roles at the time of their creation (see Grubb Institute, 1977). Also, while the duties of the Chief Probation Officer are not defined by statute, the appointment of this person must be approved by the Secretary of State (Probation Rules 1984, r. 28). They are accountable to the probation commitee and 'responsible for the direction of the probation service in the area, for its effective operation and the *efficient use of its resources*' (Probation Rules 1984, r. 30. Italics added). Chief Officers are then in the difficult position of implementing government policy, being accountable to the local probation committee and balancing this against the traditional culture of members of the organisation.

In the past, the service was considered to be adequate because it led to certain results (rehabilitation); the increase in research has cast considerable doubt on this. The state, prompted by the change of climate post-1979, could no longer rely on the judgements of professionals who were not thought effective as defined by the prevailing political discourse: criminals needed punishing. Given the constitutional autonomy of the executive from the judiciary, the government – who have increasingly considered their interests aligned with those of the state – could not direct probation officers' employers (the magistrates) and therefore concentrated on their professional managers. They, like their other state counterparts (now increasingly in Higher Education), have resorted to a centre–periphery management model and direct from a managerial 'core' to the 'front-line'. This results in accountability being stressed over autonomy and control over facilitation. If this is not the aim, it is the consequence of such changes. However, this 1960s style of management requires that the managerial directions are in tune with the organisational culture. They are not. Probation officers complain of increasing form-filling to service senior management, and senior probation officers, who were originally intended for professional supervision and carried their own caseload, have a managerial function which also involves 'servicing up' to senior management. It is widely believed, therefore, that management is not enabling, as historically they were intended to do, but controlling work. Probation officers respond in the belief that an industrial model of objectives and targets has only a limited application to their work, and published works criticise and counter-criticise 'management by objectives' (Parry-Khan, 1988; Coker, 1988).

The use of effectiveness as a criteria for probation work is more reliant on exogenous, rather than endogenous conditions. For instance, in providing alternatives to custody, there is a reliance on the decisions of magistrates in following the recommendations of social enquiry reports. While there can be little doubt that there has been success in this respect (see Roberts and Roberts, 1982), it is a strategy up against an increasing prison population. Even while alternatives to custody proliferate, the 'take up' by courts may still remain low, as shown by the results of the second phase of the Inner London Probation Service Demonstration Unit (1988). In Cohen's (1985) phrase, the 'net is widening'. Similarly, in talking about community-based alternatives to custody, the service inherits a government policy which promotes acquisitive individualism and yet talks about communities. Crime prevention retains a plausible and constructive element, as Vivien Stern notes: 'To create community spirit and community identity must be a major objective of crime policy' (1987, p. 224). Yet, if we have no 'society', just 'families' and 'individuals', the notion of community to the government in the 'sense of fellowship or sharing has no meaning and indeed, ought not to have' (Morris, 1988, p. 6). In the face of this, all that may be attainable is 'the oils of *gemeinschaft* on the waters of *gesellschaft*' (a phrase attributed to Professor Robert Pinker during a Social Policy Conference in Eastbourne, 1984).

CONCLUSION

The service is under siege and so too, therefore, is the professional status of its members. It has not been possible to chart all the changes and their effects – this is beyond the limits of this chapter. The service grew under state-sponsored activity in an environment where dominant political discourses were favourable to the ethos upon which the professionalism of its members was based. With an emphasis on 'economy' the service would appear to offer something to the present government. However, current political discourse favours punishment; a notion not in harmony with the ethos. While policy can be mediated by the perspectives of its implementers (see Young, 1977; Smith, 1977), increased central control and now the possibility of electronic monitoring severely limits this. The criteria of efficiency is difficult (if not impossible) to apply to a public sector organisation where the goals of 'profitability' guided by 'market mechanisms' are absent. As noted, the Green Paper talks of 'another organisation' for punishment in the community – one of the private security companies perhaps? The failure to see this political component in the rise of the service makes both the organisation and the professional status of its members peculiarly vulnerable; this being the case with public sector human service workers in general. The resulting lack of control over the work task, although compounded by managerial reactions, mainly occurs:

> not because, as frustrated social workers are sometimes convinced, the leadership pursues misguided tactics, but because there exists external conditions which are antithetical to the development of the form of institutionalised control under which the occupation is paramount and autonomous. (Johnson, 1972, p. 32)

Senior management react to one set of conditions, probation officers to another. To resort to an overly bureaucratic approach will only achieve a procedural and not substantive accountability in such circumstances. A service which started with firm roots in Victorian philanthropy, now finds itself facing a considerable challenge from a philosophy unsympathetic to its traditional image and ways of working. With electronic tagging on the horizon, its continuation of adaption to changing conditions no longer seems a possibility; whilst to maintain its social work ethos in a politically hostile environment looks increasingly more difficult.

NOTE

I would like to thank Ian Levitt, Bill Whittaker, Rob Mawby, Dick Hobbs and Delyth Rennie for their comments on earlier versions of this essay. My thanks also to the editors – Pam and Claire.

REFERENCES

ACOP, CCPC, and NAPO (1987) *Probation – The Next Five Years: A Joint Statement by the Association of Chief Officers of Probation*, Central Council of Probation Committees and the National Association of Probation Officers', London: ACOP, CCPC, NAPO.

ACOP (1988) *More Demanding than Prison – A Discussion Paper*, Wakefield: ACOP.

ACOP (1989) 'The Community and Crime: A Strategy for Criminal Justice. The Response of the Association of Chief Officers of Probation to the Government Green Paper', Wakefield: ACOP.

ALEXANDER, L. (1980) 'Professionalization and Unionization: Compatible After All?', *Social Work*, vol. 86 (4), pp. 819–35.

AUDIT COMMISSION (1989) *The Probation Service: Promoting Value for Money*, London: Audit Commission.

BEAN, P. (1976) *Rehabilitation and Deviance*, London: RKP.

BOCHEL, D. (1976) *Probation and After-Care: Its Development in England and Wales*, Edinburgh: Scottish Academic Press.

BOTTOMS, A. and McWILLIAMS, W. (1979) 'A Non-Treatment Paradigm for Probation Practice', *British Journal of Social Work*, vol. 9 (2), pp. 159–202.

BOX, S. (1987) *Recession, Crime and Punishment*, London: Macmillan.

BRODY, S. (1976) *The Effectiveness of Sentencing*, Home Office Research Report no. 35, London: HMSO.

CARLEN, P. and POWELL, M. (1979) 'Professionals in the Magistrates' Courts: The Courtroom Lore of Probation Officers and Social Workers', in H. Parker, (ed.).

CHRISTIE, N. (1982) *Limits to Pain*, Oxford: Martin Robertson.

CLEGG, S. and DUNKERLEY, D. (eds) (1977) *Critical Issues in Organizations*, London: RKP.

COHEN, S. (1985) *Visions of Social Control*, Oxford: Polity Press.

COKER, J. (1988) *Probation Objectives: A Management View*, Norwich: Social Work Monographs.

COLLIER, P. and TARLING, R. (1987) 'International Comparisons of Prison Populations', *Home Office Research Bulletin*, no. 23.

CORRIGAN, P and LEONARD, P. (1978) *Social Work Practice Under Capitalism*, London: Macmillan.

CURRAN, J. (ed.) *The Future of the Left*, Cambridge: Polity Press.

DAVIES, M. (1976) 'A Tale of Two Perspectives: Defensive or Developmental', *Probation Journal*, vol. 23 (3), pp. 86–9.

DAVIES, M. and WRIGHT, A. (1989) *The Changing Face of Probation*, Norwich: Social Work Monographs.

DAY, M. (1987) 'The Politics of Probation', in J. Harding (ed.).
DOWNES, D. (1983) *Law and Order: Theft of an Issue*, London: Fabian Tract no. 490.

EPSTEIN, I. (1970) 'Professionalization, Professionalism and Social Work Radicalism', *Journal of Health and Social Behaviour*, vol. 11, pp. 67–77.
FIELDING, N. (1984) *Probation Practice: Client Support Under Social Control*, Aldershot: Gower.

FOUCAULT, M. (1969) *The Archaeology of Knowledge*, London: Pantheon.
FOUCAULT, M. (1977) *Discipline and Punish: The Birth of the Prison*, London: Allen Lane.
FULLWOOD, C. (1987) *The Probation Service: From Moral Optimism, Through Penological Pessimism into the Future*, Manchester: Greater Manchester Probation Service.
GARLAND, D. (1985) *Punishment and Welfare: A History of Penal Strategies*, Aldershot: Gower.
GARLAND, D. and YOUNG, P. (eds) (1983) *The Power to Punish*, London: Heinemann.
GRUBB INSTITUTE (1977) *A Framework for the Analysis of Roles in the Probation and After-Care Service*, London: Grubb Institute.
HALL, S. (1974) 'Drifting into a Law and Order Society', Cobden Trust Memorial Lecture.
HALL, S. (1980) 'Popular Democratic *vs* Authoritarian Populism', in A. Hunt (ed.).
HALL, S. and JACQUES, M. (eds) (1983) *The Politics of Thatcherism*, London: Lawrence & Wishart.
HARDING, J. (ed.) (1987) *Probation and the Community: A practice and policy reader*, London: Tavistock.
HAXBY, D. (1978) *Probation: A Changing Service*, London: Constable.
HOME OFFICE (1961) *Report of the Inter-Departmental Committee on the Business of the Criminal Courts* ('The Streatfield Committee'), Cmnd 1289.
HOME OFFICE (1962) *Report of the Departmental Committee on the Probation Service* ('The Morison Committee'), Cmnd 1650.
HOME OFFICE (1970) *Report of the Advisory Council on the Penal System: Non-Custodial and Semi-Custodial Penalties* ('The Wootton Report') London: HMSO.
HOME OFFICE (1972) *Report on the Work of the Probation and After-Care Department 1969–1971*, Cmnd 5158.
HOME OFFICE (1984) *Probation Service in England and Wales: Statement of National Objectives and Priorities*, London: Home Office.
HOME OFFICE (1987) *Efficiency Scrutiny of Her Majesty's Probation Inspectorate*, ('The Grimsey Report') London: Home Office.
HOME OFFICE (1988) *Punishment, Custody and the Community*, Cm 424, London: Home Office.
HOME OFFICE (1989) *National Standards for Community Service*, London: Home Office.
HOWARD LEAGUE (1987) 'Justice 2000: Criminal Justice For a New Century. The Draft Report of a Working Group', London: The Howard League.

HUDSON, B. (1987) *Justice Through Punishment: A Critique of the 'Justice' Model of Corrections*, London: Macmillan.
HUMPHREY, C. (1986) *The Implications of the Financial Management Initiative for the Probation Service*, Manchester: Greater Manchester Probation Service.
HUNT, A. (1980) *Marxism and Democracy*, London: Lawrence & Wishart.
HURD, D. (1988) Speech to the 105th Conservative Party Conference at Brighton, Wednesday 12th October.
INNER LONDON PROBATION SERVICE (1988) *Report of the Inner London Probation Service Demonstration Unit, Phase Two (1985–1988)*, London: ILPS.
JARVIS, F. V. (1972) *Advise, Assist and Befriend: A History of the Probation and After-Care Service*, London: NAPO.
JOHNSON, T. (1972) *Professions and Power*, London: Macmillan.
JONES, D. (1986) *History of Criminology: A Philosophical Perspective*, New York: Greenwood Press.
JORDAN, B. (1984) *Invitation to Social Work*, Oxford: Martin Robertson.
KEYNON, S. and RHODES, P. (undated) 'A Study of Job Satisfaction in the Probation and After-Care Service', Loughborough University.
KING, D. (1987) *The New Right: Politics, Markets and Citizenship*, London: Macmillan.
KING, J. (ed.) (1969) *The Probation and After-Care Service*, (3rd ed.) London: Butterworth.
KING, J. (ed.) (1979) *Pressure and Change in the Probation Service*, Cambridge: Cropwood Conference Series No 11.
LEESON, C. (1914) *The Probation System.*
LEYS, C. (1984) 'The Rise of the Authoritarian State?' in J. Curran (ed.).
LLOYD, C. (1986) *Response to SNOP: An Analysis of the Home Office Document (SNOP) and the Subsequent Local Responses*, Cambridge: Institute of Criminology.
MATHIESON, D. (1979) 'Change in the Probation Service: Implications and Effects', in J. King (ed.).
MATHIESON, D. (1987) 'This is the Heart of Probation', *Justice of the Peace*, 18 July, pp. 458–60.
McWILLIAMS, W. (1985) 'The Mission Transformed: Professionalisation of Probation Between the Wars', *Howard Journal*, vol. 24 (4), pp. 257–74.
McWILLIAMS, W. (1986) 'The English Probation System and the Diagnostic Ideal', *Howard Journal of Criminal Justice*, vol. 25 (4), pp. 241–60.
McWILLIAMS, W. (1986) 'Understanding Organisations: Analysis of the Probation Service', in *Research, Information and Practice in the Probation Service, Proceedings of the Second National Probation Research and Information Exchange Conference*, Sheffield: Midlands Regional Staff Development Unit.
MONGER, M. (1964) *Casework in Probation*, London: Butterworth.
MORRIS, T. (1988) 'Punishment Custody and the Community', *Criminal Justice*, vol. 6 (4), pp. 5–6.
NATIONAL ASSOCIATION OF PROBATION OFFICERS (1981) *The Provision of Alternatives to Custody and the use of the Probation Order*, London: NAPO.
NATIONAL ASSOCIATION OF PROBATION OFFICERS (1987) *Community-Based Through-Care: The Case for Withdrawal of Seconded Probation Officers from Prisons*, London: NAPO.
PARKER, H. (ed.) (1979) *Social Work and the Courts*, London: Edward Arnold.

PARRY-KHAN, L. (1988) *Management by Objectives in Probation*, University of East Anglia, Norwich: Social Work Monograph.
PEASE, K. (1981) *Community Service Orders: A First Decade of Promise*, London: Howard League.
PITTS, J. (1988) *The Politics of Juvenile Crime*, London: Sage.
POINTING, J. (ed.) (1986) *Alternatives to Custody*, Oxford: Basil Blackwell.
RADZINOWICZ, L. (ed.) (1958) *The Results of Probation*, London: Macmillan.
RADZINOWICZ, L. and KING, J. (1979) *The Growth of Crime: The International Experience*, Harmondsworth: Penguin.
RAYNOR, P. (1985) *Social Work, Justice and Control*, Oxford: Basil Blackwell.
RICHMOND, M. (1917) *Social Diagnosis*, New York: Russell Sage.
ROBERTS, J. and ROBERTS, C. (1982) 'Social Enquiry Reports and Sentencing', *The Howard Journal*, vol. 21, pp. 76–93.
SCULL, A. (1977; *Decarceration: Community Treatment and the Deviant – A Radical View*, New Jersey: Prentice Hall.
SCULL, A. (1983) 'Community Corrections: Panacea, Progress or Pretence?' in D. Garland and P. Young (eds).
SMITH, G. (1977) 'The Place of "Professional Ideology" in the Analysis of Social Policy', *Sociological Review*, vol. 25 (4), pp. 843–65.
STERN, V. (1987) 'Crime Prevention – The Inter-Organizational Approach', in J. Harding (ed.).
THOMSON, D. (1987) 'The Changing Face of Probation in the USA', in J. Harding, (ed.).
VASS, A. (1984) *Sentenced to Labour: Close Encounters with a Prison Substitute*, St Ives: Venus Academica.
VASS, A. (1988) 'The Marginality of Community Service and the Threat of Privatisation', *Probation Journal*, vol. 35 (2), pp. 48–51.
WALKER, H. and BEAUMONT, B. (1981) *Probation Work: Critical Theory and Socialist Practice*, Oxford: Basil Blackwell.
WALKER, H. and BEAUMONT, B. (1985) *Working with Offenders*, London: Macmillan.
WILLIS, A. (1966) 'Alternatives to Imprisonment: An Elusive Paradise?' in J. Pointing (ed.).
WRIGHT, M. (1987) 'What the Public Wants: Surveys of the General Public, Including Victims', *Justice of the Peace* 14 February, pp. 105–7.
YOUNG, A. (1976) 'A Sociological Analysis of the Early History of Probation', *British Journal of Law and Society*, vol. 3 pp. 44–58.
YOUNG, K. (1977) ' "Values" in the Policy Process', *Policy and Politics*, vol. 5 (3), pp. 1–22.

10 Partnership in a Local Juvenile Justice System: The Case for Marginality

Kate Lyon

INTRODUCTION

The *'alternative custody' scheme* for serious young offenders reported on here illustrates the difficulties that a voluntary organisation encounters when it seeks to work in collaboration with statutory services in the juvenile justice field. It would seem that joint ventures between state and non-state agencies are likely to increase, given the emphasis of recent reports on the value of inter-agency collaboration: Barclay Report (National Institute for Social Work 1982); Wagner Report (HMSO 1988; Griffiths Report (HMSO 1988) and the proposal that private agencies might be used in the provision of some forms of social control put forward in the Green Paper *Punishment, Custody and the Community* (1988). The research findings suggest that relationships between voluntary and statutory organisations are far from problematic and that current difficulties will be magnified if the move towards this kind of inter-agency collaboration is to continue.

The project in question is designed for 'heavy-end' offenders in a Petty Sessional Division where both a high number of juvenile offenders and a high custody rate were seen to be cause for concern. It was established in 1985 as a joint venture between a social services department and a voluntary agency and arose from the voluntary agency actively seeking a partnership with the local authority in order to effect change in the juvenile justice system. Urban Aid funding provided the necessary incentive for the local authority and the two organisations joined in a partnership with the shared aim of providing an alternative to custody and bringing influence to bear on other agencies involved in the processing of young offenders.

PARTNERSHIP WITHIN A JUVENILE JUSTICE SYSTEM

The promotion of voluntary agency services for young offenders through the provision of government funding can be seen as the continuation of a tradition established in the last century in the creation of the Reformatory and Industrial Schools. What is new is the requirement that such services be based on collaborative schemes or partnerships between the voluntary agencies and local government. Such collaborative ventures it is argued serve to improve services and reduce the conflicts that exist between agencies whose priorities differ but which are required to work within the same system.

Terms such as collaboration, consultation, participation and partnership are used freely and often synonymously to describe relationships between separate agencies working within various welfare systems. The concepts themselves are elusive and their imprecise nature goes some way to explaining both their current popularity and why they have been embraced by those across the spectrum of political ideology. The principle of partnership is not confined to juvenile justice: for instance, other partnerships exist in the area of services for pre-school children (Pugh, 1985) and in community development projects (Broady and Hedley, 1988). But the concepts fail to acknowledge power differentials between different agencies and within the total social control system – 'the social', in Donzelot's term (1980). Power differentials become even more visible where partnerships are extended to service-users as well as to other service-providers. While there are those who would argue for the involvement of users (Hadley and Hatch, 1981), through 'citizen participation' (Arnstein, 1969), most schemes that are based on the partnership principle seem to find this aspect almost impossible to achieve (Broady and Hedley, 1988).

There are restraints on partnership in welfare organisations, whether voluntary or statutory, which arise from their dual accountability to the state and to professional values. Among child care professionals, for instance, there is the increasingly visible tension between social care and social control (Glastonbury *et al.*, 1985). Within juvenile justice the swing towards control is all too apparent and is well documented (Thorpe *et al.*, 1980; Burney, 1985; Hudson, 1987; Harris and Webb, 1989).

Second, voluntary agencies experience additional restraints on partnership. As Brenton (1985) points out, the increased reliance of voluntary organisations on government funding and the constrictions of charity law set limits on how far the voluntary organisations can affect policy. In addition government funding implies some degree of external control and is likely to inhibit developments within the organisation which could permit greater participation. Indeed Brenton draws attention to ' "the band-wagon effect" where voluntary organisations energetically subscribe to the policies upon which finance is currently contingent'. And the possibility of being co-opted into the penal system may be the price that has to be paid by voluntary organisations, with state funding exchanged for state control (Ryan and Ward, 1989).

There are particular difficulties with ideas of partnership when they are set within the context of agencies of social control. In setting up joint schemes intended to provide alternatives to custody (through the DHSS Initiative (LAC 83, 3) or Urban Aid funding) the intention was that non-state agencies should work with the statutory services. This can create difficulties for voluntary organisations which are constrained by their articles of constitution and status as charities from making the kinds of radical structural changes necessary in the organisation, both nationally and at the level of an individual project if full partnership is to be sought with other agencies. As voluntary organisations exist at present it does not seem possible that they are able, even if they are willing, to relinquish control in their relationships with other agencies and indeed with clients (Adams, 1981). Similarly, statutory services have their own purposes and their organisational structures and processes may be particularly resistant to collaboration with other agencies.

The purpose of the research was to examine the working of a partnership between a voluntary agency and statutory services in a local juvenile justice system. In addition to looking at relationships between service-providers it also explored whether partnership existed with service-users, since this aspect of partnership looms large in the literature. It was limited to six months which meant that there was some urgency to the task of developing a working definition of partnership. Definitions of the concept in the literature are often unclear, perhaps because, as Mittler and Mittler (1983) suggest, it may best be described as 'an ideal, a goal towards which we should be working'. The definition adopted as the starting-point was that offered by Pugh *et al.* (1987) in their work on pre-school centres: partnership is

> a working relationship that is characterised by a shared sense of purpose, and mutual respect and the willingness to negotiate. This implies a sharing of information, responsibility, skills, decision-making and accountability.

From these and other authors working mainly in the field of child care it seemed that partnership raises issues for social work professionals about

(1) the personal/professional values it embodies
(2) the style of practice it requires
(3) the organisational issues that it raises

In sociological terms the focus was on professional and occupational culture, patterns of interaction, and organisational structures which facilitate or inhibit partnership. The congruence between attitudes of project staff, other service-providers and service-users was explored but increasingly my attention focused on organisational structures and processes.

METHODOLOGICAL ISSUES

The methodology selected was that of ethnography, and as with any small-scale research which attempts to provide a rounded picture of 'how something works' there were problems of validity and reliability if only because the project was changing even during the six months research period, partly in response to changes elsewhere in the local juvenile justice system. Data-gathering included observation of the working of key structures in the local juvenile justice system such as juvenile court, meetings of the Juvenile Liaison Panels, the project's Referral Panel case conferences and 'shadowing' project staff in their work. Information was also gathered from documents and files, from interviews and from just 'hanging about'.

There were problems of access partly because of the low numbers of young people in the project at the start of the research which was a reflection of the decline in the age group. The main access problem however was the refusal of the Chief Clerk to the Justices and members of the Juvenile Panel to be interviewed. No clear reason was given for a lack of response to requests for interviews but it seemed to be related to the commitment on the part of magistrates to preserving their independence.

The position I adopted as that of *observer-as-participant* (Gold, 1958), a stance of comparative detachment. This stance was very uncomfortable at times and increasingly I found myself feeling peripheral to the project – in other words found myself in a marginal position. This served to heighten perceptions of the project and the project workers themselves as marginal within the local system. Interview responses from members of other agencies showed clearly that, with the exception of those few professionals who shared the project's values, it is seen as marginal and possibly misguided. By employing *reflexivity* (Hammersley and Atkinson, 1983) I used my own experience as a researcher to explore the experience of project staff.

SUBSTANTIVE ISSUES

The Project

A retrospective analysis of court data undertaken before the project was established demonstrated a high incidence of juvenile offenders officially processed and prosecuted, a low rate of cautioning and a very high rate of the use of care or custody orders in the local system. Established in 1985 the project is intended for 'heavy-end' offenders aged fourteen to seventeen. It offers a *Specified Activity Condition* as part of a supervision order under Section 12.3.c of the 1969 Children and Young Persons Act, as amended by Section 20 of the 1982 Criminal Justice Act, and since revised by the 1988 Criminal Justice Act. It is funded jointly by the social services department and a voluntary agency with an Urban Aid grant which is due to finish soon, at which point it is expected but not certain that the social services department will assume responsibility for the statutory funding.

The aim of the project is to reduce the numbers of young people entering custody or care by offering a community-based alternative. Its objectives are to maintain young offenders in the community by use of individually tailored programmes of activities. These programmes are designed to encourage young people to accept responsibility for their actions and to change their attitudes and behaviour in relation to offending. There is a parallel and equally important objective of influencing other agencies in their work in order to divert serious young offenders from custody.

The values of project staff have been heavily influenced by those of the Lancaster model of Thorpe *et al.* (1980) of community support of juvenile offenders, and they are members of the Association for Juvenile Justice, often playing key roles in their local branch. Their overall aim is to reduce, if not prevent the use of custody for serious young offenders, but although the project has had an impact on custody rates for young offenders they have had to adopt what is described by social services staff as a more 'realistic' stance. Project staff believe that a 'custody-free zone' in the locality is not achievable and they recognise that sentencers sometimes use the project for young people whose offending behaviour is not serious enough to warrant a custodial sentence, while continuing to send some young people to custody. In other words, project staff are not always successful in convincing sentencers that they offer a credible alternative to custody for heavy-end offenders. It may be that the explanation lies also in the hypothesis put forward by Burney (1985) in her examination of the working of the 1982 Criminal Justice Act that measures designed to influence a particular court may instead 'help to reinforce punitive sentencing attitudes rather than change them'.

Staff are committed to bringing influence to bear on other parts of the juvenile justice system and to this end they monitor Social Inquiry Report recommendations and set up meetings at the start with other welfare professionals, the police and magistrates. Monitoring forms an important part of the project's work: the staff produce annual digests of statistics on juvenile offenders and the project's Annual Report is widely disseminated. While a few representatives of the other agencies appreciate the information that the project supplies, notably in the Juvenile Liaison Bureau, social services and probation, there are others who find the statistics confusing. And so far there has been no approach to the project by magistrates to discuss these data.

Relationships with Service-Users: The Young People and Their Parents

Programmes are individually tailored to the perceived needs of the young person and all consist of three major components: counselling for offending behaviour, reparation, and supervision within the community. The offending behaviour part of the programme is the most important in the package and has become more important over the years, partly because the other two components have proved difficult to put into action. I suspect that both reparation and supervision in the community are retained largely because they are seen to confer credibility in the eyes of sentencers. When the project was initially planned strict supervision in the community was proposed with tracking of offenders as a means of enforcing this supervision. Whether this proposal was intended to make the scheme more attractive as an alternative to custody for 'heavy-end' offenders, for which funding was made available, or whether it was a serious proposal is hard to decide. With the appointment of staff to the project who were proponents of the *minimalist* approach the balance within the project's objectives shifted from *control* in the community to *maintenance* in the community.

The style of project staff in their interactions with users is described as 'non-judgemental and non-confrontational', although the young person is confronted with his or her offending behaviour. Project workers are committed to the view that most offending by young people is situational and opportunistic, and that it is sufficient to maintain them in the community until they 'grow out of crime' (Rutherford, 1986). Their position is that it is not part of their brief to attempt to compensate for years of deprivation experienced by users as the result of their position within the class system. Therefore they make no attempt to offer *treatment*, although they will help users with educational tasks, such as literacy. For much the same reasons project staff do not offer partnership to parents and they resist being drawn into attempts to control what the parents see as the young person's general bad behaviour. This is despite some parents expressing a desire to be more involved. Project staff involve parents in the assessment process, and at the mid-way and final reviews of the young person's programme, but regard any extensive work with parents as the responsibility of the probation officer or social worker who is the supervising officer.

Despite the fact that partnership with users is increasingly adopted as an aim by voluntary agencies, staff in this project are not in partnership with users although they do use partnership styles of relating to users. Indeed, given the disparity in age, status, experience and authority between the two, and the very short duration of the programme (between 24 and 36 sessions) it would be unrealistic to offer anything else. Moreover, any offer of partnership could well totally confuse the young people whose experience to date will have been that of the lack of power of adolescence, made worse by disadvantage. There is also the danger that other agencies might suspect project staff of collusion if partnership with users became an important aspect of the project. The staff are acutely aware of the need to avoid accusations of collusion, whether with the young people against the police, or by allowing the police inappropriate access to young people while they are in the project, and have drawn up guidelines for their interactions with police.

Comments by users, both past and present, illustrated their surprise and pleasure at the way in which project staff interacted with them, summed up by one young person who said 'it was quite fun over there'. Users were aware of the aim of the project. One put it concisely: 'it's to keep you out of trouble. I did woodwork.' Among those who had successfully completed programmes there was recognition that they had been given the chance to grow out of crime. For the few who had re-offended there was a fatalism common to many caught up in the criminal justice system that 'nobody can help you, you've got to do it for yourself'.

The project seems to provide a relatively benign experience for users. There are those such as Hudson (1987) who argue that adopting the minimalist approach has 'justified a neglect of offenders and their problems that is far from benign' and that concentrating on the offence plays into the hands of the New Right. Certainly, among the staff there were doubts about whether concentration on gate-keeping in the system and offending behaviour in the programme had deflected their attention from useful work that could be done with users, even in a short period of time. Help that is focused on acquiring some of the skills and access to services that more fortunate adolescents take for granted would be a step towards 'doing good' (Cohen, 1985). If there were more commitment to partnership with users and parents it could lead to short-term *just welfare* work. But apart from counselling for offending behaviour, the staff are less concerned with what they do with and for the young people than with their credibility with powerful juvenile justice sub-systems. This concern illustrates the dilemma that exists for voluntary organisations from whom the state 'sub-contracts' services where the service is part of the state's control apparatus. In order to stay in business the project has to convince sentencers that it offers a viable alternative, judged by the sentencers' values of punishment and not the minimalist values of the project. Where there is emphasis on the offence there is corresponding de-emphasis on the person which ignores the user's circumstances and seems to accept the deep divisions in our society. Hudson (1987) points out that many welfare professionals despite 'reaffirming rehabilitation' by giving practical assistance to clients, are nonetheless 'giving unwitting support to the justice model, law and order ideology' because they lack a vocabulary with which to make clear their challenge. Where a project is established, as in this example, in order to bring about change in an area with high custody rates, the first and most urgent task is that of systems management. In my opinion the project has still to resolve the question of whether, and at what stage in its development, it can or should offer such a challenge.

Relationship with Service-Providers: Other Agencies

Although the concept system is employed to describe the ways in which juvenile justice 'happens', what exists is far from being a system. Rather than demonstrating the characteristics of the cybernetic model (Beer, 1979) from which it is derived, what exists is what Jackson and Keys (1984, after Ackoff, 1974) describe as a way of managing 'messes'. It includes the police and prosecution, the defence, the courts and correctional services (Feeney, 1985), each with different purposes and different value systems. Thus conflict is bound to arise between these disparate sub-systems. Pullinger (1985) points out that communication and feedback, crucial in the interdependence posited by the model, is affected by the hierarchical positions of the sub-systems involved. It is not simply a question of power: Jackson and Keys (1984) point out that organisations 'have responsibilities to their own purposes . . . and to the purposes of the larger systems of which they are parts'. These responsibilities may often seem to conflict and the solution proposed by Ackoff (1974) is 'interactive planning' involving as many of the sub-systems as possible. But this presumes willingness to engage in such planning on the part of the constituent sub-systems, and in the criminal justice system it flounders on the reality that it is made up of a collection of autonomous units. Rather than seeking to work as a single whole, the sub-systems protect their autonomy because, as Pullinger (1985) points out '(i) there is strong and justified belief that the advantages of decentralised control outweigh those of control from the centre; and (ii) the parts pre-date the whole, and often have a strong wish to remain independent (as, for example, in the case of the judiciary)'. To date the project has found it difficult to open up communication channels with the major juvenile justice services.

Clear examples of conflict were provided in the two local Juvenile Liaison Panels. The occupational culture of the police, even those who work in the Juvenile Bureau, is often at variance with that of project staff. The language used by some police officers was sometimes deliberately provocative and two out of the four police officers I interviewed admitted to games-playing in the meetings which served to minimise the power of the non-police members. The meetings are held in the police station and are conducted in such a way as to maximise police control over the proceedings with a great deal of stage-craft in the passing to and fro of files. Similarly, ritual in the juvenile court (Parker *et al.*, 1981), particularly when used by the justices' clerks, emphasised that project staff attend with the consent of the magistrates, not by right.

The local juvenile justice system is not a closed system, rather it is open and connected with the environment within which it operates and with the nexus of control in our society of which the juvenile justice system is a part. With magistrates and police as the most powerful members of the local system, the other sub-systems form the lower part of the hierarchy of credibility. The project is of such recent origin that it is recognised internally and externally to be virtually powerless. The fact that it has had an effect on custody rates is seen simply to be because it offers another option to sentencers. Its status is that of a peripheral organisation, marginal to long-established agencies of social control, and it is tolerated because it offers no challenge to the status-quo.

The project has struggled, with some limited success, to maintain its gate-keeping criteria and avoid net-widening by excluding offenders who would otherwise be dealt with by a non-custodial penalty. However as Burney (1985) points out, the 1982 Criminal Justice Act's provisions are contradictory and 'enshrine the ambivalent attitude of society and the criminal justice system as a whole to the young offender'. At times it seemed to project workers that the local magistrates use a specified activities condition when it is in its 'welfare mode', to use words of a probation officer, rather than as a community-based alternative to custody. This should not come as a surprise. As Parker *et al.* (1981) have pointed out, the 'permissive' nature of the 1982 Criminal Justice System was unlikely to change the 'bifurcation' (Bottoms, 1983) which differentiates between the 'ordinary' and the 'serious' offender.

If the systems model is not a productive paradigm, is partnership any more useful as an organising construct? Far from being in a partnership, the project finds itself in an uneasy relationship with both court and police. Partnership implies some notion of equality and non-state organisations do not have equal status within the juvenile justice system. However, it must be acknowledged that there are very few schemes that achieve close working relationships with courts and police, and even where they exist – for instance, in Basingstoke (Rutherford, 1986), and Northampton (Northampton JLB, 1988) – relationships may not go as far as partnerships. Even with social services, who jointly fund the project, there is evidence of partnership only with particular members of the social services department, that is those who share the project's commitment to keeping young people out of custody and residential care, the majority of whom are far removed from decision-making structures within the department. For most social services personnel, at every level of the hierarchy, the project is seen as either irrelevant to their work because low numbers of juvenile offenders cannot compete with urgent statutory responsibilities, or disappointing in its insistence on excluding less serious offenders with whom social workers would welcome assistance. The early work undertaken by project staff to educate social services staff about the absolute undesirability of custody for young people seems to have fallen on stony ground, or at least to have lost some of its persuasiveness. And while procedures have been established within the department to reduce the numbers of young people going into custody or care there is ambivalence on the part of social services management illustrated by a continued commitment to a large residential establishment within the county. The department may simply be trying to keep its options open, and may be unwilling to tie up resources in a particular project at a time when funding is uncertain and when there may be political initiatives which require rapid response elsewhere. The change in local government responsibilities from service-provision to the management of services supplied by non-state organisations attendant on the Griffiths Report (1988) is one example of the pressure on local government to avoid long-term financial commitments.

The picture of relationships with probation is better. Relationships between project staff and probation officers reflect their shared values, easy patterns of interaction, and sufficient but not too much organisational structure to facilitate free communication and joint work. It has been suggested that the project might work more closely with probation by extending its activities to the older 17–21 age group currently the target of Home Office policy. A move in this direction would ensure continued viability which is of concern to the project with the contraction in the age group it currently serves. But it might also increase the risk of co-option into the (adult) penal system. The Green Paper proposes raising the upper age limit for the juvenile court to eighteen but argues for 'some flexibility' in deciding whether offenders in the age range 16 to 21 should be dealt with by juvenile or adult court. Such decisions would be based on the perceived maturity of the offender and would be made by magistrates or the Crown Prosecution Service. The suspicion here is that maturity would reflect the nature of the offence and little else, and could give rise to more 'vertical integration' (Thorpe, *et al.*, 1980) between the juvenile and the adult criminal justice systems.

It would seem that there is a disjunction between the systems model espoused by the project and the partnership model on which it was established. And neither accommodates its status as a voluntary organisation. The situation the project is in provides an example of the impotence of voluntary organisations in relation to larger, more powerful statutory agencies identified by Brenton (1985), which the Barclay Report (1982) describes as sometimes akin to a master–slave relationship. An alternative construct is necessary to make sense of the position the project is in – that of *marginality*.

MARGINALITY

The concept of marginality was first introduced by Park in 1928 (Park, 1967), and Stonequist in 1935 (Stonequist, 1961) subsequently expanded it into the social-psychological concept of marginal man, applying it to the difficulties of Jewish ghetto-dwellers who sought assimilation into a Gentile world. The marginal individual is one who exists on the borders of two groups that exert contradictory demands. Marginality encourages innovation and unconventional ways of thinking and acting which can enthuse and reward. But it takes its toll with feelings of alienation, isolation and anomie. Merton's (1957) later working of marginality, although presented within the context of reference group theory, was specifically concerned with marginal individuals and he did not recognise the cultural constructs implicit in Stonequist's original formulation. Later use of the concept did extend its use to groups, including migrants, ghetto-dwellers, the submerged poor, and women, all of whom experience difficulties in recognising their collective situation and in organising politically. The position of project staff within the local system is not dissimilar and they see themselves as excluded from genuine discourse with any other than a few like-minded welfare professionals.

One of the issues the concept highlights as crucial is the inability to choose between two groups. This is a submerged concern for project staff who claim they have no wish to be incorporated into the culture of other parts of the juvenile justice system, but at the same time are aware of a need to break in. Their commitment to resisting net-widening and inappropriate referrals to the project keeps them at a distance from members of other sub-systems, and they are very aware of the dangers of being co-opted. While partnership with users does embody democratic values which can serve to counter the extension of social control into the community partnership with other agencies carries the danger of co-option because partnership requires a degree of compromise between parties. The powerlessness of project workers suggests that they would be required to compromise their position rather more than the other parties, and it can be argued, after Stonequist, that assimilation rarely offers a threat to the mainstream.

Marginality, in contrast, although uncomfortable, might

confer some benefits and provide protection against the changes that seem imminent, particularly privatisation within the criminal justice system. Marginality's encouragement of innovative and unconventional thinking will be crucial in a climate where the swing towards punishment attendant on the 'burial of rehabilitation' (Cohen, 1985) is apparently inexorable. By avoiding closure which would surely follow from incorporation into the system, the project staff can adopt Lerman's (1975) 'strategy of search' and maintain the *least-harm* position that it advocates. It may also allow the project to continue to present Pratt's (1985) 'competing contradiction' which challenges the emphasis placed on punishment by the more powerful agencies within a local system. At the same time the concept permits the acknowledgement of the potentially malignant effects of the 'pure' minimalist stance which takes for granted the hopeless position of disadvantaged 'social junk' (Spitzer, 1975). There is an advocacy role to be played which offers 'a shield' (Ryan and Ward, 1989) to the powerless users of schemes such as the project, which is a bonus for those fortunate enough to have avoided the destructive experience of custody.

By remaining outside, project staff can be 'watch-dogs, policing the boundaries' (Erikson, 1964), and while relatively powerless they are also more free to engage in alternative discourses, one of the most powerful of which may be the professional. Professionals, Cohen (1985) reminds us, 'are not directly or necessarily acting in the best interests of the state', they are rather in Gouldner's (1979) 'morally ambiguous' relationship to the state. It is hard to judge whether this ambiguity can be retained if the move towards greater involvement of non-state agencies continues. Evidence offered by Ericson, McMahon and Evans (1987) from Canada suggests that there is more rather than less state control in the '*apparent* decentralisation' often implied in the increasing use of voluntary agencies. They argue that control is increased through 'the conditions of contract, and attendant monitoring and auditing functions'.

Project staff recognise some of these issues, although, trapped as they are between two competing models, they sometimes experience low morale and feelings of impotence. The two paradigms – partnership with its emphasis on collaboration with other agencies, and the juvenile justice model with its emphasis on gate-keeping – are contradictory. The latter is in danger of being hijacked by the justifications it provides for more, rather than less, punishment. For the project one possible solution to magistrates' continued use of custody for serious young offenders is to strive to improve credibility by offering more of the same: more emphasis on offending behaviour and more supervision in the community. The Green Paper *Punishment and Custody in the Community* (1988) provides justification for supervision in the community for adults and this is likely to strengthen the use of non-custodial penalties for juveniles and young people. Another solution might be for the project to seek to broaden its scope and there has been discussion of extending its services to young people currently taken into residential care for 'welfare reasons'. But this could give rise to the dangers of 'publicisation' (Ericson *et al.*, 1987) where the use of voluntary agencies by the state expands, with increasing numbers of individuals subject to social control, in a process of net-widening. With publicisation both the state and the voluntary sector acquire more power but the latter is subject in turn to increased control by the state, with corresponding loss of what is seen to be the strength of the voluntary sector, its flexibility and willingness to experiment. Perhaps an equally troubling result of increased use of non-states agencies may be that whatever (little) interactive planning currently exists could be eroded by a piecemeal approach to juvenile justice practice by central government. Where schemes are negotiated between central government and a range of separate non-state agencies, then relationships with other services within the juvenile justice system may be overlooked.

Marginality may protect against increasing 'commodification' (Ryan and Ward, 1989) which presents users as commodities rather than as people with needs and rights, and which carries attendant dangers of competition and cost-cutting between schemes seeking funding in the privatised social control market place envisaged by the Green Paper.

If project staff were to accept that marginality, while uncomfortable, is not synonymous with failure then they could seek ways of maximising its advantages for the project and its users. This may be regarded as an unduly optimistic vision and any Marxist analysis would look behind the symbolism and draw attention to the contradictions involved. My view is that contradictions are undoubtedly there and cannot be ignored but that recognising this does not have to preclude attempting to use the flexibility that exists in marginality. In other words, project staff could engage in resistance (Foucault, 1984).

CONCLUSION

The project by itself cannot change the face of juvenile justice in the local system. With users it could adopt more of a partnership way of working which could bring about some change in the young people's situations, and perhaps more successfully empower them. Outside the project it can continue its gate-keeping and monitoring activities, so as to prevent as many young people as possible from entering custody, although there will still be young people who are sent down, despite this alternative. But it cannot hope to challenge the most powerful local sub-systems without the support of other welfare professionals, those in the upper echelons of their respective organisations who are themselves having to respond to political initiatives which are changing the basis of their work. By acknowledging its marginal position in a way that seeks to maximise its impact on the local juvenile justice services, the project can maintain the flexibility that the position confers and use it to the benefit of young people.

The concept of marginality illuminates the complex situation of a scheme which is both handicapped by its powerlessness *vis-á-vis* very powerful juvenile justice services and constrained by the model of partnership which, without radical change in the dominant institutions, both local and national, is doomed to failure. But by maintaining a marginal position while continuing to work within the local juvenile justice system the project can 'carve out spaces' (Ryan and Ward, 1989) which will be of benefit to young people and keep alive the alternative discourse underpinning the principle of partnership.

REFERENCES

ACKOFF, R. L. (1974) *Redesigning the Future – A Systems Approach to Societal Problems*, Chichester: John Wiley.

ADAMS, R. (1981) 'Pontefract Activity Centre', in R. Adams, S. Allard, J. Baldwin and J. Thomas *A Measure of Diversion?*, National Youth Bureau, Leicester.

ARNSTEIN, S. (1969) 'A Ladder of Citizen Participation', *Journal of the American Institute of Planners*, vol. 35, 4, pp. 216–24.

BEER, S. (1979) *The Heart of Enterprise*, Chichester: John Wiley.

BOTTOMS, A. (1983) 'Neglected Features of Contemporary Penal Systems', in D. Garland and P. Young (eds), *The Power to Punish*. London: Heinemann.

BRENTON, M. (1985) *The Voluntary Sector in British Social Services*, London: Longman.

BROADY, M. and HEDLEY, P. (1988) *Working in Partnership: Community Development in Local Authorities*, London: Bedford Square Press.

BURNEY, E. (1985) *Sentencing Young People: What Went Wrong with the Criminal Justice Act 1982*, Aldershot: Gower.

COHEN, S. (1985) *Visions of Social Control*, Oxford: Polity Press.

DEPARTMENT OF HEALTH AND SOCIAL SECURITY (1983) *Circular LAC, 83, 3.*

DONZELOT, J. (1980) *The Policing of Families*, London: Hutchinson.

ERICSON, R. V., McMAHON, M. W. and EVANS, D.G. (1987) 'Punishing for Profit: Reflections on Privatization in Corrections', *Canadian Journal of Criminology*, 22, 4, pp. 355–87.

ERIKSON, K. T. (1964) *Wayward Puritans*, Chichester: John Wiley.

FEENEY, F. (1985) 'Independence as a Working Concept', in D. Moxon (ed.), *Managing Criminal Justice*, HMSO.

FOUCAULT, M. (1977) *Discipline and Punish: The Birth of the Prison*, Harmondsworth: Allen Lane Penguin.

FOUCAULT, M. (1984) *The History of Sexuality: An Introduction*, Harmondsworth: Allen Lane Penguin.

GLASTONBURY, B., COOPER, D. and HAWKINS, P. (1985) *Social Work in Conflict*, London: Croom Helm.

GOLD, R. (1958) 'Roles in Sociological Field Observation', *Social Forces*, vol. 36, pp. 217–23.

GOULDNER, A. (1979) *The Future of the Intellectuals and the Rise of the New Class*, London: Macmillan.

HADLEY, R. and HATCH, S. (1981) *Social Welfare and the Failure of the State*, London: George Allen & Unwin.

HAMMERSLEY, M. and ATKINSON, D. (1983) *Ethnography: Principles in Practice*, London: Tavistock.

HARRIS, R. and WEBB, D. (1989) *Welfare, Power and Juvenile Justice*, London: Tavistock.

HOME OFFICE (1988) *Punishment, Custody and the Community*, Cm 424, HMSO.

HMSO (1988) *A Positive Choice* (Wagner Report).

HMSO (1988) *Community Care: an agenda for action* (Griffiths Report).

HUDSON, B. (1987) *Justice through Punishment*, London: Macmillan.

JACKSON, M. and KEYS, P. (1984) 'Towards a System of Systems Methologies', *Journal of the Operational Research Society*, 35, 6, pp. 473–86.

LERMAN, P. (1975) *Community Treatment and Social Control*, London: Routledge & Kegan Paul.

MERTON, R. (1957) *Social Theory and Social Structure*, London: Free Press.

MITTLER, R. and MITTLER, H. (1983) 'Partnerships with Parents: an overview', in P. Mittler and McConachie (eds), *Parents, Professionals and Mentally Handicapped People: Approaches in Partnership*, London: Croom Helm.
NATIONAL INSTITUTE FOR SOCIAL WORK (1982) *Social Workers: Their Role and Tasks* (Barclay Report) NISW, London: Bedford Square Press.
NORTHAMPTON JUVENILE LIAISON BUREAU *The Fifth Annual Report for 1988*, Northampton.
PARK, R. (1967) *The City*, University of Chicago Press.
PARKER, H., CASBURN, M. and TURNBULL, D. (1981) *Receiving Juvenile Justice*, Oxford: Blackwell.
PRATT, J. (1985) 'Juvenile Justice, Social Work and Social Control: The Need for Positive Thinking', *British Journal of Social Work*, 15, pp. 1–24.
PUGH, G. (1985) *Partnership Paper*, 3, National Children's Bureau.
PUGH, G., APLIN, G., De'ATH, E. and MOXON, M. (1987) *Partnership in Practice: Working with Parents in Pre-School Centres*, vols. 1 & 2, National Children's Bureau.
PULLINGER, H. (1985) 'The Criminal Justice System Viewed as a System', in D. Moxon (ed.), *Managing Criminal Justice*, HMSO.
RUTHERFORD, A. (1986) *Growing out of Crime*, Harmondsworth: Allen Lane Penguin.
RYAN, M. and WARD, T. (1989) *Privatization and the Penal System*, Open University Press.
SPITZER, S. (1975) 'Towards a Marxian Theory of Deviance', *Social Problems*, 22, 5 (June).
STONEQUIST, E. (1961) *The Marginal Man*, New York: Russell & Russell.
THORPE, D. H., SMITH, D., GREEN, C. J. and PALEY, J. H. (1980) *Out of Care: The Community Support of Juvenile Offenders*, London: Allen & Unwin.

11 Victims, Crime Prevention and Social Control

Sandra Walklate

INTRODUCTION

Clarke (1987) suggests that the 1950s and 1960s were decades in which the main thrust of criminal justice policy focused on how to treat the offender rather than how to protect the community from crime. This period is also frequently viewed as a time in which, whilst individuals may have suffered criminal victimisation, there appears to have been little publicly expressed fear of crime. Interpreting this historical period in this way may, or may not, be accurate, but it does reflect a fashionable process in the policy arena: that of invoking images of the past to inform policy directions of the present. One such image, subsequently developed by Clarke (1987), has been that of the community. This chapter will be concerned to examine the extent to which initiatives in crime prevention presume a certain image of the community, and particularly with the way in which that image makes certain assumptions about the victim of crime. An understanding of these images will be offered by reference to the processes of social control and the political possibilities of penetrating those processes.

RESPONSES TO CRIME

There are a number of possible ways to categorise responses to criminal victimisation. Smith (1986) offers a categorisation of public response which distinguishes individual reactive, protective, prevention responses from collective reactive, protective, prevention responses (p. 152). Lewis and Salem (1986), in discussing the fear of crime, suggest that policy initiatives designed to prevent this have been 'top-down' in style, whether they be policies of coercion, cooperation, or empowerment. As with most categorisations it is possible to examine both of these and pinpoint limitations in or improvements to them. Rather than enter into such a detailed examination, I would like to draw attention to two features shared by these analytical frameworks.

The first feature concerns their presumed understanding of the nature of criminal victimisation. They focus primarily on the public; that is, crime that is conventionally understood as criminal and that is consequently understood as the focus for crime prevention. The second feature they share is implied by the first. The implicit support for a conventional view of criminal victimisation lends support to a conservative view of crime prevention. This does not mean that some of the mechanisms highlighted by Smith (1986) and Lewis and Salem (1986) are not useful in themselves; it does mean that they reflect, potentially, only a partial understanding of the possible responses to criminal victimisation. The categories adopted here will follow more closely the spirit of those adopted by Elias (1986). Elias, in talking about crime reduction rather that crime prevention (a label also preferred by Hope and Shaw, 1988), chooses three headings: victimisation avoidance, enforcement crackdowns, and community crime reduction programmes (p. 182). The labels adopted here, namely, victim blaming, offender blaming, and community blaming, whilst more emotive, are intended to bring to the surface the political implications associated with the crime prevention/reduction programmes under discussion. Each of these strategies will be discussed in turn, but for the purposes of this chapter the main emphasis will be on community-blaming crime prevention strategies.

VICTIM BLAMING

Victim blaming is perhaps more usually associated with a critical identification of the way in which the criminal justice process and the wider public handle the victim of rape or sexual assault. This handling presumes a victim-precipitation model of criminal victimisation which has been translated in the courts as 'contributory negligence' (see Jeffreys and Radford, 1984). The notion of victim-precipitation, however, has deep roots which reach into the way in which the victims of crime in general may be viewed (and may view themselves). Victim blaming strategies presume that the key to understanding criminal victimisation lies in the 'precipitative' behaviour of the individual, the community, or the environment. From this viewpoint a key preventive strategy becomes 'target hardening': reducing the opportunities for criminal victimisation to occur; that is, reducing the opportunities for crime which occur as a result of victim precipitative behaviour – going out alone after dark, not fitting window locks, uncared-for public space. The purpose here is not to deny that human beings consider it 'good sense' to avoid going out after dark (which women and the elderly do: see Hough and Mayhew, 1983; Kinsey, 1984; Jones, MacLean and Young, 1986), or that fitting security devices may prevent attempted burglaries becoming real ones (Hough and Mo, 1986), or the 'good sense' in creating an improved environment (Coleman, 1985) or some combination of all of these (Forrester, Chatterton and Pease, 1988); but to draw attention to what such strategies presume about crime, victims and crime prevention.

'Target hardening' is a specific feature of 'situational crime prevention'. Kinsey, Lea and Young (1986) suggest that there are two limitations inherent in this approach to crime prevention. The first is a tendency towards architectural determinism: that is, to see behaviour in general, and criminal behaviour in particular, as the product of opportunities presented by physical structures. The second is a tendency to view crime prevention increasingly as a question of technical expertise: fit the infra-red burglar alarm and the problem is solved. There is, however, a third tendency, which surfaces more clearly when the effects of 'target hardening' individuals are considered, but is also present in the other elements of target hardening discussed here. These strategies, whether focused on individual action, behaviour or property, place the responsibility for crime prevention on the victim. This not only has the effect of heightening the victimisation process – individuals see themselves not only as potential victims but potentially responsible for preventing their own victimisation. It also avoids embracing an understanding of the structural dimensions to criminal victimisation which have been most clearly demonstrated by feminist work and more recently by the 'left realist' local crime surveys. This avoidance has a number of consequences.

First, focusing on risk management behaviour, for example

women avoiding the streets after dark, avoids addressing the private dimension of domestic violence, sexual assault, rape and possibly other crimes. This is not intended to imply that there is not a gender dimension to street crime (see Worrall and Pease, 1986), but it is intended to imply that in missing the gender dimension to criminal victimisation, approaching crime prevention in terms of risk management behaviour is limited in its effect. It presumes a narrow understanding of what constitutes the criminal. In addition, the 'target hardening' of property has resulted in a number of incidents recently in which this has been so effectively embraced that the fire brigade have been unable to rescue individuals from their homes in the event of fire. Whilst this form of 'target hardening' might constitute an extreme response to the threat of criminal victimisation, it nevertheless epitomises the alienating potential of putting all the eggs in the situational basket; this, like some eggs, may have distasteful consequences.

None of this suggests that in some circumstances it does not make good sense for individuals to take individual preventive action. It is clear, however, that writ large such actions miss key structural dimensions to much criminal victimisation, misunderstanding much of what is known about the cause of crime, and may have costly consequences for individual victims of crime.

OFFENDER BLAMING

Offender blaming as a form of crime prevention takes at least two forms: the prevention of recidivism (rehabilitation), and the mobilisation, real or virtual, of support for what Elias (1986) refers to as 'enforcement crackdowns'.

The prevention of recidivism or rehabilitation comes in a number of shapes and sizes; the concern here is to comment on more recent initiatives which incorporate the victim into the process. Mediation and reparation projects of various sorts invoke the support of the victim in a number of different ways, and lack of space inhibits a fuller appreciation of the nature and development of these initiatives. (For an overview of such initiatives in this country, see Marshall and Walpole, 1985; for a general introduction to these developments, see Mawby and Gill, 1987, and Walklate, 1989; for evaluation of specific projects, see Blagg, 1985, and Launey, 1985.) The purpose here is merely to draw the attention of the reader to the way in which the involvement of the victim (either directly or indirectly) is being seen as a way to 'punish' and/or control the offender, and also as a possible way to avoid further offences being committed by raising the offender's awareness of the impact of his or her offence. Mechanisms of this sort sit at the 'soft' end of attitudes towards offenders. The second form of offender blaming usually calls for a tougher approach.

Elias (1986) suggests that the Victims Committee of the International Association of Chief of Police, and Victim Advocates for Law and Order (VALOR) are good examples of victims' groups in the United States which adopt a style calling for more prosecutions, convictions and punishment. The United Kingdom has a vociferous 'hang 'em and flog 'em' brigade and the Victims of Violence organisation comes closest to representing victims of crime from a viewpoint such as this.

Particular crackdown strategies may have the support of victims' organisations, as with police campaigns against drug abuse on Merseyside and the Wirral Parents Against Drug Abuse organisation, but the support of victims is more usually invoked symbolically. It is this latter strategy which has been successfully exploited by the Tory Party in the 1980s in the way in which law-and-order issues have been put on the political agenda. Part of this campaign has encouraged a view that the answer to the crime problem is a tougher approach to punishment, and has discouraged the view that wider social problems are in any way connected with criminal behaviour. (The impact of this strategy is addressed, in part, by Box, 1987.) The question is, do either of these offender blaming strategies work?

Again space inhibits a full answer to this question. However, it is fair to suggest that whilst some evidence supports the view that factors such as personality, attitudes and moral sense predispose some individuals to commit crime, and that therefore focusing on the individual offender, offence, and victim may have some impact for some people, there is more evidence to suggest that the incidence of crime is primarily to do with wider social processes. Consequently, offender blaming strategies writ large have little potential effect on the general incidence of crime. For example, whilst self-help groups for offenders of domestic violence do exist, offender blaming, like victim blaming, has focused on the public rather than on the private dimensions to criminal victimisation. In addition there is a racial dimension to offender blaming strategies expressed most forcibly in the way in which young blacks are effectively 'police property' (Lee, 1981). The cumulative effect of these strategies masks as legitimate the nature and extent of criminal victimisation, avoiding the possibility that the cause of crime stretches beyond the individual offender. It may be suggested that some of the more recent initiatives considered above have the additional potential of also exploiting the status of the victim.

COMMUNITY BLAMING

Hope and Shaw (1988) state that during the 1980s there has been an increasing tendency to widen the responsibility for crime prevention to include the community. They suggest that there have been two reasons for this: an increasing awareness of the fear of crime which is believed to have a deleterious effect on community life, and the increasing awareness that many people are affected by crime. The two policy strategies which have emerged in response to this increased awareness – neighbourhood watch schemes and multi-agency cooperation – both invoke notions of the community.

What is meant by the community in this context is not always clear, but what is embraced by these initiatives is a long-established understanding of the spatial patterning of crime. The criminal victimisation survey has done much to confirm this patterning, as Reiss (1986) points out. However, as he goes on to say, this evidence is collected from individuals who are then presumed to reflect a community view. There is, of course, no necessary guarantee of this.

Willmott (1987) refers to 'community' as a 'seductive word' and suggests that it is useful to distinguish between the 'territorial community', meaning people who live in a particular area; the 'interest community', meaning those people who have something more in common than territory alone; and the 'attachment community', meaning people who have a sense of belonging to a place (p. 2). These different definitions of community have some bearing on the discussion to follow.

The 'mobilisation of informal community controls' which are directed 'in the defence of communities against a perceived predatory threat from outside' (Hope and Shaw, 1988, p. 12) has, following the lead from the United States, taken the form in the UK of the neighbourhood watch scheme. There are two strands of thought which stress the positive potential of neighbourhood watch schemes as a strategy against crime. The first stresses an opportunity reduction view of crime through the importance of having 'eyes and ears on the street'. (There is some evidence to suggest that surveillance does deter burglars: see Bennett and Wright, 1984.) The second stresses the importance of creating and harnessing social cohesion; the common goal of crime prevention leading to greater civility and trust between neighbours and a subsesquent reduction in the fear of crime. The tension between these two strands of thought is most obviously displayed when the variation in implementation and effectiveness of these schemes is examined.

The support for neighbourhood watch has been overwhelming. In 1987 there were over 29 000 registered schemes (Hope, 1988, p. 146). In analysing this support on the basis of evidence from the 1894 British Crime Survey, Hope suggests:

> Where the strongest spontaneous support for Neighbourhood Watch resides is in those communities where people are sufficiently worried about crime, where they feel the need to do something about it, and where they feel positively towards their neighbours and the community in general. (p. 159)

He goes on to add that the social characteristics of those willing to involve themselves in these schemes are similar to those willing to be involved in more general voluntary activity: white, middle-aged, lower-middle/middle class. These findings concur with more specific findings concerning the circumstances in which these schemes may achieve some of their objectives: among white, middle-class home-owners (see Bennion *et al.*, 1985; Donnison, Skola and Thomas. 1986; and Bennett, 1987). In these circumstances neighbourhood watch is most likely to achieve the goal of fear reduction rather than crime reduction. Rosenbaum (1988) challenges whether fear reduction is, of itself, a legitimate goal and goes on to ask whether the answer is to 'try harder' in those areas where neighbourhood watch is less popular. This is where the tension between the two strands of thought discussed earlier emerges.

From the evidence above it seems reasonable to suggest that neighbourhood watch is popular in areas where the actual risk from crime is relatively low and where crime is seen as an external threat to the community – in other words, in those areas which dovetail with the definition offered earlier by Hope and Shaw (1988). Generally, in those areas where the incidence of and risk from crime is higher, neighbourhood watch is less popular. In these areas it is likely that crime is not seen as some external threat to the community but is a problem internal to it. Under these circumstances people may see or hear what is going on but their beliefs about crime do not lean towards neighbourhood watch since this is premised on a level of trust between neighbours which may not exist. Rosenbaum (1988) suggests that in these circumstances a multiple strategy approach is probably appropriate.

The most popular multiple strategy approach to date in the UK has been multi-agency cooperation. Hope and Shaw (1988) define multi-agency cooperation in the following way:

> inasmuch as crime within local communities is likely to be sustained by a broad range of factors – in housing, education, recreation, etc. – the agencies and organisations who are in some way responsible for, or capable of, affecting those factors, ought to join in common cause so that they are not working at cross purposes or sustaining crime inadvertently. (p. 13)

Sampson *et al.* (1988) identify two approaches which have been used to understand the nature of such multi-agency cooperation: the benevolent and the conspiratorial. Their own work points to the importance of developing

> a more socially nuanced understanding which is alive to the complexities of locality-based crime prevention initiatives and of power differentials running between different state agencies, as well as to the competing sectional interests within existing communities. (p. 478)

There are indeed dilemmas to be faced by agencies participating in such initiatives; they may be less than democratic (i.e. dominated by the expert status of the police: Kinsey, Lea and Young, 1986), and they may compromise the role of agencies in other areas of their work (social workers and young people, the probation service; see Blagg *et al.*, 1988). The question here, however, is concerned with what multi-agency policing can achieve for the community with respect to criminal victimisation and the fear of criminal victimisation.

At one level it is clear that the emergence of victim support schemes has relied on inter-agency cooperation: from the referral of the victim by the police (though this is not the only source of referral for victim support schemes) to the initial help in accommodation, administration, or the mutual use of volunteers from the probation service in certain areas. (This has been a feature of victim support, for example, on Merseyside.) This form of inter-agency cooperation has not had as its main aim crime prevention; though subsequent advice offered to victims may have a preventive element.

The preventive approach within multi-agency policing has focused largely on either the technology of crime prevention or on the control of offenders (see the development of intermediate treatment as an example of this latter strategy), and in so doing has not necessarily embraced an understanding of the impact that this has on victims of crime or an understanding of crime which moves beyond targeting particular kinds of crime or responding to locally defined nuisances (see Blagg *et al.*, 1988; Sampson *et al.*, 1988). This, however, is not the necessary implication of multi-agency policing as defined.

Blagg *et al.* (1988) point to the ways in which the neglected features of inter-agency cooperation can be explored in a preventive manner by such cooperation. They state:

> But what is most striking is the contrast between the neglect of domestic violence as a site upon which to enact measures of crime prevention (in other words, to regard such violence as 'crime') or to invoke the concept of inter-agency cooperation, when set against the elaborate liaison apparatus which is arranged around child protection. (p. 217)

Implementing such a process would require not only encouraging such incidents to be defined as crime but also would require the inclusion of the less formally recognised community groups and women's groups. This suggestion does not mean, necessarily, that domestic violence would be effectively prevented or policed (this is patently not the case with child abuse, for example), but it does entail a more radical interpretation of mult-agency cooperation. Such an interpretation bears some comparison with the notion of 'community safety' as discussed by Bright (1987).

The framework offered by Bright (pp. 49–50) includes a number of strategies; for the involvement of local councils, for services for victims of crime, for protecting groups most at risk (women, ethnic minorities, children), for different residential areas and finally for schemes involving the police. This framework embraces a number of critical issues in the context of community crime prevention. First, it starts from the premise that tackling criminal victimisation and the fear of crime is the responsibility of a broad base within the community: formal agencies, informal agencies, and community networks. This implies that it is necessary to ensure community participation by creating the circumstances in which that participation is fully representative and thereby facilitated. Second, it declares a definition of crime which incorporates an understanding of criminal victimisation through an appreciation of those dimensions which are more usually neglected by community crime preventing – namely, age, race, and gender. Third, it emphasises a genuinely cooperative approach to crime prevention which moves towards ideas of empowerment (see above, and Lewis and Salem, 1986).

It is clear, then that there are a number of different strands to community blaming with which this discussion is concerned. Neighbourhood watch, and multi-agency cooperation as conventionally understood, are limited by the fact that they tend to be police-led and to operate with a focus on property crime, street crime, or nuisances. They are also initiatives which have primarily a territorial interpretation of the community in which crime is either seen as a threat external to the community (neighbourhood watch) or, where it is recognised that crime is an internal problem, may result in the further stereotyping of that community (see Sampson *et al.*, 1988). Neighbourhood watch and multi-agency cooperation also tend to operate in a 'top-down' style, often neglecting less formal groups and certainly glossing over the difficulties of creating social cohesion (informal social control) which Shapland (1988) argues already exists in some communities and whereby the solution to criminal victimisation, it is felt, will be found. It is only through the notion of 'community safety' and the question of the neglected features of multi-agency cooperation that it has been possible to identify an alternative approach to community crime prevention, which also appears to come closest to embracing all three definitions of community offered by Willmott (1987).

Outlining the assumptions of community-based initiatives in this way is not intended to deny that neighbourhood watch in some areas may serve to alleviate the fear of crime, or that inter-agency cooperation may result in some progress for some sections of a community. It is clear, however, that in transferring the responsibility for crime prevention from the individual to the individual community, the main thrust of these initiatives only offers a partial approach to tackling criminal victimisation and its impact.

COMMUNITY RHETORIC AND SOCIAL CONTROL

The main concern of what follows is to offer an understanding of why recent initiatives in crime prevention have focused on the community in the form that they have. None of this is intended to undermine the findings that some community-based initiatives may have some sort of impact on conventional crime or may make some sections of the public 'feel better' about the threat of crime. As Rock (1988) suggests, initiatives led by NACRO (the safe neigbourhood unit) and by the Land Use and Resource Centre (led by Professor Alice Coleman) seem to work. What is much more uncertain is why.

At one level the commitment and involvement of particular individuals in particular projects become the controlling mechanisms which ensure the success or failure of those projects. (Much the same observation could be made concerning the development and effectiveness of mediation and reparation projects.) The success of such projects therefore is as much attributable to those participants as it is to the validity of the overall community approach. However, since there is little consistent or reliable evidence that the community approach to crime prevention works, it is necessary to look beyond the participants to understand why this approach persists.

Given the general thrust of government policy since 1979, it is possible to suggest that the appeal of community crime prevention is a reflection of the general appeal of the notion of the community painted on that broader canvas. The combined strategy of 'rolling back the state' and the fiscal requirement to reduce public expenditure has led policy in the direction of the community as a potentially cheaper alternative to state initiatives. Whether, in reality, 'value for money' and 'efficiency' are achieved by this strategy, is, of course, open to considerable debate. The rationale for such initiatives, however, is not solely based in economics. The expression of such economic ideals is underpinned by a set of political ideals which place great emphasis on encouraging individuals and communities to take responsibility for a whole range of activities in order to reconstruct a society bound together by shared norms (likened by Lea, 1987, to Durkheim's conception of mechanical solidarity). This begins to deepen our understanding of the persistence of the image of the community.

The economic, then, is overlaid by two more processes: the political and the ideological. The political dimension runs through a number of issues which involve victims of crime: from the way in which (at this point Home Office based) criminal victimisation surveys may be used; to the emergence of the Criminal Injuries Compensation Board; the financial backing given to the National Association of Victim Support Schemes; and the development of mediation and reparation projects as well as community-based crime prevention schemes. The 'official' backing given to this range of initiatives (referred to by Miers, 1978, as the 'politicisation of the victim') has arguable been achieved as a result of the politically neutral and largely conventional image of the victim which pervades them. Political parties (more recently those on the right) can be seen to be doing something about the problem of crime and the needs of victims of crime without challenging the prevalent stereotypical assumptions of what a crime victim looks like.

A further dimension to this is evident in the political desire to promote the 'freedom of the individual'. In the context of crime prevention this means that individuals, and individual communities, are free to choose whether or not to take the responsibility for crime prevention. This emphasis fails to recognise, of course, that individual freedom might also be curtailed by such initiatives, that some are 'freer' than others to buy sophisticated burglar alarm systems, and ultimately fails to recognised that some sections of the population are 'freer' than others from criminal victimisation. This emphasis on the individual discourages embracing a view of criminal victimisation which recognises the deeper implications of the economic framework within which we operate; victimisation by corporations for example. Failure to address questions such as these is not just a case of deliberate political machination. Nor is the observation intended to undermine some of the potential good effects that the initiatives outlined above may have and already do have for some victims of crime. It is intended to draw attention to the way in which these initiatives have succeeded and been successful with a structurally neutral image of the victim. Such an image not only serves political ends but also ideological.

Some time ago, Bottoms (1983) drew attention to the way in which the development of community strategies in response to crime had been affected by the 'powerful motif' of the victim. Referencing some of the developments already cited above, Bottoms goes on to argue that the social control theorising of Scull (1977) and Cohen (1985) does not handle this motif easily:

> these developments in various non-criminal spheres are not necessarily sinister, which should perhaps make us at least pause before painting too blackly the 'penetration' and 'community absorption' which Cohen identifies as key aspects of community corrections. Indeed this public-private admixture can even be seen in some other aspects of the criminal justice system itself, in contexts where there is no implication of the state acting in any overbearing or improper fashion – the victim support schemes are a clear illustration. (Bottoms, 1983, p. 192)

The extent to which Bottoms would now make this same observation concerning victim support schemes, given the changes that have occurred in their funding since 1983, is perhaps open to some debate. The more fundamental point concerning this 'motif of the victim' seems to be not so much how it fits with the specific concerns of 'penetration' or 'absorption' but how this motif constitutes a significant strategy of avoidance. This strategy of avoidance works to encourage a conventional and structurally neutral view of criminal victimisation.

In the context of the foregoing discussion of crime prevention it has been clear that whilst some crime prevention initiatives have the potential of being interpreted with a view to incorporating a structurally informed view of victimisation, this has been for the most part a minority view. In some respects the issue of crime prevention is not peculiar in this respect; there is a wider reluctance to embrace the sexist, racist, and ageist structure of our social system as a whole. This wider reluctance, and the specific avoidance strategy exemplified within crime prevention images of the crime victim, ultimately serve to maintain a particular social order; and may indeed add to the repertoire of strategies available to control offenders (via mediation and reparation) and encourage particular views of the role of communities within those wider mechanisms of social control.

The tendency to individualise the problem of criminal victimisation (whether individuals or individual communities) involves economic, political and ideological processes. The question remains as to the extent to which these strategies can be penetrated by alternative policy directions.

CRIME PREVENTION: LOOK LEFT OR RIGHT?

The denial that unemployment is related to crime pervades the majority of the community initiatives discussed here. It comes as no surprise, then, to observe that those communities in which crime is seen as an internal threat rather than an external one are also those communities in which there are other social problems, like unemployment, poor housing, etc. These are also the communities in which neighbourhood watch has been less successful. This denial is also a feature of the response to crime by the political right. If the understanding of what constitutes the criminal is broadened to include racial harassment, domestic violence, sexual harassment, and then the activities of large corporations, the delimiting and narrow focus of crime prevention strategies in general becomes more acute. The question remains, however, as to whether left-wing strategies would look any different.

In many respects the political left and right share the same dilemmas in the issue of crime prevention as those faced by the right. The discussion of the notion of community safety above clearly suggests that a radical position on crime prevention does not necessarily involve any novel strategies. The discussion of the notion of community safety clearly suggest that, in a radical position on crime prevention, the concept of community is still important. How that community is to be approached, harnessed and encouraged in its organisation towards crime prevention is, however, clearly different. In the context of understanding criminal victimisation, the 'left realists' within criminology have made much of putting the victim at the centre of their agenda. It is worth considering some of the observations to be made from this position with respect to crime prevention.

Lea (1987) states that:

> The maximization of democratic participation is ultimately the solution both to the problem of what is crime and to the problem of how to deal with it. (p. 369)

He further argues that an important feature of a realist approach to crime prevention would be to involve a real plurality of agencies, both formal and informal, centrally and locally organised. These would work on the basis of the contradiction of interests that would exist between them, which would force a re-evaluation and resolution of conflicts on a regular basis. In this way he suggests the relationship between institutions and communities could be reworked. Matthews (1987), while usefully critical of the concept of community, goes on to argue that left realism needs to examine the potential of a diverse range of community involvement in crime. He states that:

> 'Community' crime control strategies can clearly be double-edged. We cannot assume that greater public participation will necessarily be progressive. Rather we need to explore the range of strategies as well as specific networks which may encourage a new form of social cohesion. (p. 397)

Young (1988) also comments on the way in which the findings of the radical victimisation surveys will have a real effect on crime prevention; though he does not translate this into specific policies. More recently Corrigan, Jones and Young (1989) have discussed the relationship between 'rights' and 'obligations' and the need for the left to tackle this thorny issue. In the context of crime prevention an argument such as this leads to the implication that if individuals have the 'right' to be free from the threat of or fear of crime, does that then obligate them to invest in all the 'high-tec' equipment in order to make any reasonable claim when this equipment fails to protect them? (a view not far from that adopted already by some insurance companies for people living in particular areas). Ultimately this line of reasoning does not seem to have the interests of the victim, or potential victim, at heart, and becomes increasingly more problematic when the position of women, children, and ethnic minorities is considered.

In spite of the problems associated with the question of rights and obligations, what is clear is that there is an obvious commitment on the left in general, and left realism in particular, to harnessing the democratic process and to developing strategies to improve the representation and participation of all groups in the community in crime prevention. This would certainly widen the focus of concern for crime prevention.

While the general tenor of such an approach is laudable, there are inevitable practical difficulties in achieving these goals. Jefferson, McLaughlin and Robertson (1988) usefully highlight the difficulties and dilemmas of implementing policies which are sensitive to the questions of participation, representation, and the community. These practical problems need to be more clearly addressed by the left, though in theory these goals should avoid the trap of merely extending the mechanisms of social control in an unacknowledged and unintended way without taking the interests of various groups into account.

One problem remains. A key issue, so far not addressed, is how 'non-criminalised problematic situations' (Lea, 1987, p. 362) – that is, in part, the activities of large corporations – can be placed on the crime prevention agenda. Again the left realist turns to the democratic process:

> The development of the categories of criminal law in any free society requires the maximum public participation in processes of democratic discourse. The distinction between what is embodied in the criminal law and what are regarded as problematic situations will always retain an element of arbitrariness outside such conditions. (Lea, 1987, p. 364)

Box (1987) and Carson (1982) discuss extending the regulatory framework in order to improve control over corporate crime. Box (1987) also points to the example of 'consumer revolts' (Thalidomide, Opren) and the need for a heightened awareness of what such 'revolts' might achieve. Without some framework of crime prevention that encompasses an understanding of these criminal victimisation processes which go on 'behind our backs', as it were, as well as those of which we are aware and are willing to identify as crime, our understanding of criminal victimisation and how to prevent it will always be partial and limited. It is easier to see what the democratic process has to offer the disenfranchised than it is to anticipate what might be gained from this by the already powerful.

CONCLUSION

Both the left and right join together in espousing the importance of democracy, the community and 'appreciating the victim'. Such an appreciation has proceeded on the right in a structurally neutral fashion, and on the left, not unsurprisingly has been more structurally informed. The ultimate problem to be resolved, both in policy terms and theoretically, is, when the victim is put at the centre of the stage, what relationship does this have with what is meant by crime and crime prevention? Put another way, how are we to tackle criminal victimisation in a way which embraces an understanding of the structural and ideological bases of what constitutes a victim?

REFERENCES

BENNETT, T. (1987) *An Evaluation of Two Neighbourhood Watch Schemes in London, Executive Summary*, Final Report to the Home Office Research and Planning Unit, Cambridge: Institute of Criminology.

BENNETT, T. and WRIGHT, R. (1984) *Burglars on Burglary*, Aldershot: Gower.

BENNION, C., DAVIES, A., HESSE, B., JOSHUA, L., McGLOIN P., MUNN, C. and TESTER, S. (1985) *Neighbourhood Watch: The Eyes and Ears of Urban Policing?*, Occasional Papers in Sociology and Social Policy no. 6, University of Surrey.

BLAGG, H. (1985) 'Reparation and Justice for Juveniles', *British Journal of Criminology*, vol. 25, pp. 267–79.

BLAGG, H., PEARSON, G., SAMPSON, A., SMITH, D. and STUBBS, P. (1988) 'Inter-Agency Co-ordination: Rhetoric and Reality', in T. Hope and M. Shaw (eds), *Communities and Crime Reduction*, London: HMSO.

BOTTOMS, A. E. (1983) 'Neglected Features of Contemporary Penal Systems, in D. Garland and P. Young (eds), *The Power to Punish,* London: Heinemann, pp. 166–202.

BOX, S. (1987) *Recession Crime and Punishment*, London: Macmillan.

BRIGHT, J. (1987) 'Community Safety, Crime Prevention and Local Authority', in P. Willmott (ed.), *Policing and the Community*, Policy Studies Institute Discussion Paper 16, London: PSI, pp. 45–53.

CARSON, W. G. (1982) *The Other Price of Britain's Oil*, Oxford: Martin Robertson.

CLARKE, M. J. (1987) 'Citizenship, Community and the Management of Crime', *British Journal of Criminology*, 27, pp. 384–400.

COHEN, S. (1985) *Visions of Social Control*, Cambridge: Polity Press.

COLEMAN, A. (1985) *Utopia on Trial*, London: Hilary Shipman.

CORRIGAN, P., JONES T. and YOUNG, J. (1989) 'Rights and Obligations', *New Socialist*, February–March, pp. 16–17.
DONNISON, H., SKOLA, J. and THOMAS, P. (1986) *Neighbourhood Watch: Policing the People*, London: The Libertarian Research and Education Trust.
ELIAS, R. (1986) *The Politics of Victimization*, Oxford: Oxford University Press.
FORRESTER, D., CHATTERTON, M. and PEASE, K. (1988) *The Kirkholt Burglary Prevention Project, Rochdale*, Crime Prevention Unit Paper 13, London: HMSO.
HOPE, T. (1988) 'Support for Neighbourhood Watch: A British Crime Survey Analysis', in T. Hope and M. Shaw (eds), *Communities and Crime Prevention*, London: HMSO, pp. 146–63.
HOPE, T. and SHAW, M. (1988) 'Community Approaches to Reducing Crime, in T. Hope and M. Shaw (eds), *Communities and Crime Reduction*, London: HMSO, pp. 1–29.
HOUGH, M. and MAYHEW, P. (1983) *The British Crime Survey: First Report*, Home Office Research Study no. 76, London: HMSO.
HOUGH, M. and MAYHEW, P. (1985) *Taking Account of Crime: Key Findings from the Second British Crime Survey*, Home Office Research Study no. 85, London: HMSO.
HOUGH, M. and MO, J. (1986) 'If At First You Don't Succeed', *Home Office Research Bulletin 21*, pp. 10–13.
JEFFERSON, T., McLAUGHLIN, E. and ROBERTSON, L. (1988) 'Monitoring the Monitors: Accountability, Democracy and Policewatching in Britain', *Contemporary Crises*, 12, pp. 91–106.
JEFFREYS, S. and RADFORD, J. (1984) 'Contributory Negligence or Being a Woman? The Car Rapist Case', in P. Scraton and P. Gordon (eds), *Causes for Concern*, Harmondsworth: Penguin, pp. 154–83.
JONES, T., MACLEAN, B. and YOUNG, J. (1986) *The Islington Crime Survey*, Aldershot: Gower.
KINSEY, R. (1984) *Merseyside Crime Survey: First Report*, Liverpool: Merseyside County Council.
KINSEY, R., LEA, J. and YOUNG, J. (1986) *Losing the Fight Against Crime*, Oxford: Blackwell.
LAUNEY, G. (1985) 'Bringing Victims and Offenders Together: A Comparison of Two Models', *Howard Journal of Criminal Justice*, vol. 24, no. 3, pp. 200–12.
LEA, J. (1987) 'Left Realism: A Defence', *Contemporary Crises*, 11, pp. 357–70.
LEE, J. A. (1981) 'Some Structural Aspects of Police Deviance in Relations with Minority Groups', in C. Shearing (ed.), *Organizational Police Deviance*, Toronto: Butterworth, pp. 49–82.
LEWIS, D. A. and SALEM, G. (1986) *Fear of Crime: Incivility and the Production of a Social Problem*, New Brunswick N.J.: Transaction.
MARSHALL, T. and WALPOLE, M. (1985) *Bringing People Together: Mediation and Reparation Projects in Great Britain*, Home Office Research and Planning Unit Paper 33, London: HMSO.
MATTHEWS, R. (1987) 'Taking Realist Criminology Seriously', *Contemporary Crises*, 11, pp. 371–402.
MAWBY, R. I. and GILL, M. (1987) *Crime Victims: Needs Services and the Voluntary Sector*, London: Tavistock.
MIERS, D. (1978) *Responses to Victimization, Abingdon: Professional Books*

REISS, A. (1986) 'Official Statistics and Survey Statistics', in E. A. Fattah (ed.), *From Crime Policy to Victim Policy*, London: Macmillan, pp. 53–79.

ROCK, P. (1988) 'Crime Reduction Initiatives on Problem Estates', in T. Hope and M. Shaw (eds), *Communities and Crime Reduction*, London: HMSO, pp. 99–115.

ROSENBAUM, D. P. (1988) 'A Critical Eye on Neighbourhood Watch: Does It Reduce Crime and Fear?', in T. Hope and M. Shaw (eds), *Communities and Crime Reduction*, London: HMSO, pp. 126–45.

SAMPSON, A., STUBBS, P., SMITH, D., PEARSON, G. and BLAGG, H. (1988) 'Crime Localities and the Multi-Agency Approach', *British Journal of Criminology*, vol. 28, no. 4, pp. 478–93.

SCULL, A. (1977) *Decarceration: Community Treatment and the Deviant – A Radical View*, Englewood Cliffs, N.J.: Prentice-Hall.

SHAPLAND, J. (1988) 'Policing with the Public', in T. Hope and M. Shaw (eds), *Communities and Crime Reduction*, London: HMSO, pp. 116–25.

SMITH, S. J. (1986) *Crime, Space and Society*, Cambridge: Cambridge University Press.

WALKLATE, S. (1989) *Victimology: Victims and the Criminal Justice Process*, London: Unwin Hyman.

WILLMOTT, P. (1987) 'Introduction', in P. Willmott (ed.), *Policing and the Community*, London: PSI, pp. 1–7.

WORRALL, A. and PEASE, K. (1986) 'Personal Crime Against Women', *Howard Journal of Criminal Justice*, vol. 25, no. 2, pp. 118–24.

YOUNG, J. (1988) 'Radical Criminology in Britain: The Emergence of a Competing Paradigm', *British Journal of Criminology*, vol. 28, pp. 159–83.

12 Left Realism in Criminology and the Return to Consensus Theory

Kevin Stenson and Nigel Brearley

The recasting of the knowledge base of social democracy has involved the use of the term 'realism' in a number of policy areas. In criminology, a social democratic, or 'left' realism has been developed by a group of intellectuals, in sympathy with the parties of the social democratic left, who seek to challenge the hegemony in left discourses of Marxist and neo-Marxist analyses of crime and the justice system. In their view, the left's misuse of notions of moral panic (Hall *et al.*, 1978), suggesting that the police, courts and mass media have exaggerated the incidence of crimes like mugging, has led to a serious underestimation of the scale of the problem of intra-class street crime for working-class people and the non-working poor. Street assaults and robberies, burglaries, sexual attacks and so on, in decayed inner-city neighbourhoods and poor housing estates are demoralising and are a key element in the social disorganisation of working-class 'communities', already suffering from a multiplicity of economic and social deprivations, including a marked vulnerability to the effects of white-collar crime (Lea and Young, 1984).

More profoundly, in adopting a philosophically realist position, left realism rejects what is alleged to be on the left an idealist and nominalist view of crime itself (Matthews, 1987, p. 371). The latter view, an outgrowth of the labelling theories of the 1960s, would reduce crime to a matter of definitions, rather than real human suffering.

Left realism was also developed as an alternative to – or perhaps a radical recasting of – the 'right' realists of American criminology, stemming from the work of J. Q. Wilson (1975) and E. Van Den Haag (1985), who called for a scaling-down of the grandiose ambitions of criminology to explain the social structural origins of crime and promote changes in structural crimogenic conditions. Rather, they encourage a sharper focus on street crime and a recognition of the necessity of punishment (Platt and Takagi, 1977; Matthews, 1987, pp. 375–9; Currie, 1985a).

The underestimation of the scale of the problem of crime by the hard left, perhaps in a misplaced and romantic defence of predatory, lawless youth, provides a strange echo of the claims by Home Office researchers that the risks of victimisation are exaggerated and that fear of crime, rather than crime itself, is the real problem (Kinsey *et al.*, 1986, ch. 3). A succession of local crime surveys in Merseyside, the London Boroughs of Islington and Hammersmith, Haringey (at Broadwater Farm) have been conducted by Richard Kinsey of the Centre for Criminology at Edinburgh and Jock Young and his colleagues at the Centre for Criminology at Middlesex Polytechnic (Kinsey, 1984; Jones *et al.*, 1986; Jones *et al.*, 1987; Painter *et al.*, 1989).

By focusing more precisely than the British Crime Surveys on differential victimisation rates in particular geographical areas and for particular social categories, left realists claim to have demonstrated that for residents in poor areas, fear of crime is not paranoid fantasy amplified by the media, but rather a well-founded estimation of risk. They claim, in addition, that overwhelmingly, across the lines of class, gender and ethnicity, the crime surveys reveal that respondents' priorities for crime control are remarkably uniform and at variance with those set by largely unaccountable police forces, which prioritise public order and their own internally generated bureaucratic goals and objectives. A truly accountable police force would respond to the priorities for crime control set by the citizens who pay them. These would emphasise the protection of the life, limbs and property of the most vulnerable; in fact the right to protection from victimisation should be considered among the core human rights of any civilised society (Young, 1987a, p. 355).

The wider political message involved in left realist proposals for crime control, including, for example, locally initiated victim/offender mediation schemes, dispute settlement projects and so on, in addition to the more familiar policing strategies (Lea, 1987, p. 366), is that they must be considered alongside other 'community building' projects in poor areas (ibid, p. 369) as part of the deeper strategy of developing effective community organisation among poorer citizens. Effective crime control can be an important precondition for the entry of the politically marginalised poor – otherwise divided along the lines of age, gender, ethnicity, religion and incremental economic differences – into the democratic process.

While sympathetic to the general thrust of left realism, we are concerned that ambiguities in the general realist position may inhibit its ability to engage effectively with the arguments about law and order on the political right. Much of the theoretical work of realists, so far, has been devoted to differentiating their position from other positions on the left; the real arguments, however, remain with the right.

This chapter will be developed in three main sections. The first part will situate the developing discourses of left realist criminology and crime control policies within the political framework set by challenges from the right. The right, both at the level of social policy discourses about law and crime, education and morality and, recently, in the form of moves to monitor the moral content of the mass media and the moral framework of local authority service provision and the school curriculum, has put the nature of the moral consensus which should underpin modern society very firmly on the political agenda. In particular, it is argued that, in response, left realism marks a significant shift away from the sociological and moral relativism of earlier forms of radical criminology in the 1970s and from the Marxist and neo-Marxist crimonologies of the hard left. The latter continue to mount a critical assault on the criminal justice system from a moral and analytical position which situates itself outside the state and the institutions of bourgeois democracy. We will not, in this chapter, be concerned with accounting for the sharpening conflicts between Marxist and social democratic criminological discourses (Scraton, 1987). Rather, from within a broadly social democratic perspective, we will be concerned with identifying and strengthening a shift towards sociological and moral consensus theory within left realism.

It will be argued that left realism cannot be understood in narrowly abstract theoretical terms, nor in terms of a series of policy prescriptions offered to solve the 'crime problem'. It is, rather, part of a complex of institutionally located political strategies, a characteristic it shares with other criminological discourses.

Second, however, the superficial unity provided by the political project of left realism and its shift towards consensus theory, are in tension with the ambiguities created by its eclectic theoretical lineage. While this eclecticism has been evidence of creativity, at this stage it constitutes an impediment to further progress. Again, this problem is not confined to criminological discourses, but must be located within the wider project of reconstructing the knowledge base of social democracy.

Third, it is argued that as left realism increasingly contests the middle ground of analysis and policy formation, its theoretical bias towards methodological individualism creates the risk that it will be drawn into the methodologically individualistic, utilitarian discourses which have long dominated state-sponsored criminology and crime control policy. In order to avoid this tendency, it is suggested that left realism exploit and develop its radical reading of Durkheim's sociology, which is founded on a methodologically collectivist critique of English utilitarianism. This redirection of left realism will be developed particularly in relation to the conceptualisation of consensus and the creation of a moral framework for programmes of crime control.

REDISCOVERING CONSENSUS, RESPONDING TO THE CHALLENGE FROM THE RIGHT

While a full exploration of the contradictions and ambiguities of right-wing discourses about crime and crime control is beyond our present brief, we must note in recent years an intensifying onslaught on the role of welfare policies in the justice system. Following assaults by American New Right intellectuals on welfarism in the American administrative apparatus, their British counterparts have argued for a return to deterrence and retribution as the key founding principles of a justice system (von Hirschi, 1976; Brewer *et al.*, 1981; Van Den Haag, 1985; Morgan 1981). Right-wing critiques of the role of welfare professionals within the justice system present them as unproductive drones, expanding their professional empires and invading the civil liberties of citizens under the guise of 'care'. Ironically, these critiques are a distorted echo of critiques of welfare, beginning in the 1960s and 1970s, from the libertarian left, first from within the labelling theory framework of interpretive sociology (e.g. Schur,

1973; Morris *et al.*, 1980) and later within the terms of Foucault's post-structuralism, or a mixture of the two rather discordant bedfellows (Foucault, 1977; Cohen, 1985; Thorpe *et al.*, 1980; Stenson, 1986).

But one of the key differences between the earlier, left libertarian and recent New Right critiques hinges around their respective underlying models of society. The left libertarians tended to reject consensualist images of society. American functionalists, for example, using organic metaphors, claimed that the health, welfare and justice systems represented, or could represent, the broader public interest in maintaining the health of the social 'body'. For the left libertarians, by contrast, society was represented as a field of competing or coexisting groups and individuals, with competing definitions of reality, normality and deviance.

Thus, one of the seminal texts within this movement was critical of depictions within conventional, state-sponsored psychiatry of illicit drug use as a social pathology and of the drugtaker as determined by forces beyond his or her control (Young, 1971). Such depictions of the deviant were characterised as absolutist, based on fixed and morally conservative notions of normality, rationality and deviance. The more useful sociological starting-point was deemed to be a relativist stance, which acknowledged the diversity of rationality and definitions of reality and morality within modern society (ibid, ch. 3).

Although under Thatcher the New Right in Britain seems to embrace a conflictual politics of confrontation, eschewing the old corporatist discourses of 'consensus' welfare state politics, it does still cling to a consensualist model of society. Whilst presenting the welfare apparatus as pursuing self-serving, sectional interests, the New Right shows faith in the ability of the institutions of the law, and a suitably reformed and purged educational system, to represent the core moral values and social rules which, for them are the foundations of an orderly society. The essential point of classifying an act as a crime is to punish and denounce its perpetrators and thus reinforce the sanctity of society's rules. In reinforcing the moral boundaries of the social order, the law provides an important social education to citizens at large (Morgan, 1981, p. 65).

This 'New Retributivist' faith in the law to function as an agency of moral education in society has, in recent years, been supplemented by a renewed emphasis, in speeches by Conservative ministers, on the need to restate and uphold a traditional familist (pro-nuclear family), universal framework of values. Moreover, these strictures now have the material force of legislation. Notoriously, section 28 of the Local Government Act 1988 prevents employees of local authorities from pursuing policies which may be seen as 'promoting' homosexual behaviour and relationships as being morally equivalent to those of heterosexuals. Moreover, section 46 of the Education Act 1986 requires that sex education in schools be given within a familist moral framework. The message is forcefully underlined in a Department of Education circular (No. 11/87) to schools about sex education, reminding teachers that any message which could be seen as encouraging children in homosexual experiment would count as the procurement of under-age persons, a serious criminal offence. Furthermore, teachers are reminded that, 'for many people, including members of various religious faiths, homosexual practice is not morally acceptable, and deep offence may be caused to them' (para. 22).

This manoeuvre represents an attempt to forge links between those who share a conservative, Judeo-Christian hostility towards homosexuality, in defence of family values, with kindred spirits in the new ethnic minority communities. Such sentiments can strike a chord with many people in the parental generation of Sikhs, Moslems, Hindus and Afro-Caribbean Pentecostalists, who are anxious to preserve patriarchal authority in the home and maintain traditional religious morality. This morality expresses not simply a nostalgic longing for the old country, but also functions as a cement to bond the wider minority community in defensive solidarity. The presentation of liberal views on homosexuality in schools may represent one more face of what could be perceived as the encroaching 'decadence' of the white, British culture which surrounds them. Moreover, we suggest that the attempt to create a state-directed moral consensus through a new conservative moral alliance is not confined to the issue of sexual morality but extends to the familiar claims that much criminal and other forms of anti-social behaviour have their origins in the collapse of stable family life and the moral authority and clear patterns of socialisation that go with it. We would argue that this attempt to reconstruct a universal or absolutist moral consensus extends to the new nationally imposed common curricula in the schools, which are prescribed by the new Education Act.

The Education Secretary, Kenneth Baker, in his address in February 1989 to a post-synod assembly of the Church of England, elaborated a theme developed the previous year by the Prime Minister, Margaret Thatcher, in her statement of the moral foundations of Thatcherism, delivered to the Assembly of the Church of Scotland. These speeches were a riposte to the moral critique of Thatcherism contained in the speeches of Anglican bishops and in the Church of England's document 'Faith in the Cities'.

In his speech, the minister reiterated a list of core values which he had enunciated in a previous speech, including the injunctions not to lie, cheat, steal and so on (*Guardian*, 2 February 1989). He claimed that these values underlie the curricular reforms of the new Education Act, but that they had been 'undermined by those whose views had become fashionable in the 1960s and who claim that in a pluralistic world all values are relative' (*Guardian*, ibid). However, there is a paradox in that within this state-orchestrated discourse, the sphere of morality is limited to the 'private' world of civil society and to interpersonal relations in particular. In a reprise of Kantian ethics, the ethical principles are presented as axiomatic, categorical imperatives and the moral agent is presented as an individual subject. This citizen as moral subject, moreover, cannot offload his/her moral responsibilities onto collective, public institutions. An active citizenship, in which conduct is motivated by altruistic goals, is to be applauded; but again, this is a matter for individual choice, responsibility and action. One consequence is that the moral evaluation of Hayekian market philosophy and government policies is declared off limits. Thus, while the Christian values placed on community and human interdependence are to be applauded, for Baker, 'it is quite another [thing] to use these ideas . . . to advance, for example, a theological critique of the privatisation of state assets' (*Guardian*, ibid). Furthermore, he criticises 'too great a willingness to take a top down view of problems, and to view state-sponsored collectivist policies as having some intrinsic moral merit, rather than seeing these merely as offering one approach among others' (ibid).

The space of the 'social' (Donzelot, 1979; Rojek *et al.*, 1988), constructed through the social and economic strategies of social democracy, is a sphere of collectively funded and organised security. It consists of the safety nets of social insurance, public transport, socialised medicine, publicly policed public space, and so on. Within the New Right framework, this field is absorbed into the interpersonal sphere of civil society, of supposedly private and voluntary relations. Furthermore, this can be seen as an attempted solution to the conflicts between organicist, hierarchical and free-market–libertarian strands of conservatism (Norton and Aughey, 1981; Eccleshall *et al.*, 1984). But the charge from Roy Hattersley and other Labour politicians is that Hayekian, libertarian, market conservatism unleashes an unrestrained egoism in the population which, in its wake, increases levels of crime.

Given policies which retreat from the state control and regulation of the provision of marketable goods and services, the only effective remaining controls are a repressive justice system, and the attempt to form the individual citizen as a moral subject. Within the New Right utopia, a reformed education system and a morally regulated mass media take care of the developing subjectivity of the child, and a justice system, based firmly on the principles of retribution and deterrence, takes care of the moral education of adults and young people. The middle ground of welfare-based, non-custodial sentencing measures and crime prevention strategies is squeezed between the extremes. These welfare-based strategies are constituent elements of the 'social', now broadly under attack from the New Right ideology (King, 1989), even if the fiscal burdens of custody prevent those measures from being displaced in practice.

A Non-Absolutist Consensus

In the face of the hitherto scarcely challenged attempt by the Right to define the moral agenda, extending it in such a way that that may even wean away ethnic minority communities previously considered to be loyal to the Left, left realism has signalled a shift away from relativism, back towards a contest for the right to define the consensual moral basis of modern society. Thus, Jock Young, whose early text *The Drugtakers* (1971), as we have indicated, operated largely within the terms of a libertarian discourse of deviancy theory, founded on the opposition between absolutism (bad) and relativism (good), has recently, in discussing the same topic, introduced a realist notion of consensus, which, without announcing itself as such, stands between absolutism and relativism. Young's view of illegal drug use has shifted from a libertarian concern with the rights to self-determination of young drug users to the concerns of an anxious parental generation:

> To argue against present systems of control is not the same as arguing against control, and however fallacious consensual stereotypes of drug use may be, there is a widescale consensus across all social groups that incoherence, impotence and early death are not social goods. (Young, 1987b, p. 449)

There is a similar shift of emphasis in acknowledging that deviancy theory may have exaggerated the capacity for rational thought and conduct on the part of the deviant (ibid, p. 448). But the clearest indication of the realists' shift away from relativism is manifest in their rejection of the claim that the legal categories of crime are purely nominal (Hulsman, 1986), representative of sectional interests and imposed by powerful minorities on an unwilling majority of the population. Whilst recognising that there may be problematic relationships between particular categories of crime and their application in an unequal society, still the major categories of legally defined crime *do* represent majority public opinion (Young, 1987b, p. 354; Lea 1987, pp. 360–1; Matthews, 1987, pp. 372–3).

The local crime surveys conducted by the realists were a technology for demonstrating the degree of consensus over crime and crime control priorities. The *coup de grâce* was the survey of Broadwater Farm in North London, the scene of severe rioting in 1985. This estate, with a large black population, had popularly been cast as generally lawless and anti-police. While there were strong criticisms of the police and other authorities, there was, nevertheless, considerable agreement across the divisions of age, gender and race, about what should be considered the main priorities for crime control. The concerns about sexual attacks on women, mugging, burglary, racist attacks, heroin dealing and drunken driving were in line with the findings of other left realist crime surveys (Young, 1987b, p. 354; Jones *et al.*, 1987). Thus the majority of people in this supposed cradle of insurrection could still be seen to share in the broad value consensus of British society.

But what distinguishes this intermediate notion of consensus from the absolutism of the Right, is its firm commitment to the ground rules of a culture of sustainable diversity:

> A central part of the realist project is to distinguish those activities which will facilitate a culture of diversity and those which destroy it. (Young, 1987b, p. 354)

This acknowledgement is crucial in that it recognises limits to the range of acceptably diverse forms of conduct. It simultaneously recognises the inevitability and functional necessity of the police, the justice and penal systems – even while there is considerable scope for a social democratic reformation of those institutions – in order to reproduce the conditions of possibility of a tolerant culture of diversity. This signals a rapprochement with other left discourses which, similarly, have been sharpening the distinction between a social democratic approach to law and order and libertarian discourses.

Essentially, the new discourses reject the libertarian view of socialism as the emancipation of the working class and other self-defined oppressed groups. Left libertarians assume that the law and its application is primarily negative and repressive in its effect and will wither away, along with other state institutions, with the coming of socialism. In those circumstances, citizens would retrieve the function of social control from alien and oppressive institutions, performing self-policing in a spontaneous form. Paul Hirst, the leading exponent of the new social democratic discourses, and an erstwhile critic of Jock Young's earlier forms of radical criminology (Hirst, 1975; 1980), presents the law as a positive force, essential in all modern industrial societies, whether socialist or capitalists (Hirst, 1986).

In fact, the law would have to be considerably strengthened in order to redirect socialism away from its unpopular and inefficient, statist, post-war forms. One leading realist, Roger Matthews, has endorsed Hirst's model of a pluralistic, decentralised society, where direct state control gives way to greater autonomy for the institutions of civil society, held in a system of checks and balances by strengthened legal controls. The law must regulate the inevitable clashes between the sectional interests of decentralised decision-makers on behalf of an identifiable *public* interest (Hirst, 1986, p. 85; Matthews, 1987, pp 382–3). It is notable that Hirst is moving towards the development of general theories and away from an earlier Marxist concern with the historically contingent character of law and justice systems. Whilst important differences remain between Hirst and Young, for example over their respective notions of rights (Young, 1987b, p. 355; Hirst, 1986, p. 62), in like manner, Young's concern with rights reflects a more general desire to elevate realism into a universal and hence generally applicable criminology.

Thus, so far, it seems reasonable to present realism as a move towards an 'intermediate', pluralist form of consensus theory, in common with like-minded others on the social democratic left. In this sense it is a counterpart to the American work of Elliot Currie (1985b). Moreover, recently, Young has stressed the continuities between modern realism and the earlier forms of radical criminology within a broader paradigm (Young, 1988). If we stress the political character and contexts of the production of knowledge, it makes sense to emphasise the continuities between different versions of the emerging social democratic consensus theory; realism cannot be reduced to its theoretical statements or research reports.

As David Garland, following Foucault (1977), argues – in discussing criminological programmes in the Edwardian period – knowledge is indissolubly related to power strategies (Garland, 1985, p. 74).

It would be premature, at this stage, to attempt a comprehensive analysis of the power/knowledge complex of left realist criminology, but we must bear in mind its technical and discursive resources in relations to its organisational basis (ibid, p. 74), As a social movement, left realism operates in a rich complex of overlapping academic/social networks in and out of the conference circuit, in the Labour Campaign for Criminal Justice, a key parliamentary policy-making lobby, in the Fabian society, in complex policy-making roles in relation to Labour-run local authorities (in Islington and elsewhere) and in relation to the more progressive, reform-oriented lobbies within the police and the Home Office.

The central thread running through these practices is a concern to seize the initiative on law and order away from the Right, back to the parties of the social democratic left, presumably in all advanced societies. However, in embracing the search for effective improvements in service delivery of policing to the poor and so forth, as Downes and Rock comment, their:

> solutions are not so very different from the more liberal proposals of Home Office officials in Britain or their counterparts (elsewhere) . . . (Their proposals) . . . display a marked affinity with those of experts from other professional positions, and there are the makings of a new professional consensus which possesses considerable authority. (Downes and Rock, 1988, pp. 309–10)

However, it would be misleading to underestimate the specifically theoretical dimensions of the left realist project. Underneath the broad political unities which are emerging in the political centre ground, there remain important differences which now constitute impediments to continued advance. In particular, there are important ambiguities in the notions of consensus and the conceptions of the human subject which underpin the realist venture.

ECLECTIC THEORETICAL LINEAGE

Young's claim that there is a broad continuity in the concerns of radical criminology, from the time of *The New Criminology* (Taylor, *et al.*, 1973) to the current left realist phase (Young, 1988), is plausible in the sense that there remains an overriding concern to develop a politically based, comprehensive theory of crime, which, unlike the narrow 'administrative criminologies' of state-sponsored criminology in Britain and the United States, does not eschew either the aetiological quest nor the rehabilitative ideal (Kinsey *et al.*, 1986, pp. 57–74). Yet we would also claim that there remains an awkward continuity of theoretical diversity. The New Criminology contained elements of the libertarian, interactionist sociology of the American labelling school (most clearly represented in Young's earlier text, *The Drugtakers*) in its concern with the analysis of subcultures and the amplifying effects of societal reaction. A central feature of that school, rooted in the American pragmatist philosophical tradition (cf. Rock, 1979), is its founding faith in the creative rationality of the human subject and its hostility to determinist, positivist and social systems explanations of human conduct. This sociological approach is a form of methodological individualism, in that the logical building blocks of society are creative, meaning endowing, human actors. 'Society' is, at best, seen in nominalist terms, as a shorthand for a field of interaction between individuals and groups of individuals.

Yet the New Criminology tries to marry this approach with a Marxist-based, structural account of the wider origins of criminal motivation and reaction to crime, in a political economy of crime (Taylor *et al.*, 1973, pp. 270–4). The latter is clearly realist in its view of society as a reality *sui generis* and hence methodologically collectivist in recognising class struggle and other structural forces which impinge on crime and crime control. These forces are irreducible to the actions of human subjects. But most interesting for our present purposes is the attempt to rescue Durkheim as a radical theorist of crime (ibid, p. 87).

We have developed our argument in relation to Durkheim at greater length elsewhere (Stenson and Brearley, 1989) and there are points of continuity between our argument and that of Pearce (1989), though unlike Pearce, we are not concerned to draw any links between Marx and Durkheim.

Taylor, Walton and Young concur with Durkheim that the forced division of labour gives rise to crimogenic frustrations, which, to be relieved, would need the development of an unconstrained meritocracy (Taylor *et al.*, 1973, pp. 74–8; cf. also Reiner, 1984, and Pearce, 1989).

While recent references to Durkheim by the realists are rare, it is clear that their current concern with creating a form of consensus which can reproduce a culture of sustainable diversity is beginning to look Durkheimian in the radical sense (Lea, 1987, pp. 365–6). Nevertheless, uneasy ambiguities remain over the precise meaning of the intermediate notion of consensus in a culture of diversity. The ground rules and values are barely described. Using the language of fundamental human rights, Young (1987a, p. 355) presents the consensus as guaranteeing a negative notion of freedom. This is familiar within the British liberal tradition and is represented as freedom from criminal victimisation. Underlying this conception of *freedom from* victimisation lies a particular, pragmatist ontology of the human subject as unitary and constitutive. That is, we have here a conception of the human subject as rational, in his/her own terms, and the author of his/her actions. As we have emphasised, this is the legacy of an attachment to the conception of creative subjectivity, inherited from symbolic interactionism. We will shortly return to the problem of the substantive content of the consensus, but let us first examine the issue of the subject.

Homo Duplex

The elements which limited Young's full acceptance of Durkheim at the time of The New Criminology have not yet disappeared. The major stumbling-block at that stage was Durkheim's construction of the individual subject, at odds with the purposive, creative and rational subject. Taylor, Walton and Young followed the standard interpretation of Durkheim's model of human nature, that the human being is a 'homo duplex', consisting of, on the one hand, biologically and psychologically driven, insatiable, egoistic desires, and on the other hand, an altruistic dimension, consisting of socially generated normative controls. They argue that, for the most part, Durkheim represents the deviant as driven by egoistic desires and hence devoid of significant levels of human reason (Taylor *et al.*, 1973, p. 89). By contrast, they, like Howard Becker and others in the neo-Chicagoan school (Matza, 1969), were still anxious to retain a recognition of that rationality.

More recently, in the landmark text of left realism, *What Is To Be Done About Law and Order?* (Lea and Young, 1984), these theoretical concerns remain. Culture is not represented in Durkheimian terms as a symbolic order with an independent force in its own right but rather, in terms familiar from the post-Mertonian subcultural theorists of delinquency (Downes and Rock, 1988, pp. 137–65), as a problem solving device,

> as the ways people have evolved to tackle the problems which face [people] in everyday life . . . in order to solve the problems posed (by structural locations), cultural solutions are evolved to attempt to tackle them: that is, people develop their own subcultures. (Lea and Young, 1984, p. 76)

Lea and Young explicitly reject positivist explanations of deviance which explain it as a pathological and mechanically necessary response to individual or social pressures and also explanations which would portray crime as the product of a continuity of criminal values, passed on through the socialisation process. Again, they emphasise the logical primacy of the individual subject, endowed with meaningful rationality (ibid, p. 78). Culture is thus only recognised insofar as it comes into the purview of individuals constructing subcultural solutions to the problems at hand. Thus they approvingly cite Ken Pryce's study of the formation of leisure subcultures (which tolerate a degree of deviant behaviour) among young blacks who reject the 'shitwork' available to them. This subcultural solution, evolved in concert by assemblies of rationally calculating egos, enables them to 'survive unemployment, racism and the few menial jobs available to them' (ibid, p. 78; and Pryce, 1977).

There are affinities here with the rationalist and existential descriptions of deviant commitment, broadly derived from the methodologically individualist American pragmatist tradition, which are offered by Box (1981) as an alternative to positivist and determinist explanations of social control and the formation of deviant personality and motivation early in life. Again the creative subject remaking him/herself anew in each situation, is logically prior to the collective dimension of culture. Perhaps left realism (in one guise) shares with this 'control theory' a contract model of society; in Box's terms, 'We all make our separate contract with society' ' (Box, 1981, p. 129).

Yet, as we have already seen, realists still believe in some conception of a general public morality at the level of the 'total society', which is conceptualised as a sphere of structural institutional forces and dominant values (Lea and Young, 1984, p. 85); but what values? Here is a telling contradiction: whereas in the most recent statements the dominant values of public morality are conceptualised in terms of the rights, freedoms and responsibilities operating in a culture of diversity, as a complex of civilised standards (Young, 1987a, p. 355), the dominant values have also been conceptualised as the egoistic, capitalist values of the stock exchange.

In an echo of Robert Merton, crime is seen as a response by the poor to relative deprivation, which attempts to realise the greedy ambitions exalted in a market society (Lea and Young, 1984, pp. 96–7). Thus the dominant value system is characterised in both egoistic and altruistic terms. This is an eminently Durkheimian characterisation, but no theory is provided which enables us to see the relationship between the subcultural level and that of the 'total society' and the supra-individual levels of culture. It is beyond the brief of this chapter to produce such a fully elaborated theory, but we hope to indicate the basic framework which might inform it. Yet, to open that door, in our third section, we must explore further the ambiguities and misunderstandings in the realists' conception of the subject.

AVOIDING UTILITARIANISM

We might question the rather altruistic, Rousseau-like assumptions about human nature which underlie Lea and Young's *What Is To Be Done About Law and Order?*. It is assumed that the impetus for egoism comes not from the individual's biological or psychological dispositions but exclusively from the dominant egoistic value system. In this sense their work embodies a culturally plastic view of human nature which, as Hawkins has argued, characterised Durkheim's early writings (Hawkins, 1977, p. 232).

More recently Young has come to recognise the importance of trying to reconceptualise the subject in terms of a new notion of citizenship in social democracy (Corrigan, Jones, Lloyd and Young 1988; and Corrigan, Jones and Young 1989). These authors counterpose a traditional, social democratic conception of the individual – as simply one of a passive mass of recipients of state services and goods – against the New Right's market conception of the individual as a rationally calculating, discerning consumer who wishes to maximise his/her choices (Corrigan *et al.*, 1988, p. 3). Arguing, in effect, for a rapprochement between the two models, they stress the need to reconceptualise the relationship between the state and the citizen in terms of a reciprocity between efficiently delivered and accountable state services and discerning, choosing individuals who must actively participate in the social sphere. Moreover, these citizens must recognize their duties as part of a contractual bargain which guarantees their rights.

Echoing the Gladstonian liberals, they argue that the role of the state is to intervene in order to redress the inequalities of the market (ibid, p. 8), and to foster a constructive meritocracy in which effort will be effectively rewarded (ibid, pp. 7–8). There is here a groping recognition of the culturally constructed nature of the individual subject/citizen (Corrigan *et al.*, 1989: 17), a recognition sidestepped by the earlier commitment to the rationalist and humanist assumptions about the human subject which underpin subcultural theory.

Furthermore, in a clear but unacknowledged reference to Durkheim's version of socialism as involving the restraint of sectional and individual egoistic desire on behalf of the collective good, they stress the moral obligation of the individual to express the 'socialness' within him/herself: 'Socialness and its obligations matter for everyone as an expression of community' (Corrigan *et al.*, 1989, p. 17). The implication here is that deviants are expressing only their egoistic nature and desires, whether that egoism is rooted in the dominant culture or in purely personal desire, thus forfeiting some of their rights. For example, people who refuse both work and *truly effective* training opportunities should not be entitled to state benefit (ibid, p. 17).

However, the shift towards a more cultural and methodologically collectivist conception of the subject is vitiated by the retention of a social contract model and what they admit is a 'limited utilitarianism', in which the guiding principle of the administration of state services should be the Benthamite criterion of what is the greatest good of the greatest number (Corrigan *et al.*, 1988, p. 6). The realist version of utilitarianism is more committed to pluralist and decentralised procedures, for example in relation to crime control (Lea, 1987, p. 366), than was the case with traditional mandarin, criminological discourses.

But this shift towards utilitarianism may not be restricted to the ethics of social administration: it may also involve, partially, a shift towards the aetiological position of utilitarian, British criminology. Young admits that the break, in the 1960s and 1970s, between radical criminology and sociological positivism 'was a deep flaw' (Young, 1988, p. 168). We have noted that he has moderated his view of the deviant as a rational subject; may this signal a shift back towards a determinist aetiology?

We must recall that what Young characterises as social democratic positivism (ibid, p. 159) has its roots in the British empiricist/associationist, philosophical and scientific tradition, which had spawned the utilitarian philosophy of the mandarin, reformist, administrative classes. The conception of the relation of the individual to society in utilitarianism is methodologically individualistic: the atomistic individual logically precedes social relations. In one version, he/she is 'homo economicus', rationally calculating the costs and benefits to action. British administrative criminology in its shift towards situational crime prevention has moved towards a 'homo economicus' view, while retaining elements of the old individualist positivism, with its search for the causes of crime in personality factors and early family experiences (cf. Clarke and Cornish, 1983).

In that second version the deviant is determined by internal and external factors pushing her/him into crime. In this case, the formation of the subject, why some children are more likely than others to end up as committed criminals, is clearly on the agenda (West and Farrington, 1977). If, as seems possible, the formation of the subject, both respectable and deviant, and the role of the family and school ascend the realist agenda (cf. Currie, 1985a), it does not necessarily have to involve a rejection of rationalism and a slide back into the traditional forms of explanation within a positivist criminology.

Durkheim remains a useful guide here. As we have argued (Stenson and Brearley, 1989), for Durkheim and for Kant there was no either/or choice between free will or determinism (Lukes, 1973, p. 74). Freedom exists by degrees and in a potential sense. While one's reason remains undeveloped, one is not free, but in the grip of one's passions and contingent circumstances (Kant, 1867, quoted in Randall, 1965). Similarly, for Durkheim (long predating Foucault) discipline, or self-mastery, is the key to freedom (Durkheim, 1961, p. 46). We suggest that this approach to rationality is less a hostage to rigid determinism, than to the big-hearted American pragmatist tradition, which democratically doles out freedom and rationality in equal proportions to all actors, high and low, deviant or respectable. The ambiguities in realism over the subject remain, and so do the difficult questions concerning democracy and the role of the expert in understanding that individual and the wider social body.

Realism, the Expert and the Divination of Consensual Morality

In the Fabian social democratic tradition, the expert was assumed to be the best equipped to make practical, 'technical' judgements about crime control, safely removed from the demeaningly turbulent political and moral realm (cf. Walker, 1987, p. 153; and Stenson, 1988). Yet a Fabian reliance on the expert is certainly not abandoned in realism. In a complex, unequal society, where there are powerful egoistic as well as 'civilised', altruistic cultural currents operating, divining the 'real' or objective nature of the consensual values is fraught with difficulty. The local crime surveys have functioned as technologies to 'reveal' the underlying consensus, which, presumably through social disorganisation and mass media distortions, has been concealed.

Durkheim himself warned that 'objective evaluation (of the moral order) and average evaluation should not be confused' (Durkheim, 1953, p, 83). The survey is not a neutral tool; its data are social constructions, in addition to being indicators of social patterns (Stubbs, 1987). Matthews registers a partial recognition of this problem in his distinction between 'direct' and (left) 'representative' realism. In the latter, investigation proceeds via 'dialectical abstraction' (Matthews, 1987, p. 376).

What this means is not that the survey is irrelevant as a technology for revealing the objective contours of the moral order in modern society, but that it, with other methods, is a creative theoretical construction which must indicate both the present complexities of the moral order under anomic conditions and the ideal moral forms which underpin a stable and more equitable, organically solidaristic society (Durkheim, 1953, p. 54). In view of this and because of the tensions within the individual citizen/subject as 'homo duplex', moral education and the formation of the subject citizen must be, as the Right have recognised, high on the political agenda.

We suggest accomplishing a more thorough break with utilitarianism, recognising the implications of Durkheim's critique of contract models of society – that there are complex institutional and moral underpinnings to the institution of the contract and the ability of the individual to enter into it (cf. Lukes, 1973, pp. 145–6). In particular, we must recognise the significance of Durkheim's attempt to provide a sociological framework for Kantian ethics (Durkheim, pp. 40–62). The duty which lies at the heart of moral life is founded on the complex web of reciprocal interdependencies which are the conditions of possibility of social life. The New Right politician's lists of universal moral values, limited and restricted to the narrow interpersonal realm as it is, has considerably greater appeal than the more conditional, fluid moral discourses of utilitarian and situational ethics. This is because it recognises the categorical and imperative quality of moral rules and that the pursuit of the 'good' can be experienced as a transcendent, desirable goal in itself (1953, p. 46).

But the New Right list of moral imperatives is ill-equipped to provide a moral basis for the interdependencies of a modern society. Individual social life is made possible by a complex of public institutions and services in both the state-funded and 'private' sectors. A truly sociologically based, social democratic ethics must recognise the moral responsibilities of this sphere and the individual's relation to it. Practically, this means that social and economic policies are primordially moral in character and can thus be a legitimate subject for moral debate. The active citizen must be equipped, as a constructed subject, to participate in this debate.

Durkheimian moral discourses have been more recently supplemented by investigations of the moral strategies incorporated in the web of disciplinary agencies involved in public health, individual health care, education, psychiatry, the caring professions, the justice system, and so on (cf. Foucault,1977 and 1979; Garland, 1985; Rose, 1985). Accounts of these strategies in terms of social control (Cohen and Scull, 1983) fail to grasp their positive as well as negative, constraining dimensions. They involve 'the promotion of subjectivity, through investments in individual lives, and the forging of alignments between the personal projects of citizens and images of the social order' (Miller and Rose, 1988, p. 172; Hirst, 1986, p. 62).

But the importance of these programmes is that they tend to be targeted at specific sections of the population, and disproportionately towards the poor. Hargreaves has, within a Durkheimian framework, emphasised the need to make the more successful majority of children a moral target and not just the deviant minority. There is a need to temper the extreme egoism of the moral agenda of schooling, with its overarching emphasis on individual achievement and reward, as experienced by high achieving pupils, with a more clearly altruistic moral programme (Hargreaves, 1979).

But to echo Durkheim, it would be a mistake to exaggerate the importance of the institutions of the state. It is important to recognise the significance of intermediate levels of social organisation and grouping between state and citizen (Reiner, 1984, p. 200). The individual is connected to the wider social collectivity not simply via the institutions of the state and local authorities, but also by a complex range of institutions within civil society. These include religious and ethnically based moral communities. Given that even a culture of diversity needs shared ground rules and values, major questions can be raised about the relationship between the individual citizen, moral sub-communities and the wider moral order (see Factor and Stenson, 1988a,b; 1989). For example, what part may these moral sub-communities, which can provide a major source of identity for the individual, play in the control of crime?

So far, realists have been predominantly concerned with crime and crime control initiatives centring on the relationship between official agencies and the local state. A Durkheimian canvas would, perhaps, be broader, particularly in our understanding of what comprises the 'social' sphere, which is quite central to a social democratic social order.

CONCLUSION

Left Realists are alive to the dangers of the social sphere becoming dominated by authoritarian forces. They stress the dangers of the police 'colonising' other public agencies of social intervention, for example in relation to crime control initiatives (Kinsey *et al.*, 1986). The involvement of untrained police officers in crime control education in schools represents a stark reminder of this (Vorhaus, 1984). Despite the dangers of a slide back into the utilitarian discourses of administrative British criminology, there remains a firm commitment to make the agencies of the public sphere, particularly the police, publicly accountable, and a similar democratic commitment to 'discover' the wishes and needs of the ordinary citizen. This marks a rejection of patronising, top-down, Fabian conceptions of the relation between the citizen and the social sphere (which we should recognise includes much more than the institutions of the local and national states).

Yet it is clear that the excitement engendered by left realism within criminology, and the disappointments at its failures to meet high expectations, indicate that it is not simply an analytic project, nor is its project restricted to piecemeal social engineering. Buried within it is a prescriptive project to create a new type of civilised, law-abiding subject. The New Right have put onto the political agenda the formation of the moral subjectivity of the citizen. Predictably, this subject is presented as constituted predominantly in the 'private' spheres of the family (cf. control theory, Hirschi, 1969), and in a public sphere, largely reduced to the market.

However, the New Right's attempt to return to an axiomatic, individualistic and religious-based morality is deeply unDurkheimian and would provide no basis for an effective education for citizenship, and crime control in particular. The dependence on religion is dangerously divisive in a multi-cultural society. There would be no effective, *collective* basis for a consensual secular morality, even if that secular morality has religious roots and continues to be nourished by them.

We suggest that an effective challenge to the Right requires an embrace of a methodologically collectivist conception of the subject and social relations. As Marquand (1988) has argued, the utilitarian assumptions of traditional British political culture have largely restricted the scope of intervention in people's lives to the externalities of behaviour. Is it not necessary, within a democratic rather than authoritarian framework, for public interventions, including the sphere of crime prevention and control, to take on the task of the moral persuasion of citizens? If so, we must stress the intrinsically social aspects of the character of the human subject and the need for a higher civic morality, which is of intrinsic value and thus irreducible to the needs and interests of the individual.

NOTE

We would like to thank Roger Matthews and Paul Rock for constructive criticisms.

REFERENCES

BOX, S. (1981) *Deviance, Reality and Society*, London: Holt, Rinehart & Winston.

BREWER, C. *et al.* (1981) *Criminal Welfare On Trial*, London: Social Affairs Unit.

CLARKE, R. and CORNISH, D. (1983) *Crime Control In Britain*, Albany: State University of New York.

COHEN, S. (1985) *Visions Of Social Control*, Cambridge: Polity.

COHEN, S. and SCULL, A. (eds) (1983) *Social Control and the State*, Oxford: Blackwell.

CORRIGAN, P. *et al.* (1988) *Socialism, Merit and Efficiency*, London: The Fabian Society.

CORRIGAN, P. *et al.* (1989) 'Rights and Obligations', *New Socialist*, 59.

CURRIE, E. (1985a) 'Crime and The Conservatives', *Dissent* (Fall).

CURRIE, E. (1985b) *Confronting Crime: An American Challenge*, New York: Pantheon.

DONZELOT, J. (1979) *The Policing of Families, Welfare Versus the State*, London: Hutchinson.

DOWNES, D. and ROCK, P. (1988) *Understanding Deviance*, Oxford: Oxford University Press.

DURKHEIM, E. (1953) *Sociology and Philosophy*, London: Cohen & West.

DURKHEIM, E. (1961) *Moral Education: A Study in the Theory and Application of the Sociology of Education*, London: The Free Press, Collier Macmillan.

ECCLESHALL, R. *et al.* (1984) *Political Ideologies, An Introduction*, London: Hutchinson.

FACTOR, F. and STENSON, K. (1988a) 'Identity Crisis', *Youth In Society*, (June).

FACTOR, F. and STENSON, K. (1988b) 'Constructing an Identity', *Youth in Society* (July).

FACTOR, F. and STENSON, K. (1989) 'Community Control and the Policing of Jewish Youth', Paper presented to the British Criminological Conference, Bristol Polytechnic, July.

FOUCAULT, M. (1977) *Discipline and Punish*, Harmondsworth: Penguin.

FOUCAULT, M. (1979) *The History of Sexuality*, Harmondsworth: Penguin.

GARLAND, D. (1985) *Punishment and Welfare*, Aldershot: Gower.

HALL, S. *et al.* (1978) *Policing the Crisis*, London: Macmillan.

HARGREAVES, D. (1979) 'Durkheim, Deviance and Education', in L. Barton and R. Meighan, *Schools, Pupils and Deviance*, Nafferton: Studies in Education.

HAWKINS, M. J. (1977) 'A Re-Examination of Durkheim's Theory of Human Nature', *Sociological Review*, vol. 25, no. 2, pp. 229–51.

HIRSCHI, T. (1969) *Causes of Delinquency*, Berkeley: University of California Press.

HIRSCHI, A. VON (1976) *Doing Justice: The Choice of Punishments*, Report of the Committee for the Study of Incarceration, New York.

HIRST, P. Q. (1975) 'Marx and Engels on Law, Crime and Morality', in I. Taylor *et al.* (eds), *Critical Criminology*, London: Routledge & Kegan Paul.

HIRST, P. Q. (1980) 'Law, Socialism and Rights', in P. Carlen and M. Collinson (eds), *Radical Issues in Criminology*, Oxford: Martin Robertson.

HIRST, P. Q. (1986) *Law, Socialism and Democracy*, London: Allen & Unwin.

HULSMAN, L. (1986) 'Critical Criminology and the Concept of Crime', *Contemporary Crises*, vol. 10, pp. 63–80.

JONES, T. *et al.* (1986) *The Islington Crime Survey*, Aldershot: Gower.

JONES, T. *et al.* (1987) *Saving the Inner City*, The first report of the Broadwater Farm Survey, London: Mddx. Polytechnic Centre for Criminology.

KING, M. (1989) 'Social Crime Prevention à la Thatcher', *The Howard Journal*, vol. 28, no. 4.

KINSEY, R. (1984) First report of the Merseyside Crime Survey, Liverpool, Merseyside County Council.

KINSEY, R. *et al.* (1986) *Losing The Fight Against Crime*, Oxford: Blackwell.

LEA, J. (1987) 'Left Realism: A Defence', *Contemporary Crises*, 11, pp. 357–70.

LEA, J. and YOUNG, J. (1984) *What Is To Be Done About Law and Order?*, Harmondsworth: Penguin.

LUKES, S. (1973) *Emile Durkheim*, Harmondsworth: Penguin.

MARQUAND, D. (1988) *The Unprincipled Society*, London: Jonathan Cape.

MATTHEWS, R. (1987) 'Taking Realist Criminology Seriously', *Contemporary Crises*, 11, pp. 371–401.

MATZA, D. (1969) *Becoming Deviant*, New Jersey: Prentice-Hall.

MILLER, P. and ROSE, N. (1988) 'The Tavistock Programme: The Government of Subjectivity and Social Life', *Sociology*, vol. 22, no. 2, pp. 171–92.

MORGAN, P. (1981) 'The Children's Act: Sacrificing Justice to Social Workers' Needs?', in C. Brewer *et al.*

MORRIS, A. *et al.* (1980) *Justice for Children*, London: Macmillan.

NORTON, P. and AUGHEY, A. (1981) *Conservatives and Conservatism*, London: Temple Smith.

PAINTER, K. *et al.* (1989) 'Hammersmith and Fulham Crime and Policing Survey', Enfield, Middlesex Polytechnic.

PEARCE, F. (1989) *The Radical Durkheim*, London: Unwin Hyman.

PLATT, T. and TAKAGI, P. (1977) 'Intellectuals for Law and Order: A Critique of the New Realists', *Crime and Social Justice*, (Fall–Winter) pp. 1–16.

PRYCE, K. (1977) *Endless Pressure*, Harmondsworth: Penguin.

RANDALL, J. H. (1965) *The Career of Philosophy*, vol. 2, New York: Columbia University Press.

REINER, R. (1984) 'Crime, Law and Deviance: The Durkheimian Legacy', in S. Fenton, *Durkheim and Modern Society*, Cambridge: Cambridge University Press.

ROCK, P. (1979) *The Making of Symbolic Interactionism*, London and Basingstoke: Macmillan.

ROJEK, C. *et al.* (1988) *Social Work and Received Ideas*, London: Routledge.

ROSE, N. (1985) *The Psychological Complex*, London: Routledge.

SCHUR, E. (1973) *Radical Non-Interventionism: Rethinking the Delinquency Problem*, Englewood Cliffs, N.J.: Prentice-Hall.

SCRATON, P. (ed.) (1987) *Law, Order and The Authoritarian State*, Milton Keynes: Open University Press.

STENSON, K. (1986) 'Foucault, Policing and the Body', Paper presented to the National Deviancy Conference, Central London Polytechnic, March.

STENSON, K. (1988) Review of Walker, N. 'Crime and Criminology, A Critical Introduction', *Sociology*, vol. 11, no. 2.

STENSON, K. and BREARLEY, N. (1989) 'Realism, Crime and Ethics', Paper presented to the British Sociological Association Conference, 1989.

STUBBS, P. (1987) 'Crime, Community and the Multi-Agency Approach: A critical reading of the Broadwater Farm Inquiry Report', *Critical Social Policy*, 20, pp. 30–45.

TAYLOR, I. *et al.* (1973) *The New Criminology: For a Social Theory of Deviance*, London: RKP.

THORPE, D. *et al.* (1980) *Out of Care*, London: George Allen & Unwin.

VAN DEN HAAG, E. (1985) *Deterring Potential Criminals*, London: Social Affairs Unit, Research Report no. 7.

VORHAUS, G. (1984) *Police in the Classroom – A Study of the Schools Involvement Programme in Hillingdon*, Hillingdon Legal Resource Centre, Hayes.
WALKER, N. (1987) *Crime and Criminology: A Critical Introduction*, New York: Oxford University Press.
WEST, D and FARRINGTON, D. (1977) *The Delinquent Way of Life*, London: Heinemann.
WILSON, J. Q. (1975) *Thinking About Crime*, New York: Basic Books.
YOUNG, J. (1971) *The Drugtakers*, London: MacGibbon & Kee.
YOUNG, J. (1987a) 'The Tasks Facing A Realist Criminology', *Contemporary Crises*, 11, pp. 337–56.
YOUNG, J. (1987b) 'Deviance', in P. Worsley (ed.) *The New Introducing Sociology*, Harmondsworth: Penguin.
YOUNG, J. (1988) 'Radical Criminology In Britain: The Emergence of A Competing Paradigm', in P. Rock (ed.), *A History of British Criminology*, Oxford: Clarendon Press.

Index